T0330387

The Political Economy of Democratic Institutions

The Political Economy of Democratic Institutions

Peter Moser

Lecturer in Economics, University of Applied Sciences of
Eastern Switzerland and University of St Gallen, Switzerland

THE LOCKE INSTITUTE

Edward Elgar

Cheltenham, UK • Northampton, MA, USA

Published by
Edward Elgar Publishing Limited
Glensanda House
Montpellier Parade
Cheltenham
Glos GL50 1UA
UK

Edward Elgar Publishing, Inc.
136 West Street
Suite 202
Northampton
Massachusetts 01060
USA

A catalog record for this book is available from the British Library

Library of Congress Cataloging in Publication Data

Moser, Peter Daniel, 1962–
    The political economy of democratic institutions / Peter Moser.
    (The Locke Institute series)
    Includes bibliographical references.
    1. Representative government and representation. 2. Democracy. 3. Majorities. 4. Political stability. I. Title. II. Series.

    JF1051 .M67 2000
    321.8'01'1—dc21
                                                                    99–088523

ISBN 1 85898 966 3

Printed and bound in Great Britain by Biddles Ltd, www.biddles.co.uk

To Martina

In framing a government which is to be administered by men over men, the great difficulty lies in this: you must first enable the government to control the governed; and in the next place oblige it to control itself.

James Madison (1788: 320)

For economic growth to occur the sovereign or government must not merely establish the relevant set of rights, but must make a credible commitment to them.

Douglass C. North and Barry R. Weingast (1989: 803)

Contents

Figures

Tables

Acknowledgments

This project on the positive theory of political institutions originated in 1992 when I became interested in studying the sophisticated principal agent relations in politics. Fortunately, I could spend the academic year 1992/93 at the Hoover Institution at Stanford University. Hoover proved to be the ideal academic environment for my research and I am deeply indebted to Barry Weingast and to Susanne Lohmann for introducing me into this fascinating research area. But also the many discussions with George Tsebelis, John Ferejohn, George Garrett and Hilton Root contributed to new ideas and clarified my thinking. Financial support for this period at the Hoover Institution was partly provided by the Swiss National Science Foundation.

The majority of the applications of positive political theory to particular issues (mostly on institutions in Europe) were developed at the University of St Gallen. There, I benefited from many fruitful discussions with, among others, Lars Feld, Martin Hagen, Heinz Hauser, Gebhard Kirchgässner, Heinz Müller, Marcel Savioz, Robert Straw and Andreas Ziegler. Particular thanks go to Claudia Hubschmid with whom I collaborated on the research presented in Chapter 9 and to Robert Straw for carefully proof-reading the manuscript.

Another group of colleagues provided me with advice and comments on different parts of this book. In this capacity, I would like to thank the group of researchers organized in NEMEU, particularly Bernard Steunenberg, Gerald Schneider and Hannelore Weck-Hannemann. Furthermore, I appreciate the comments by Peter Bernholz, Jakob de Haan, Thomas Havrilesky, Simon Hug, Dennis Mueller, Manfred Neumann, Friedrich Schneider, Ludger Schuknecht, Roland Vaubel and many others to whom I apologize for not mentioning. Some of the arguments presented in this book were published for the first time in the form of articles: Hubschmid and Moser (1997); Moser (1996b, 1997b, 1999a, 1999b). While I have reworked the material to present it in book form, I would like to thank the editors and anonymous referees of the following journals: *European Economic Review*, *European Journal of Political Economy*, *Journal of Common Market Study*, *Public Choice* and *Swiss Review of Economics and Statistics*. Last but not least, the editorial help by Charles Rowley at the Locke Institute helped to improve the manuscript substantially.

Most of all, I would like to thank Martina, Lukas, David and Anna for their patience and for their continuous insistence that life is much more than just research. And they are completely right.

Peter Moser
Chur, January 2000

1. Introduction

In democracies, a majority of the people determines policy either by directly voting on issues or indirectly by choosing their representatives. Democratic mechanisms serve to limit the divergence between the actions of political officials and the preferences of the people. Yet these mechanisms come at a cost. Democracies are limited in providing durable policies, because, first, today's voter cannot bind future ones, and second, because in many circumstances no policy commands a majority against all other possible proposals. In principle, a majority can replace public policies and has an incentive to do so if it faces time-inconsistent constraints (Kydland and Prescott, 1977) – for example when a tax base is elastic *ex ante* but becomes completely inelastic *ex post*, as for a levy on accumulated capital (Fischer, 1980) – or if today's majority has different preferences than the majority that enacted the status quo.

In addition, if a policy choice comprises more than one issue, there exists almost always a proposal that can defeat the status quo which makes coalitions vulnerable and changes likely (Condorcet, 1785; McKelvey, 1976; Schofield, 1978). This potential for change contrasts with the requirements of a market economy that there should be well-defined and stable property rights. The state's role is to define and enforce these rights. Individuals who perceive that property rights once created are respected and enforced by the state will be more inclined to make investments. If, however, rights are viewed as insecure, for example because of the fear of substantial tax increases or outright confiscation of property, expected private returns from investments are lower, which reduces growth of the economy. Perceived insecurity of property rights and time-inconsistent policies thus impede development, and can result in a no-growth equilibrium trap in which a society cannot alter the status quo, despite radical changes in announced policy (Weingast, 1995).

There is not only abundant empirical evidence that well-defined private property rights substantially increase the income of societies (Easton and Walker, 1997; Hall and Jones, 1997; Sachs and Warner, 1997) but furthermore that such rights must be perceived as stable. For example, Svensson (1998) in a cross-country analysis of 101 countries found that governments in unstable and polarized political systems tend to invest little in the legal infrastructure, resulting in lower levels of domestic investment. Brunetti (1998) reported that higher volatility of policies is related to lower average growth rates. Also, Rodrik (1991) pointed out that the success of policy reform may depend in no small part on the private sector's expectation of policy reversal. This dilemma is apparent in the democracies of Eastern Europe, as well as in many developing countries.

Beginning from the proposition that decisions taken by majority rules are generally unstable and not binding for future voters, and so are insufficient for the required security of a private market economy, the thesis is that political institutions that limit the policy discretion of majorities provide the sought sources of stability. Of course, stable policies are not sufficient for economic growth to occur, rather it is necessary that these institutions credibly commit political actors to sustain open markets based on private property rights. Empirical evidence supports the view that majority rule decisions alone are insufficient for economic growth and that democratic decision rules do not guarantee an escape out of the no-growth equilibrium trap (North, 1990; Przeworski, 1991; Alesina and Perotti, 1994; Borner, Brunetti and Weder, 1995; Brunetti and Weder, 1995; Root 1996).

1.1   INSTITUTIONS AND STABILITY

Political institutions are a principal source of stability. This is one common thesis of the literature reviewed in Part I of this study and the analysis of the checks and balances in the Swiss political system in Part II. Political institutions are defined as humanly devised constraints on simple majority rules. Of course, the majority rule is itself a constraint but because this study focuses on democracies, it is assumes that the simple majority rule is given and additional constraints only are analysed. Political institutions include rules of the political game set at the constitutional level, the organizational structure of legislatures and administrative and judicial procedures. Such institutions shape the incentives faced by political actors, for example by restricting the type of policy comparison via agenda-setting rights and other procedural rules, by granting partial or complete veto possibilities, and by influencing the distribution of information. An appropriate configuration of institutions can lead to a stable policy choice that cannot be replaced by any other policy proposal. For this type of equilibrium Shepsle (1979) introduced the term 'structure-induced equilibrium' and a wide variety of such equilibria have been found (Romer and Rosenthal, 1978; Shepsle, 1979, 1986a; Gilligan and Krehbiel, 1987; Hammond and Miller, 1987; Shepsle and Weingast, 1987a; Baron and Ferejohn, 1989a; Tsebelis, 1995a; Part II, this volume).

1.2   INSTITUTIONS AND POLICY CHOICE

The existence of a structure-induced equilibrium implies that different institutional arrangements give rise to different policies, that is, public policies depend not only on the preferences of the constituencies, but also on political institutions. An analysis of these institutions seeks to reveal the properties of the supply function of political actions and thereby complements the interest group approach to politics (Olson, 1965; Stigler, 1971; Peltzman, 1976; Becker, 1983; Potters and Sloof, 1996). Because some interest groups are more likely to form than others, a fundamental bias arises in the demand for public policy. For example, this is reflected in protectionist international trade policy (Hillman, 1989). In the interest group approach, such demand for self-interested policy is then simply translated into political outcomes. The same is the case in the rent-seeking literature which looks at how resources are used to influence potential allocation (Nitzan, 1994). However, the interest group and rent-seeking approach cannot readily be applied to make clear predictions if several groups compete with each other or to explain the often discontinuous changes in public policies. The claim is that legislative and other political institutions can explain which coalition of groups are more likely to succeed in having their sought policies implemented, how groups can maintain their benefits over time (by shaping institutions in order to affect the choices in the future), and why policy changes occur at some particular time and not at others (Weingast, 1981; Weingast and Moran, 1983; Ferejohn, 1986; Gilligan, Moran and Weingast, 1989; the essays in Crain and Tollison, 1990; and for institutional effects on fiscal policy, see Pommerehne, 1978, 1990; Alt and Lowry, 1994; Kiewiet and Szakaly, 1996; Matsusaka, 1995; Feld and Kirchgässner, 1998). This approach is used in Part III of this study in order to analyse legislative choices in the European Union (EU). The investigation reveals that the European Parliament (EP), which is traditionally regarded as weak, can influence policy choices under certain conditions.

1.3 INSTITUTIONS AND REGULATORY BEHAVIOR

A third line of research focuses on the implications of stability-enhancing institutions for regulatory behavior. In situations in which an agency or bureaucracy interprets and executes a statute, the individuals within the agency or bureaucracy are in effect permitted to make the first policy choice. This policy prevails unless preempted by legislative action. Whenever legislative structures induce stability, that is, whenever legislative equilibria exist, the agency can take advantage of this and select its most preferred policy within the set of stable outcomes. Consequently, the magnitude of agency discretion depends not only on informational advantages but also on legislative institutions, including decision rules and party organizations (for US legislative institutions, see Calvert, McCubbins and Weingast, 1989; Ferejohn and Shipan, 1989, 1990;

Eskridge and Ferejohn, 1992; Hammond and Knott, 1996; for parliamentary systems see Steunenberg, 1994a, 1996; Tsebelis, 1995a). In Part IV of this study, this argument is applied to a specific agency, namely to central banks. In contrast to the previous literature, which regarded agency discretion as costly for legislators, this study claims that in the case of central banks, some discretion is politically beneficial because it insulates central banks from political pressure. However, only countries with checks and balances are able to credibly provide independent central banks and reap the benefits of such independent banks.

1.4   RELEVANCE FOR ECONOMISTS

The subject of the research reviewed and extended in this study is political institutions. The research program – sometimes labeled 'positive theory of political institutions' – seeks to explain how political institutions work, in what respects they constrain political actors and why they prove binding in practice.[1] This field belongs traditionally to political science. Why should this subject be of interest to economists? There are two answers to this question – a methodological and a pragmatic one.

First, economic methodology is a tool that can not only be applied to study market transactions but also to analyse political choices. Microeconomics, including the economic theory of organizations (Milgrom and Roberts, 1992; Holmstrom and Tirole, 1989; Williamson 1985, 1989), and particularly game theory, proved to be very fruitful for investigations of political decisions. These tools have been used not only by economists but have become a standard instrument for political scientists. Many important contributions are published in leading journals of political science. These tools have been adapted to the particular subjects of research and thereby have been further developed. Economists should be aware of these improvements in rational choice analyses because these advances may help them to improve their analyses of economic choices and of economic institutions.[2]

The second reason for the relevance of this research for economists is more pragmatic. Although many economists like to advise politicians, economists have started to realize that their advice is only followed if it is politically attractive, and this is not often the case. For policy advisors to have more impact they have to be focused on rules or institutions, as has long been advocated by Buchanan and Tullock (1962), and further developed by Frey and Kirchgässner (1994) and Brennan and Buchanan (1985). However, in order to follow this advice, economists have to know how political institutions work, which is exactly the purpose of this research program.

NOTES

1. There is also a broad literature on the normative theory of political institutions based on the path-breaking work by Buchanan and Tullock (1962) and Buchanan (1971). A more recent contribution to this literature is Mueller (1996).
2. A good example of a methodological transfer of tools developed in the analyses of political institutions to economies is Miller's (1992) study of managerial dilemmas in hierarchies.

PART I

Legislative institutions and public policy:
A survey of the literature

Introduction to Part I

The majority rule is probably the most studied decision rule by social choice scholars, either by using spatial or axiomatic approaches. The spatial approach derives the results using geometry or calculus, while the axiomatic approach assumes that individual preferences satisfy certain basic rationality axioms from which the results are derived (for a survey of spatial models, see Enelow and Hinich, 1984; Krehbiel, 1988; Miller, Grofman and Feld, 1989; Shepsle and Weingast, 1994; for axiomatic models, see Schwarz, 1986, Sen, 1986; Kelly, 1988; examples of text book treatments are Ordeshook, 1986, chapters 2 and 6; Mueller, 1989, chapters 5 and 20; Bernholz and Breyer, 1994, chapters 11 to 13; Frey and Kirchgässner, 1994, chapter 5; Shepsle and Bonchek, 1997). Spatial models are relied on because they are better suited for empirical work. Spatial models are often referred to as *positive political theory* (Riker and Ordeshook, 1973).

Chapter 2 describes the methodology of spatial models which are used to illustrate the major results of majority rule decisions. Section 2.2 discusses the major property of majority rule decisions that whenever several dimensions are involved an equilibrium almost never exists. Consequently, any policy choice is vulnerable, that is, there is always a majority that prefers a different policy. Section 2.3 reviews extensions of the simple model that incorporate different assumptions about behavior, information and preference distribution, and introduce dynamic aspects. This literature points out the extent of the instability in majority rule decisions. The effects of institutional constraints on majority rule decisions are analysed in Chapter 3 and a review of major applications of this theory is presented in Chapter 4.

2. Collective decisions under simple majority rules

2.1 METHODOLOGY

The spatial analysis of simple majority rules is based on a few basic ingredients. It is necessary to characterize the nature of the choices, the preferences of the decision makers, to make assumptions about their behavior, and about their informational situation, and finally to define the equilibria concept (Krehbiel, 1988: 260–6).

The objects of choice are represented as points in a multidimensional space, denoted R^m, where m is the number of dimensions. The simplest example are two dimensions. Suppose that legislatures have to decide how much money to appropriate for defense and social programs which simultaneously determines taxes. This choice is illustrated in Figure 2.1, where x_1 and x_2 denote the dimension of defense and social spending, respectively. Consequently, any point $x = (x_1, x_2)$ on the plane is a potential legislative choice. Each legislator is endowed with a utility function over X, $U^i(x)$, with an ideal point in the space, denoted as $x_i = (x_{i1}, x_{i2})$, that is $U^i(x_i) > U^i(x) \ \forall \ x \neq x_i$. The ideal points of the three legislators A, B and C are depicted in Figure 2.1 as x_A, x_B and x_C respectively. These points represent their most preferred combination of spending and implied taxes. Utility declines the further away an alternative is from the ideal point, and it is usually assumed that the decline of utility increases the larger the distance from the ideal point. Such utility functions are called concave.

The utility function for legislator A takes the form:

$$U_A(x) = -[a_{11}(x_{A1} - x_1)^2 + 2a_{12}(x_{A1} - x_1)(x_{A2} - x_2) + a_{22}(x_{A2} - x_2)^2]^{\frac{1}{2}}$$

(2.1)

where a_{11} and a_{22} represent constants that weight the two issues and a_{12} determines the interaction between the two issues. Such utility functions are referred to as weighted Euclidean distance functions. The utility function in (2.1) allows legislators to be more sensitive to a policy change regarding one issue than to the other issue ($a_{11} \neq a_{22}$), and for preferences to be nonseparable ($a_{12} \neq 0$), which implies that a legislator's most preferred point on any given dimension is affected by policy changes in other issues. Unless mentioned, the arguments that follow are not affected by assuming separable preferences ($a_{12} = 0$) and equal weights ($a_{11} = a_{22}$). With such assumptions, each legislator is indifferent among spending combinations that are an equal distance from his or her ideal point and the indifference curves are circles. Such indifference curves through the status quo (q) are drawn in Figure 2.1. The points inside these indifference curves are each legislator's *preferred-to set*, defined as the set of alternatives strictly preferred by legislator i to q, $P_i(q) = \{x \in X \mid U^i(x) > U^i(q)\}$. Finally, the *contract curve* is the locus of tangents of the indifference curves of two legislators and corresponds to the Pareto-optimal points for those two persons. Since indifference curves are circles in Figure 2.1, the contract curves are straight lines connecting two ideal points, for example $x_A x_C$.

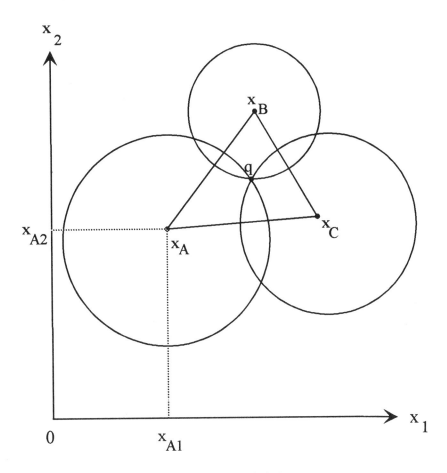

Figure 2.1   Preferences in two-dimensional choice space

The assumptions about the behavior of the decision makers differ in the literature. The simplest models assume *sincere voting*; voters vote for their most preferred alternative on each pair of alternatives with which they are confronted with. In other models, voters are assumed to be forward looking or *sophisticated*, that is voters know the future sequence of votes, look ahead and anticipate the future consequences of the issue currently under consideration.

With regard to the assumptions about information, the early models of spatial choice assume that political actors are fully informed about each other's preferences and about the structure of the game. More recent contributions have relaxed this assumption either by assuming that legislators have a subjective probability estimate about the preferences of the other actors or that the outcome of a policy choice is uncertain.

The dominant form of equilibria in the early models is analogous to a stable outcome. The models concentrate on the institutional features that render the outcome stable without analysing the behavior that leads to such outcome. More recent game-theoretic models focus on actions or strategies that lead to stable outcomes, defined as variations of the Nash equilibrium: this type of equilibrium is defined as a combination of strategies such that each actor cannot improve the outcome by choosing a different strategy, given everyone else's behavior.

2.2   PURE MAJORITY RULE: MAIN RESULTS

Spatial models assume that there is a constant group of individuals with stable preferences that make decisions by pairwise comparison using the simple majority rule. Given these stable preferences, does the majority rule procedure lead to a stable outcome or equilibrium? The results differ substantially depending on which assumptions are used regarding the number of dimensions, the behavior, the informational structure and the equilibria concept. Most important, however, is the impact of institutional assumptions which are discussed in Chapter 3. It is useful to distinguish between two sets of assumptions: the number of dimensions and whether the members behave sincerely or sophisticatedly (Table 2.1).

For the one-dimensional choice space, Black (1958) proved that if the preferences of all voters are single-peaked, the ideal point of the median voter is a *median point* (or *Condorcet winner*, named after Condorcet who discovered the cycling property of voting under majority rule in 1785). At least half of all ideal points are to the right or equal to it and at least half of the ideal points are to the left or equal to it. With an odd number of voters, this position is a unique equilibrium that is a stable outcome which cannot be replaced by any alternative. With an even number of voters, the equilibrium is usually not unique, but the closed interval of median points. The median voter theorem holds for sincere and sophisticated voters.

Table 2.1   Equilibrium under simple majority rule

	Voters are sincere	Voters are sophisticated
One dimension	*Median voter theorem* Equilibrium is the ideal point of the median voter	*Median voter theorem*
Several dimensions	An equilibrium almost never exists *Global cycling result* If no equilibrium exists sincere voting can lead anywhere in the space	An equilibrium almost never exists With sophisticated voting cycling is restricted to the uncovered set

If the choice space comprises two or more dimensions an equilibrium almost never exists. An equilibrium exists only in the special case when there is *a median point in all directions*. Every line through this point divides the ideal points such that at least half are on or to one side of the line and half are on or to the other side of the line (Plott, 1967; Tullock, 1967; Davis, DeGroot and Hinich, 1972). Because this condition is extremely stringent, it is said that majority-rule equilibrium almost never exists.[1]

If no equilibrium exists, pairwise comparison leads to a cycle. With spatial preferences, the cycling is not constrained but global, as McKelvey (1976, 1979) and Schofield (1978) formally established. McKelvey's global cycling theorem states that – given Euclidean preferences, two or more dimensions in the choice space, three or more voters, the absence of a median in all directions and sincere voting – any arbitrary point x_m in the space can be reached by a sequence of proposals such that every proposal is majority-preferred to the previous proposal in the sequence. This theorem implies that anything *can* happen under majority rule. With no equilibrium, there exists an agenda that will lead sincere voters to any point.

The instability of majority rule decisions is illustrated in Figure 2.2. The three shaded petals are the set of policy alternatives that are preferred by a majority of the decision makers to the status quo q. This set of points is called the *win set of q*, and is defined as $W(q) = \{y \in X \mid \mid y\,P_i\,x \mid \geq \mid x\,P_j\,y \mid \}$ where $\mid y\,P_i\,x \mid$ is the number of legislators who prefer y to x. Notice that any point in the win set is dominated by some other points in the space. Except for very special circumstances, the win set is nonempty ($W(x) \neq \emptyset$, $\forall\,x \in X$) for any point x in the choice space X, which defines the instability of pure majority rules. To be more concrete, suppose that legislator A is the agenda setter in the example of Figure 2.2. The global cycling theorem implies that she can design an agenda that yields sincere majority choices from q to her ideal point x_A through a sequence of majority votes although x_A is not in the win set of the original status quo (q). Such an agenda is $V = (q, y_1, y_2, x_A)$. Beginning at q, the first vote is between q and y_1. Since legislators A and B prefer y_1 to q, y_1 wins the vote. The next vote is between y_1 and y_2. y_2 is preferred to y_1 by legislators A and C, and therefore becomes the new status quo. Finally, legislator A can confront a proposal that represents her ideal point x_A to y_2. The proposal x_A is preferred to y_2 by legislators A and B, and therefore wins the vote.

The instability of pure majority rules implies that the allocation of agenda rights is decisive for the outcome. If, for example, the right to set the agenda

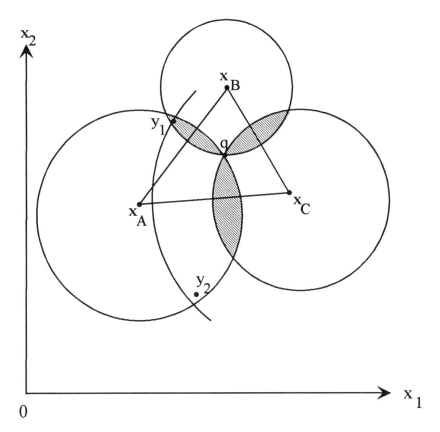

Figure 2.2   Global cycling in two-dimensional space

is transferred from A to B, B can reach her ideal point x_B by an analogous sequence of majority votes, therefore, the delegation of agenda rights is usually constrained such as to limit the advantage of the agenda setter. Examples of agenda delegations are discussed in detail in Chapter 3.

The instability of majority rule decisions and the implied dominating influence of the agenda setter is not constrained to the spatial context. In contrast, the major results were derived using the axiomatic approach. However, these theorems all establish the possibility of a cycle. It remains, of course, an empirical question how often a set of preferences arise that lead to a cycle. In general, when no restrictions are placed on the types of preference orderings decision makers may have, the likelihood of a cycle is high and increases as the number of alternatives or the number of voters rise (Ordeshook, 1986: 57–8; Mueller, 1989: 81–2). A sufficient but strict condition to ensure a simple majority rule equilibrium is the existence of a majority with identical preferences (Kramer, 1973). Less restrictive is the result established by Caplin and Nalebuff (1988). If a consensus exists, defined as a concave function of voters' ideal points, then an equilibrium exists according to a 64 per cent majority rule. The assumption of consensus ensures that the decision group is not polarized. To the extent that the issues to be decided involve redistribution, preferences tend to be polarized which increases the likelihood of instability.

2.3   PURE MAJORITY RULE: SOME EXTENSIONS

The instability and global cycling of majority rules seem at odds with the high degree of stability observed in politics, as pointed out by Tullock (1981) and shown empirically by Stratmann (1996). Different approaches have been used to deal with the conflict between theoretical predictions and observations. One avenue has been to search for *a preference-induced equilibrium* by restricting the dimension or the distribution of preferences (as discussed in section 2.2) or by modifying further assumptions of the model. What happens if legislators vote sophisticatedly instead of sincerely? What happens if legislators are uncertain about the positions of proposals or if candidates are uncertain about the positions of voters in a representative democracy?[2] The other avenue is to analyse institutional constraints in specific majority voting situations and to determine which factors lead to stability and can be used to predict the outcome. This is the approach taken by the concept of the *structure-induced equilibrium* and is discussed in Chapter 3. In between is a literature that focuses on the instability that emerges from a multiperiod time frame. These models analyse how today's majority can bind tomorrow's majority via its policy choice. In the following section, the implications of sophisticated voting, uncertainty and multiperiod choices on the outcome of pure majority decisions are reviewed.

2.3.1   Sophisticated Voting

Sophisticated voting is best illustrated for a finite amendment agenda[3] such that decision makers know the voting sequence in advance. Figure 2.3 depicts a voting tree for a two-stage game in which voters have to choose first between the status quo q and the proposal x, and second between the winner of this first vote against proposal z. It is assumed that a majority prefers q to z, z to x and x to q, such that no Condorcet winner exists. Since sophisticated voters look forward, their decisions in the first vote depend on the correctly anticipated decision in the second vote. In the last stage, nobody has an incentive to vote other than sincerely, hence q wins against z and z against x in the second vote; therefore, the first vote between q and x is in fact a vote between q and z, since z is the sophisticated voting equivalent of voting for x. Given the assumed preferences, q is the (subgame perfect) equilibrium. Notice that if voters behave sincerely, z would be the equilibrium.

Sophisticated behavior constrains majority rule outcomes relative to sincere behavior. Shepsle and Weingast (1984) proved that, from any initial point q, there is an agenda that can lead sophisticated voters to only those points that are not covered by q – and no longer to any points in the space as with sincere voting. All points outside this *uncovered set* are covered by q. The relation 'x

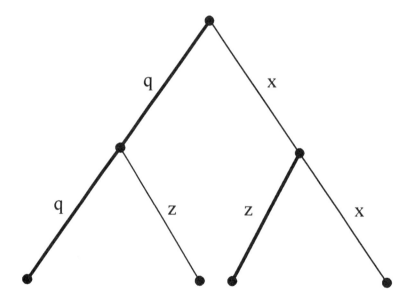

Figure 2.3   Voting tree for a two-stage game

is covered by q' is defined in the following way: q defeats x, $q \in W(x)$, and all points that defeat q also defeat x, $W(q) \subset W(x)$ (Shepsle and Weingast, 1984: 58; for the definition of a fixed and finite agenda, see Miller, 1980; Ordeshook and Schwartz, 1987; and Cox, 1987). Consequently, an agenda setter cannot mislead forward-looking voters to an alternative that is defeated by the status quo and by any alternative that defeats the status quo directly.

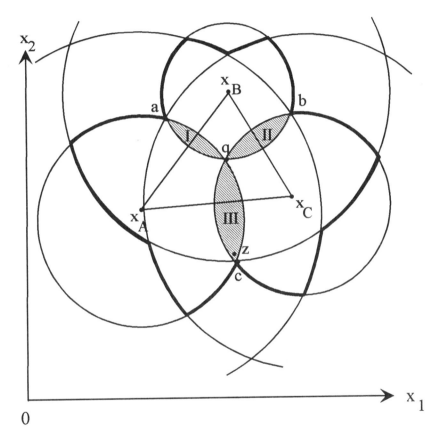

Figure 2.4   Uncovered set of q

In Figure 2.4 the uncovered set is drawn for the same three voters as in Figure 2.1. The three petals, labeled I, II, III, comprise $W(q)$. The area inside the bold surface is the set of points that q does not cover. It is constructed as the union of the win sets of the extreme points a, b and c which are the points in $W(q)$ most distant from q in each direction: $UC(q) = W(a) \cup W(b) \cup W(c)$. Points outside $UC(q)$ are covered by q and therefore will lose against q if voters are sophisticated. For example, if legislator A is the agenda setter how could she reach her ideal point x_A? She has to introduce an alternative z, such that the agenda is $V = (q, x_A, z)$ with the following sequence: q versus x_A and the winner against z. x_A is the equilibrium if a majority prefers x_A to z and z to q in the second stage. Notice that it is not necessary that x_A defeats q. If the legislators vote for q in the first vote, they know that q will lose in the second stage against z. Since they prefer x_A to z they vote strategically in the first stage and choose x_A. Legislator A can successfully realize her ideal point as the equilibrium choice if she chooses z close to c inside $W(q)$. Of course, legislators B and C are worse off in x_A than in q, but as long as B and C do not cooperate, the decisive legislator B votes for x_A and against q because otherwise z would win which B dislikes even more than x_A. Consequently, sophisticated voting behavior does not increase the likelihood of there being an equilibrium but it does constrain cycling to the uncovered set of the initial point q. This set is still large, especially if q is far away from the Pareto set.

2.3.2   Uncertainty

A second approach to explain stability in majority rule decisions has been to incorporate uncertainty (for a survey of early contributions, see Calvert, 1986). The typical application in these models are elections in which voters do not choose between policy proposals but between (usually two) candidates. Uncertainty enters into these models in two ways. First, voters are uncertain for which policy candidates stand and, second, candidates are uncertain about voters' choices. The approach that incorporates uncertainty about candidates' positions is summarized by Enelow and Hinich (1984, 1989) (for recent empirical evidence, see Enelow and Hinich, 1994 and Iversen, 1994 for West European democracies). Uncertainty leads voters to economize on information and to concentrate on a few political labels to identify the expected policy position of candidates. These expectations may vary from voter to voter. Such predictive dimensions (as, for example, left–right or degree of support for environmental protection) reduce multidimensional issues to a few dimensions. For a single predictive dimension, the median voter result applies; for multiple predictive dimensions, the requirements for a median in all directions to exist are again very severe.

The second approach to incorporate uncertainty is to assume that the candidates can choose any point in the policy space but that they are uncertain about how voters vote, that is, that voters' choice is influenced by factors unknown to the candidates (Coughlin, 1992). These models are called 'probabilistic voting models'. The probability that voter i votes for a candidate is a function of the utility this voter associates with the platforms of all candidates

$(U_1^i, U_2^i, \ldots U_n^i)$. For a contest between two candidates, the probability that voter i chooses candidate 1 (P_1^i) is

$$P_1^i = f(U_1^i, U_2^i), \text{with } f_1 > 0, \, f_2 < 0. \tag{2.2}$$

The probability function transforms the utility into probability mountains. Assume that both candidates want to maximize their expected number of votes or plurality and that they present their positions simultaneously. In this case, they try to maximize the sum of these individual probability functions. Under certain conditions there exists a unique equilibrium outcome and both candidates offer the same platform.

A probabilistic description of voters' choice behavior seems at first sight appropriate whenever candidates have incomplete information about voters' preferences or whenever there are random factors that can affect voters' decisions. The requirements for the existence of an equilibrium in probabilistic models seem much less severe than for deterministic voting models in which voters vote with certainty for the candidate closest to his or her ideal point. However, there are two problems associated with this approach, a theoretical and empirical one. First, for a unique equilibrium to exist it is required that the voting probabilities are strictly concave (changing less than proportional) in the loss resulting from the candidates' own policy platforms and strictly convex (changing more than proportional) in the loss resulting from the other candidates' platforms. As Kirchgässner (1996b) points out, these conditions are much more demanding than usually perceived because the strong concavity/convexity assumption has to hold globally. For example, it requires extreme left-wing voters to react stronger to small moves of the right-wing candidate than to changes of the left candidate, which contradicts the empirical evidence.

Second, probabilistic voting models often come up short in terms of testable implications. One empirical prediction of probabilistic models is that both candidates announce the same policy platform (policy convergence), which is at least to some degree in conflict with political reality. To account for policy divergence, it has to be assumed that candidates are at least partially policy-motivated. Then, they not only care about winning the election but also about the policy platform with which they win the election, assuming that they keep their promises if elected (Wittman, 1983; Hansson and Stuart, 1984). In this case however, the conditions for the existence of an equilibrium become again stricter (Lindbeck and Weibull, 1993).[4]

2.3.3   Policy Choice and Stability

A different and additional source of instability is introduced by models of collective decision making which focus on the dynamic inconsistency of preferences for policy outcomes from one period to the next (Glazer, 1989, 1993; Persson and Svensson, 1989; Alesina and Tabellini, 1990; Tabellini and Alesina, 1990; Gersbach, 1993; Besley and Coate, 1998; for empirical evidence, see Crain and Tollison, 1993). These models focus on the choice of one policy issue but comprise two or more time periods. Instability occurs because the current median voter is uncertain whether he or she will be the median voter in the next period, or because the current government has only a limited probability of being reelected in the future. Consequently, today's policies are vulnerable to reversals tomorrow. The inability of present-period decision makers to write a binding contract with the decision maker in the next period is the basic problem in these analyses.[5] As long as current policy makers can affect some variables that enter in the successors' decision problem, they can affect the policy carried out by their successors. Therefore, current decision makers select a different and possibly suboptimal policy to what they would have chosen if they knew they were the decision makers in the future.

Public debt is a standard example with which current decision makers can influence future decisions. If the conflict is about the level of public expenditures (Persson and Svensson, 1989) a conservative government that expects to be replaced by a liberal government in the next election will implement a fiscal policy that features lower taxes and higher deficits than the conservative government would otherwise prefer. The reason is that it wants to control the ability of the future liberal government to embark on a higher spending program. If competing parties disagree about the desired composition of public goods, and there is a positive probability that the opposition party wins the next election, then there is a bias toward larger public debt levels whichever party is in power (Alesina and Tabellini, 1990; Tabellini and Alesina, 1990). Facts can also be created for future policymakers by choosing long-term ('durable') projects even if these projects are more costly than otherwise equivalent short-term projects (Glazer, 1989; Crain and Oakley, 1995). More generally, by favoring policies with high initial costs but low future costs, future policymakers have less incentive to cancel the policy (Glazer, 1993). In contrast, if current policy makers cannot enjoy future benefits, they invest less than otherwise. Garfinkel (1994) argues that this might be beneficial if this behavior reduces military spending and diminishes international conflicts.

Consequently, policy makers that face the problem that their decisions may be reversed in the future, try to reduce the discretion of future policy makers. If they cannot rely on institutional constraints to mitigate this problem, they have an incentive to use their policy choices to influence the behavior of their successors. This latter strategy is costly, however, since it usually requires deviation from the first best policy.

2.3.4 Summary

In this chapter, the conditions that lead to unstable collective choice, based on a pairwise comparison by majority rules, have been reviewed. A large number of scholars have tried to solve the obvious conflict between theoretically predicted instability and observed stability of collective decisions in many democracies. The approaches discussed relax informational or behavioral assumptions and emphasize the prevalence but also the limits of the instability in majority rule decisions. Introducing sophisticated voting does not induce an equilibrium but only limits the area of cycling. Uncertainty about who the future decision makers will be is an additional source of instability even in one-dimensional policy choices. Only if decision makers follow a particular probability function in their majority rule decisions does an equilibrium in more dimensional choices exist.

NOTES

1. This result follows from the application of Arrow's general impossibility theorem ([1951], (1963)) to simple majority rule in the spatial context.
2. A further extension not discussed here is whether logrolling would escape the cycling problem. This is not the case. As Bernholz (1973, 1974) established, the existences of a logrolling situation implies intransitive social preferences and thereby the absence of an equilibrium.
3. In an amendment agenda, the winner of the previous vote is always pitted against the next alternative.
4. A different explanation for why party platforms do not converge is provided by Snyder (1994). He argued that incumbent officeholders can increase their chances of reelection by choosing different party platforms. If voters can distinguish the parties, legislators representing a constituency with preferences similar to the party platform are almost sure to be reelected. If the position of the parties were indistinguishable, the reelection chance for all legislators would be 1/2.
5. Time inconsistency in these models is caused by changes in preferences while the usual time-consistency problem arises because the same government faces different constraints in two periods.

3. Institutional constraints and stability

In the literature reviewed in Chapter 2, scholars analysed the effects of majority rule decisions by formulating their models as generally as possible: participants compare points in n-dimensional space pairwise by the majority rule. Proposals by any member are possible and preferences are common knowledge. With only the majority rule explicitly specified, some scholars have searched for preference orderings that produce a stable point. As Ostrom (1986) correctly pointed out, the result that such points almost never exist is only proven for this very specific arrangement in which the majority rule is not constrained by any other configuration of rules or institutions, and may no longer be true when other rules are fully specified.

This observation gives rise to a substantive, albeit imprecise distinction between preference-induced equilibrium and structure-induced equilibrium. A preference-induced equilibrium is a stable point that is chosen by a collective choice based on an unconstrained or pure majority rule due to a specific preference configuration. Structure-induced equilibrium (SIE) (introduced by Shepsle, 1979) refers to stable points that are induced because the majority rule is constrained by additional rules (or structures). Examples of such constraints are a predetermined voting sequence and the requirement that each issue dimension has to be considered separately. Both requirements limit the set of outcomes that can be compared at each stage. Additional structure is created by allocating precisely defined agenda and veto rights to a subset of participants. Of course, in both equilibrium notions the interaction of rules and individual preferences determine the outcome. However, the research agenda of the SIE pays special attention to the particular decision structure and procedure, and thereby allows spatial models to offer theoretical explanations for observable phenomena.

The equilibrium concept of the SIE is that of a stable policy that cannot be defeated by the application of the given decision rule. In terms of cooperative game theory, points belonging to the SIE are also points in the core. However, the focus of the SIE is on institutional features that render a policy stable. For example, a median in all directions is in the core but not in the SIE, because the stability of this point is not induced by constraints on the majority rule. Furthermore, the concept of the SIE can and has been used in noncooperative game theory (early contributions are by Baron and Ferejohn, 1989a and

Weingast, 1989a). A status quo is a SIE if 'taking no action' is the optimal (Nash) strategy for all players.

The aim of this chapter is to review the effects of some types of constraint on majority rule decisions, which are common in many existing institutions. It focuses on voting sequence, issue-by-issue voting, and on the allocation of agenda and of veto rights and analyses their effect on the outcome of legislative choices. Selected applications of this theory to real world institutions are discussed in Chapter 4.

3.1 VOTING SEQUENCE

The global cycling result implies that a person who has the exclusive right to set the agenda can lead sincere voters to any point in the space including the agenda setter's ideal point. If voters are forward looking, the final outcome is restricted to the uncovered set of the status quo which may or may not include the agenda setter's ideal point. However, it is unlikely that members of a decision group would tolerate the concentration of power in an agenda setter. One way to protect themselves is by constraining the admissible agenda or voting sequence. Notice that the model that produces global cycling assumes that the agenda is built forward; the status quo is voted on first and the most recent proposal is voted on last. Most existing legislatures embody agenda mechanisms that are constructed backward. Alternatives are voted on in the reverse order in which they are placed on the agenda and the status quo is voted on last. An agenda built backward is more constraining than an agenda built forward (Shepsle and Weingast, 1984: 71). Referring to Figure 2.4, building forward from the status quo q, the sophisticated outcome is contained in uncovered set of q, $UC(q)$. Building backward, the winning alternative must defeat q in the last vote, therefore, it must be in win set of q, $W(q)$ which is a subset of $UC(q)$.

3.2 ISSUE-BY-ISSUE VOTING

Members of a decision body who consider complex matters often simplify the discussion by breaking issues into subparts, debating each part separately from the others. Thereafter, the germaneness rule permits discussion only on the specific issues and precludes the introduction of new ones that the members might consider simultaneously. The Swiss Constitution, for example, requires that constitutional amendments include only one issue (see Chapter 6).

Depending on whether voters are sincere or sophisticated and on whether their preferences are separable or not separable, issue-by-issue voting has the following effects, as summarized in Table 3.1.

Table 3.1   Effects of issue-by-issue voting

	Preferences are separable	Preferences are not separable
Voters are sincere	The issue-by-issue median is the unique stable outcome, unaffected by voting order	A unique stable outcome exists, but the outcome depends on the voting order and whether issues can be reconsidered
Voters are sophisticated	The issue-by-issue median is the unique stable outcome, unaffected by voting order	In general, no stable outcome exists If issues cannot be reconsidered, a stable outcome may exist but depends on the voting order

The case for separable preferences is illustrated in Figure 3.1 which portrays three voters' ideal points, x_A, x_B and x_C, some circular indifference curves for those voters and a status quo point q. This configuration of preferences fails to yield a Condorcet winner, because there is no median in all directions. Now suppose that the voters must first vote on issue 1(x_1), and then on issue 2(x_2). The dashed line l_1 that passes through q corresponds to the admissible proposals that the voters can consider in the first stage of voting. It is assumed first that voters are sincere, that is, they do not anticipate issue 2 while voting on issue 1. With separable preferences, the induced preferences on l_1 are single-peaked. By charting a perpendicular line from x_i to l_1, the points on l_1 closest to voter i's ideal point are determined. y_1 is the median point on issue 1 and corresponds to voter B's ideal preference on that issue, x_{B1}. After the vote on issue 1, issue 2 is considered. All admissible motions lie on the line l_2 that goes through y_1. Voter A's ideal policy on issue 2, x_{A2}, corresponds to the median point on issue 2 and the policy y_2 is the median point on both lines, called the 'issue-by-issue median.' Neither reconsideration of issue 1 nor a change in the voting order alters this result. Hence, although the separable preferences of the participants are such that under simple majority rule alone no equilibrium exists, sincere voting on one issue at a time in sequence induces a stable outcome.

Sophisticated behavior does not change this result as long as preferences are separable (Kramer, 1972). Suppose the same voting order as before, first voting on issue 1 then voting on issue 2, sophisticated voters look forward to the second vote on issue 2. Here, everyone votes sincerely such that x_{A2} is the chosen policy on issue 2, independent of the choice on issue 1. In the first vote

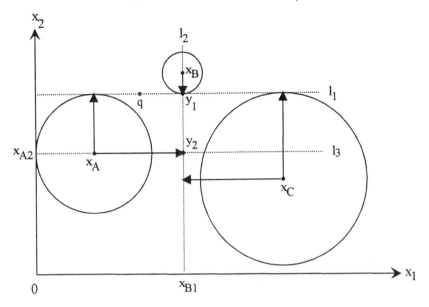

Figure 3.1   Issue-by-issue voting with separable preferences

on issue 1 all motions lie on the line l_3 because everyone knows that x_{A2} will be chosen in the second vote. Again x_{B1} is the median policy and y_2 is the issue-by-issue median also with sophisticated behavior.

What happens if preferences are *not* separable? Consider Figure 3.2 which depicts again three voters with rotated elliptical indifference contours. Such indifference contours reflect nonseparable preferences since the utility-maximizing choice in one dimension depends on the choice of the other dimension. Imagine, for example, that the legislators have to decide how much money to spend for private and public transportation. While some persons may regard these investments as substitutes (as more money is spent on public trans-portation, they want to use less for roads), persons representing the interests of public transportation may want to spend more money on it, the more is spent on private transportation, in order to keep public transportation competitive.

Suppose that the voting proceeds again from the status quo point q first on issue 1 and then on issue 2. As before, because the preferences are convex the induced preferences on the line l_1 are single-peaked but they depend on the specific form of the indifference contours and on the location of l_1. Hence each voter has a conditional ideal point on each issue: the ideal point on one issue depends on the value that the other issue may take (Enelow and Hinich, 1984: 135). Specifically, for voter A, the lines $x_{A1}(x_2)$ and $x_{A2}(x_1)$ are those two

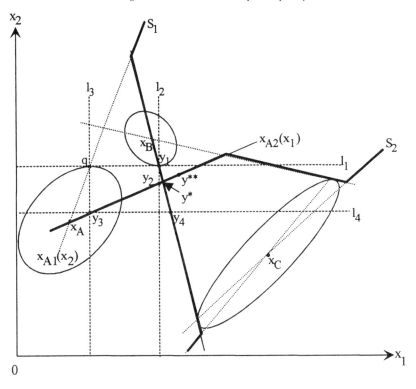

Figure 3.2   Issue-by-issue voting with nonseparable preferences

conditional ideal points for issues 1 and 2, respectively. Finally, the bold lines S_1 and S_2 denote the locus of all median conditional ideal points for any given x_2 and x_1 respectively.

 With sincere voting and the mentioned procedure, voter B's most preferred point on l_1, y_1, is chosen in the vote on issue 1. y_1 is at the intersection of l_1 with S_1. In the vote on issue 2 constrained to the line l_2, y_2 is the median point. However, if the order of voting is reversed (voting first on issue 2, then on issue 1), y_3 is the median preference in the first vote on issue 2: B's most preferred point on l_3 lies north of q, C's most preferred point south of y_3. In the second vote, with y_3 the new status quo, the median point on the line l_4 is y_4. Hence, without separable preferences on the issues, the voting order can affect the outcome. If issues can be reconsidered, neither y_2 nor y_4 are stable: y_2 is not the median preference with respect to issue 1 and y_4 is not the median preference with respect to issue 2. Only the intersection of S_1 and S_2, at y^*, is a stable point from which no further movement is possible. Such a stable point always exists under sincere issue-by-issue voting (Ordeshook, 1986: 254–6). However, it is unlikely that starting from the status quo this point is reached in the first round of voting, rather several rounds of voting are necessary to reach the issue-by-issue median y^* with sincere voting.

Of course, sincere behavior with nonseparable preferences is unrealistic because the choice on one issue affects the optimal choice on other issues. Assume that voters are sophisticated in the sense that they have perfect foresight (Denzau and Mackay, 1981). If the vote is first on issue 1 then on issue 2 sophisticated voters will anticipate that a vote on issue 1 determines a specific point on issue 2, given by S_2, the locus of all median conditional points on issue 2 for given x_1; therefore, they will look for the best choice on S_2. In Figure 3.2, this corresponds to y^{**} which is the most preferred point on S_2 for the median voter (B). In general, y^{**} is not at y^*, the intersection of S_1 with S_2, because in y^*, an indifference contour of B is tangent to the horizontal line through y^* (not drawn), while in y^{**}, a indifference contour is tangent to S_2. As with sincere voting, the outcome depends on the voting order.

Notice that in contrast to separable preferences, S_1 and S_2 are not straight lines; therefore, there is no guarantee that preferences are single-peaked implying that cycling along S_i can occur (Ordeshook, 1986: 263–6). Hence, with nonseparable preferences and sophisticated behavior an equilibrium may not exist. However, an equilibrium is more likely with issue-by-issue voting than under an unconstrained majority rule. For an equilibrium to exist in the former case, preferences have to be single-peaked with respect to the lines S_i while for unconstrained majority-rule voting preferences have to be single-peaked in all directions.

The example of issue-by-issue voting reveals clearly that details of procedure and specific assumptions can be critically important in determining whether outcomes are stable or not. If preferences are separable, issue-by-issue voting induces an equilibrium. If they are not separable, an equilibrium is not guaranteed to exist but intransitivity is limited to the line S_i.[1]

3.3   PROPOSAL RIGHTS

Besides an exogenously determined voting sequence, and the breaking of more dimensional decisions into one-dimensional subparts, the allocation of proposal rights decisively determines the equilibrium in majority rule choices. The global cycling theorem implies that if no median in all directions exists, then, if there is a person with a monopolistic right to make proposals, she can reach her ideal point if voting is sincere, or she can reach her most preferred point inside the uncovered set of the status quo if voting is sophisticated. Of course, the never-ending struggle over policy outcome would just be replaced by a never-ending

Table 3.2   Effects of proposal rights

	Closed rule	Open rule
With gatekeeping	*One dimension* The outcome is the agenda setter's most preferred point in the win set of the status quo The SIE is the interval between the median voter's ideal point and the ideal point of the agenda setter	*One dimension* The outcome is the agenda setter's most preferred point in the win set of the status quo The SIE is the interval between the median voter's ideal point and the point at which the agenda setter is indifferent to the median voter's ideal point
	Two dimensions The outcome is the agenda setter's most preferred point in the win set of the status quo The SIE is only the agenda setter's ideal point	*Two dimensions* The outcome is either the status quo or a point that is in the intersection of the win set of the status quo and the win set of the proposal by the agenda setter The SIE is large and depends on the predicted legislative outcome
Without gatekeeping	*One dimension* The same outcome as in the one-dimensional case with gatekeeping	*One dimension* No influence by the agenda setter. The outcome is the ideal point of the median voter which is the only SIE
	Two dimensions The same outcome as in the two-dimensional case with gatekeeping	*Two dimensions* No influence by the agenda setter. The outcome is a point inside the win set of the status quo, and no SIE exists
		Baron and Ferejohn Agenda setter can obtain disproportionate benefits if voters are impatient and a majority can impose cloture

struggle for agenda control. In reality, proposal rights are more constrained than is implicitly assumed in the cycling theorem. In the following analysis of the effects of proposal rights, it is assumed that all persons are sophisticated and that the status quo is voted on last. Furthermore, it distinguishes between one- and two-dimensional choices.

Proposal rights include two attributes: first, the right to block any proposals and thereby maintaining the status quo (gatekeeping right). Examples of gatekeeping rights are committees in the US Congress (see Chapter 4, section 4.1) and, to some extent, the Commission of the EU (see Chapter 8). More generally, in a bicameral system with both chambers having equal rights, each chamber has gatekeeping rights because it can decide not to consider an issue brought forward by the other chamber. Second, proposal rights include the right to make proposals which are considered subsequently either under a *closed rule* (nobody else is recognized to make a proposal) or under some kind of *open rule* that allows proposals by other persons to be considered after the agenda setter has introduced her proposal. Proposal rights in legislative decision making are typically granted to legislative committees, groups of legislators, the executive or in direct democracies to groups of citizens. Closed rule considerations were predominant in the US Congress prior to the 1970s and are still used in the ratification of international treaties.

The four possible combinations of proposal rights are depicted in Table 3.2. In the following section, there is a discussion on the effects of agenda rights; first for one-dimensional and second, for two-dimensional choices.

3.3.1 One-dimensional Choices

Following the presentation in Denzau and Mackay (1983), Figure 3.3 illustrates the effects of agenda control for one-dimensional choices. x_M and x_A represent the ideal points of the median voter and of the agenda setter respectively, q the status quo, and $x_M(q)$ the point on the policy line where the median voter is indifferent to q. Hence, all points in the interval $[q, x_M(q)]$ defeat q, and therefore are elements of the win set $W(q)$. The agenda setter A is indifferent between the median point x_M and $x_A(x_M)$, and between q and $x_A(q)$. Moreover, a *legislative* or *voting outcome function*, $L(q, y, M(y))$ is defined, which maps a status quo, the proposal of the agenda setter (y), and the set of feasible amendments ($M(y)$) into an expected outcome. This function is the agenda setter's forecast of the consequences of making a specific proposal. If the agenda setter prefers q to what she anticipates would result if she makes a proposal, then she will make

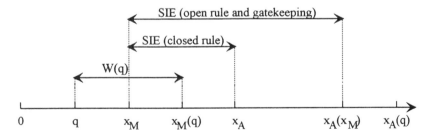

Figure 3.3 Agenda setting in one-dimensional choices

no proposal and with gatekeeping power, q prevails. In this case, q is an element of the SIE. More precisely, a SIE exists if there is a point $x \in X$ such that x is preferred to the outcome that would result if the agenda setter makes a proposal; $x \in P_A(L(q, y, M(y)))$ (Shepsle, 1986a: 115).[2]

Under the closed rule assumption, the agenda setter can make a credible take-it-or-leave-it offer relative to the status quo or reversion point and no amendments are possible: $M(y) = 0$. This model was first analysed by Romer and Rosenthal (1978). Starting from q in the example of Figure 3.3, the agenda setter chooses her most preferred position in $W(q)$ which is $x_M(q)$. More generally, if q is in the interval $[x_M, x_A]$ the agenda setter cannot move policy closer to her ideal point, and therefore will keep the gates closed. Each point in this interval is an SIE. If q is smaller than x_M, the agenda setter proposes her most preferred point in the SIE which is also in $W(q)$; if q is larger than x_A she proposes her ideal point. These results also hold if the agenda setter can be forced to make a proposal to which no amendments are permitted because she can always keep the status quo by proposing it. Notice that the further away the status quo or reversion point from the ideal point of the median voter, the larger is the potential influence of the agenda setter (Romer and Rosenthal, 1978).

Under an open rule with gatekeeping rights, once the agenda setter makes a proposal, any amendments along the policy dimension X are allowed: $M(y) = X$. With any voting sequence, the voting outcome $L(q, y, X)$ is the median point x_M. Hence, the agenda setter will only make a proposal if she prefers x_M to q, otherwise she will keep the gates closed. Consequently, the SIE under open rule and gatekeeping power is larger than under closed rules; it is the set of points in the interval $[x_M, x_A(x_M)]$. However, if the agenda setter can be forced to open the gates and amendments are allowed, the influence of the agenda setter disappears, and x_M is the outcome.

3.3.2 Two-dimensional Choices

The absence of an equilibrium in more than one dimension is responsible for different effects of proposal rights. In addition to the assumption that voters are sophisticated, and that the status quo is voted on last, this study follows Weingast (1989a) in supposing that the proposal of the agenda setter is voted on second to last. Figure 3.4 illustrates a situation with three legislators and their ideal points denoted as x_A, x_B and x_C. Person A has again the proposal rights.

As in the one-dimensional situation, the influence due to proposal rights is absent if the agenda setter can be compelled to make a proposal which is considered under open rule. In this case, the outcome can be anywhere in $W(q)$ and, in contrast to one-dimensional choices, no SIE exists.

Under a closed rule, and independent of a gatekeeping right, the SIE comprises only the most preferred point of the agenda setter in $W(q)$. In

Figure 3.4, the SIE is the ideal point of person A. If the status quo is not at x_A, the agenda setter can always make a successful proposal and increase utility.

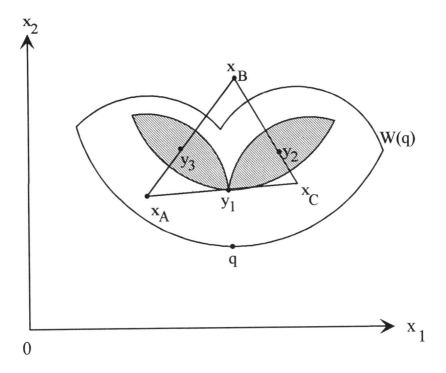

Figure 3.4   Agenda setting in two-dimensional choices

If amendments are possible, the size of the SIE increases dramatically. Even if only one amendment is allowed, the agenda setter can no longer be certain of improving on the status quo. Suppose that she proposes y_1. With the assumed voting sequence, any successful amendment y must beat both q and y_1, that is $y \in W(q) \cap W(y_1)$. In general, this is not a very restrictive condition, as Figure 3.4 suggests: It leaves a large number of opportunities for amendments that benefit other voters at the cost of the agenda setter. Thus, any point in the shaded region, like y_2 could result. If the proposer has the right to keep the gate closed, she has an *ex ante* veto and can only defend the status quo. Since it is difficult for her to predict the legislative outcome once she has made a proposal (no SIE exists), and particularly since the agenda setter is uncertain whether the outcome is worse than q, the agenda setter has an incentive to keep the gates closed even if q is far from her ideal point. In general, the agenda setter will only make a proposal if it increases her utility and makes it impossible for

B and *C* to build a coalition and choose a point that defeats *q* and y_1 and makes *A* worse off than at q.[3]

Obviously, there is a severe commitment problem in such situations: potentially, all three legislators can be made better off if they could enter enforceable agreements. However, even if *A* and *B* agree to choose policy y_3, there remains the enforcement problem, because *A* can always renege and subsequently enter a coalition with *C*. To render reneging impossible, *A* can partially give up the proposal rights. Assume that *A* transfers the proposal right along dimension x_2 to *B* and keeps only her rights along dimension x_1. Such a bargain could be institutionalized within a committee system, with two committees having different jurisdictions and dominated by legislators with different preferences. Such a structure of the decision making enforces y_3: the only possible changes along x_1 are to the disadvantage of the responsible gatekeeper *A* and are therefore blocked, and changes along x_2 are impossible because *B* cannot find the support of a majority to improve the situation.

3.3.3   *Ex Post* Veto

While the *ex ante* veto (gatekeeping right) cannot assure very much for the agenda setter if amendments to her proposals are permitted, an *ex post* veto is more valuable (Shepsle and Weingast, 1987a, 1987b). Shepsle and Weingast argue that in the US Congress, the bicameral conference in which bicameral differences are resolved gives the committees the possibility of vetoing legislative decisions. In the EU, the Commission has the right to withdraw its proposal at any stage of the decision making giving the Commission an *ex ante* veto. Such a veto gives the agenda setter not only the possibility to protect herself against welfare-reducing changes in the status quo once she has made a proposal but confers offensive capacities as well. Referring to Figure 3.4, suppose that the proposal of the agenda setter y_1 stimulates the amendment y_2. Because $y_2 \notin P_A(q)$, with the *ex post* veto, if y_2 passes, then the agenda setter will veto it and reinstall q. A vote for y_2 is in reality a vote to maintain the status quo. But all voters prefer y_1 to q, therefore y_1 will defeat all amendments like y_2. In sum, the *ex post* veto ensures that the final outcome will either be q or an element of $P_A(q)$.

3.3.4   Impatience

All the models discussed so far have come to the conclusion that the influence of an agenda setter is severely limited under an open rule and vanishes completely if the setter can be forced to make a proposal such that she can no longer defend the status quo. Baron and Ferejohn developed a bargaining model (1989a, 1989b) that suggests that even under an open rule the proposer reaps disproportionate distributional benefits in equilibrium even if there are no *ex post* powers as in Shepsle and Weingast (1987a). Since Baron and Ferejohn's model is one of the first with an explicit game-theoretic formulation,[4] their model is briefly outlined here and an illustration given of the equilibrium under open rule for a three-member legislature.[5]

Baron and Ferejohn model a legislature that has to divide a dollar among its members using simple majority rule. In the case of three members (*A*, *B*, *C*), the choice space is three-dimensional. A proposal $x = (x_A, x_B, x_C)$ denotes allocations of the dollar to each of the legislators. Legislators are risk-neutral and seek to maximize their expected share of the dollar. Legislators may be impatient; they may prefer to have a fixed portion of the dollar in session 1 to having the same portion in session 2. Members are thus assumed to have a common discount factor $\delta \leq 1$ which reflects either time preferences or the probability of reelection.

Under Baron and Ferejohn's simple open rule, an unlimited number of proposals may be considered in the course of the game, and a proposal may change the allocation in any dimension of the choice space. Thus, no pure majority rule equilibrium exists if the majority rule decisions were completely unstructured. Baron and Ferejohn based their game on the following structure (see Figure 3.5). First, the agenda setter (*A*) makes a proposal (x_A). Then, each of the other members of the legislature (*B* and *C*) has an equal probability (1/2) of being recognized to make a motion, either to invoke cloture or to propose an amendment. If cloture is moved and it is approved by a majority, the proposal is voted on and, if approved, the dollar is divided. Given complete information, cloture is only moved if it and the proposal pass. If an amendment is offered it

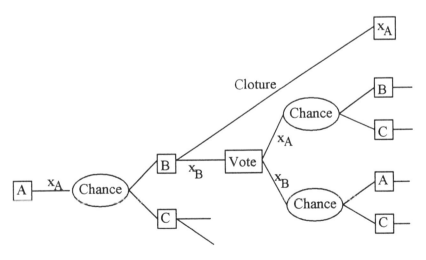

Figure 3.5   Procedure in the Baron–Ferejohn model

must be voted against the proposal immediately; an amendment to the amendment is not permissible. The winner of this vote becomes the proposal in the next session and another member is recognized.

Given this structure, Baron and Ferejohn characterize the stationary subgame-perfect equilibrium. An equilibrium strategy describes which motion each member should make if recognized and how to vote when any possible motion is put to a vote. Strategies are subgame-perfect if it is the interest of each person to follow the specified strategy at every stage that may be reached in the game. Strategies are *stationary* if strategies do not depend on the history of the play, that is a member will behave identically in two identical subgames even if the preceding events differ.

For the simple open rule, the stationary subgame-perfect equilibrium has the following properties: if there is no or relatively little discounting, the agenda setter (A) makes an offer to enough other members to form a majority. With a probability of 1/2 this offer is accepted, and with probability of 1/2 the proposal is defeated by an amendment and the agenda setter loses any procedural advantage. For example, in the three-member case with no discounting, A offers one other voter, say B, 2/5 and keeps 3/5 for herself. This payoff to B must be just sufficient to induce B to approve the proposal if he is recognized. For B to accept A's proposal, the expected value of being the agenda setter must be 2/5, because if B is recognized he is in exactly the same position as the agenda setter and therefore obtains the same expected value as the agenda setter.

The expected value for the agenda setter, V_A, must satisfy the following expression:

$$V_A = \frac{1}{2}\frac{3}{5} + \frac{1}{2}\delta\left(\frac{1}{2}0 + \frac{1}{2}\delta V_A\right). \qquad (3.1)$$

Assuming that the offer of 2/5 to B is just sufficient, that is, B accepts and the play ends if B is recognized. This occurs with a probability of 1/2. If C is recognized, he makes an amendment that offers nothing to the agenda setter and 2/5 to B.[6] This offer is accepted if B is recognized in the next session, otherwise A is recognized again and an identical subgame begins that must have the same value, namely V_A. Solving for V_A yields 2/5 for $\delta = 1$, hence, A's proposal is an equilibrium strategy.

If there is more discounting (δ gets smaller), the agenda setter wishes to include more voters in the winning coalition in order to increase the likelihood that her proposal is accepted. However, she can give each member less because of their impatience; they are willing to accept less in this session instead of holding out for a larger share in the next session. In the three-member case, if $\delta = 0.6$ the agenda setter gives 0.27 each to the other two voters and keeps 0.46

for herself. Although the coalition is larger with $\delta = 0.6$ than with $\delta = 1$, A's agenda rights allow her to gain 46 cents of the dollar in the case with impatience which is more than she gets in the case of no discounting (40 cents).

Baron and Ferejohn's model suggests that even under open rules, the right to propose is valuable and that the winning coalitions often exceeds a bare majority. There are two sources for the proposal power. First, the impatience and, second, the procedural assumption that a majority can end the debate. If cloture requires unanimity, the distribution is equal as the discount factor converges to one.

3.4   VETO RIGHTS

As revealed in the case of the *ex post* veto by the agenda setter, granting veto powers to several players increases the size of the SIE. Veto institutions are widespread in collective decision making and include not only institutional veto players as, for example, bicameral parliaments or executives with veto powers, but also parties in a government coalition (see Chapter 4, section 4.1). As Cox and McKelvey (1984) and Tsebelis (1995a) have proved more generally, policy stability increases with the number of veto players, the more different are their policy positions (lack of congruence) and the smaller the difference within the group that constitutes a veto player (cohesion).

Following Tsebelis (1995a), the argument is illustrated in Figure 3.6, which depicts the ideal points of three players, x_A, x_B and x_C and a status quo q in a two-dimensional context. If, for example, A and B are veto players (that is, they have to approve any decisions) then only a point inside the win set of players A and B, $W_{AB}(q)$ will be chosen. If in addition A and B can make amendments, then only points in $W_{AB}(q)$ that are on their contract curve (the line $x_A x_B$) will be the outcome of the decision (points between v and u). If the status quo is on $x_A x_B$, no policy change is possible. Hence, the SIE comprises the line between x_A and x_B. If player C is also a veto player then any points inside the triangle $x_A x_B x_C$ are elements of the SIE and no change is possible. The SIE comprises a larger area not only the more veto players there are but also the more different their policy positions are. The contract curve $x_A x_B$ or the triangle $x_A x_B x_C$ expands the more dispersed are the ideal points of these players.

So far, veto players were considered to be single individuals rather than a collection of individuals. What happens if these veto players are composed of individuals with circular indifference curves who decide by simple majority rule? For this case, the concept of the *yolk* proves helpful. The yolk can be used to predict how a group decides by the simple majority rule. Although a median in all directions within the group is unlikely to exist, the median lines pass typically near the center of the distribution of the ideal points of the group

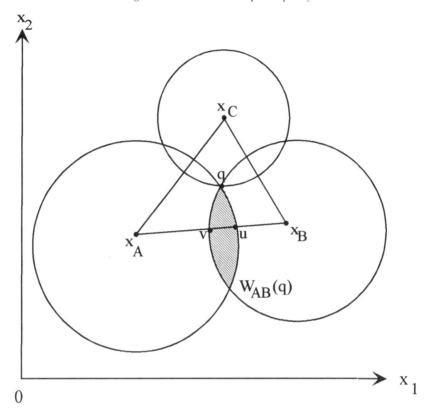

Figure 3.6   Individual veto players and stability

members. Therefore, in a two-dimensional context, a yolk is defined as the
region bounded by the circle of minimum radius r and center c such that it
intersects every median line. A median line partitions the ideal points so that
no more than half of them lie on either side of the line (Ferejohn, McKelvey and
Packel, 1984; McKelvey, 1986; Miller, Grofman and Feld, 1989). If d stands
for the distance of the status quo q from the center of the yolk, then the win set
of q for the considered group is included in the circle with the radius of $d + 2r$.
In other words, a majority of the heterogeneous group prefers q to all points that
are $2r$ further away from the center than q. Referring to Figure 3.7, if veto
players A, B and C are groups of persons with their centers of the yolk at x_A,
x_B and x_C respectively, then, in contrast to the case with individual veto players,
q can be beaten but only by points inside W_{ABC}, the heavily drawn area in
Figure 3.7. The limits of the win set W_{ABC} are defined by circles through the
center of the yolk with the radii equal to the distance between q and the center

plus twice the radius of the corresponding yolk ($2r_A$, $2r_B$, $2r_C$). Notice that the larger the yolk the larger the win set and the less stable the policy choices. Consequently, if the preferences within the veto players are similar or symmetrically located around the center, then the size of the yolk is small, therefore raising stability.

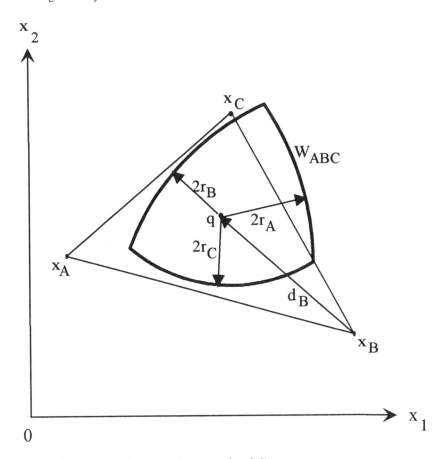

Figure 3.7   Collective veto players and stability

3.4.1   Summary

The discussion in this chapter suggests that the structure of the decision-making process is of particular importance. Voting sequence, the breaking of complex matters into subparts, the allocation of agenda control and the extent of agenda rights, as well as the distribution of veto rights, contribute to stable and consistent policy choices, and thereby overcome the instability of pure or unconstrained majority rule decisions. Furthermore, and more important for applied work, the structure of a decision process is decisive in predicting policy choices. This allows the evaluation of decision rules and the comparison of different decision structures. This issue is taken up in Chapter 4, in which a selective review of applications of this theory to existing legislative institutions is made.

NOTES

1. However, even if sophisticated voting issue by issue according to a prespecified voting order with nonseparable preferences induces an equilibrium, this is no longer true if any issue can be reconsidered after each vote. In this case, global instability prevails again. Here, sophisticated voters have a severe information problem because even perfect information about voters' preferences may not enable voters to forecast the outcome that will be reached on later issues since no equilibrium exists (Enelow and Hinich, 1984: 150).
2. It is assumed that the agenda setter is a single person, therefore, the preferred-to set is used. If the right to set the agenda is given to a group, $W(q)$ instead of $P(q)$ has to be used in the above definition which then corresponds to the formulation in Shepsle (1986a).
3. Formally, the proposal y must be in $PA(q) \cap W(q)$, and must make B or C better off than a point in $PB(q) \cap PC(q) \cap PB(y) \cap PC(y)$. The size of the SIE in situations such as in Figure 3. 4 has not been determined in the literature. Related is the approach by Hammond and Knott (1996).
4. However, Baron and Ferejohn are not the first to apply game theory to questions of legislative choice: see Kramer (1972) for an early game-theoretic spatial model, and, for game-theoretic models with incomplete information, see for example Austen-Smith and Riker (1987) and Gilligan and Krehbiel (1987).
5. The focus of their model is broader than that discussed here. Their model identifies precisely how different institutional arrangements, like open or closed rule, affect the distribution of benefits among legislators and influence the size of the winning coalition.
6. Notice that in this case, C is in exactly the same position as A and, given the assumption that A had chosen optimally, C will make a permutation of A's proposal such that C gets 3/5, B the 2/5 and A nothing.

4. Legislative institutions and policy choices: selected applications

The theoretical debate about majority rule decisions as reviewed in Chapters 2 and 3 had only a limited impact on the first generation of rational or public choice analyses of legislative institutions. In the early applications which were almost exclusively focused on the US Congress, majority rule cycles, so much emphasized by formal theorists, did not seem to play an important role, while features of legislative structure and process which were neglected in the early formal models were much emphasized in applied research (Fenno, 1973; Ferejohn, 1974; Fiorina, 1974, 1977; Shepsle, 1978, 1986b and for a comprehensive survey, see Weingast, 1989b and Shepsle and Weingast, 1994).

In the first half of the 1980s, the inconsistency between theoretical models and the applied literature was mitigated by the institutional enrichment of the analysis of majority rule decisions, as outlined in Chapter 3. The concept of the structure-induced equilibrium based on a politics-of-distribution perspective offered a new way to analyse structures and procedures in real world legislatures and a large number of studies were produced. Primarily, the main focus was still on the US Congress with its dominating committee system and its weak parties. Later, these models were adapted to include political parties, applied to more European-style parliamentary governments, and most recently used to analyse the decision rules of the EU. Furthermore, the concept of the structure-induced equilibrium proves not only valuable in analysing legislative choices but has become an important tool in studying regulatory policy making. In such a situation, an agency (for example a bureaucracy, the government, a central bank or even a court) is allowed to make the first policy choice which may be reversed by the legislators if they wish and are able to do so.

The aim of this chapter is to present and discuss applications of the concept of structure-induced equilibrium to legislative decision making (section 4.1) and regulatory policy making (section 4.2). The survey is selective insofar as it concentrates on those applications that have had a major impact on the theoretical discussion. Furthermore, it does not address in particular the literature on asymmetric information. In some of these models, debate and threats become important signals in a world of imperfect information (Austen-Smith and Riker, 1987; Matthews, 1989; Austen-Smith, 1990; Banks, 1991). Moreover, institutional arrangements may reflect incentives to acquire and disseminate information which provides a different and additional argument for legislative structures than the need to solve distributional issues (Gilligan and Krehbiel, 1989; Krehbiel, 1991). Some of these arguments will be referred to in the discussion of the committee system.

4.1 LEGISLATIVE POLICY MAKING

The basic three assumptions of the spatial approach to legislative choice are:

1. The preferences of the legislators are *heterogeneous*. Due to differences in constituents' characteristics, different responsiveness to distinct interest groups, and maybe due to different personal notations of good policy, policy preferences of the legislators are heterogeneous.
2. The issues considered are usually more dimensional. Otherwise, the position of the median legislator is decisive and gains from logrolling are absent.
3. The majority rule is a binding constraint. Acting alone, a legislator cannot succeed, rather he or she must find the support of a majority in order for a proposal to become law.

As Weingast and Marshall (1988) pointed out, the combination of diversity and majority rule requirement generates gains from exchange and cooperation among legislators. This is illustrated in Figure 4.1 which depicts the by now familiar example of three legislators with different policy preferences and their indifference curves through the status quo q. A pair of these legislators can improve their utility if they replace q with a policy in their respective win set. For example, legislators A and B could agree on policy y_1 which makes both better off than q, but the challenge they face is how to enforce their exchange. After having replaced q with y_1, each legislator, A and B, can improve his or her utility by forming a new coalition with C. B and C, for instance, could agree on a policy in $W_{BC}(y_1)$, say on y_2, and A has a similar incentive to form a coalition with C. Consequently, the existence of cycles implies unstable coalitions, and rational coalition partners discount the potential gains from a proposed trade by the probability of reneging. The gains from exchange can only be fully realized if these exchanges can be enforced. Indeed, as Weingast and Marshall (1988) elaborated, the enforcement problem becomes even more severe if exchanges are not simultaneous (it is not always possible to package all the deals into one bill), and the flow of benefits are not contemporaneous (a polluted river is cleaned up at some point in time while subsidized health care for the poor is an ongoing expenditure).

The insufficient enforcement of legislative exchanges in an unstructured legislature suggests that legislators will search for ways to ensure the delivery

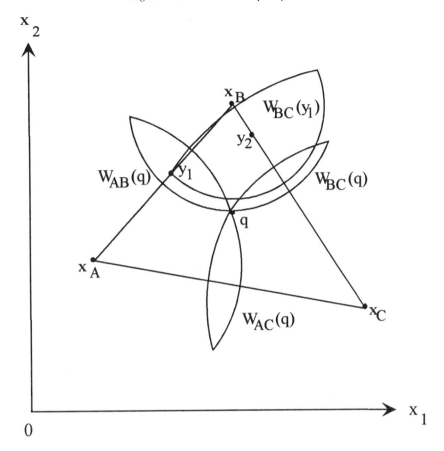

Figure 4.1 Gains from trade for legislators

of the benefits of exchange. The first question is whether repeated interactions alone generate incentives strong enough such that the potential loss of reputation induces legislators to keep their promises. That repetition can generate honest behavior has been argued in many contexts (for example, in market exchange by Klein and Leffler, 1981; in organizations by Kreps 1990; in political contexts by Bernholz, 1978 and Axelrod, 1984; and in game theory by Fudenberg and Maskin, 1986). However, these results rely on the assumptions that: (1) everybody knows who cheated; (2) the payoffs are stable and; (3) the persons remain the same. As Weingast and Marshall (1988) argued, these conditions are not met in politics (neither are they always fulfilled in market exchange, see Kirchgässner 1996a). In many situations, it has to be determined who cheated, persons and payoff change, and information about the past behavior of other persons is costly to acquire. Particularly, legislators face the uncertainty of reelection and cannot bind future legislative sessions. Reputation does not work perfectly in such circumstances. Institutions can improve the efficacy of reputation mechanism by providing governance structures that complement the reputation mechanism in preventing opportunistic behavior – a point on which the economics of organization is also based (Coase, 1937; Alchian and Demsetz, 1972; Jensen and Meckling, 1976; Klein, Crawford and Alchian, 1978; Williamson, 1979, 1985; Grossman and Hart, 1986; Hart and Moore, 1990).[1]

In the face of these problems legislators will devise institutional solutions that 'cope with the need for exchange, the problem of enforcing deals, the problem of extending the life of a deal, and the necessity for making deals robust to unanticipated events' (Shepsle and Weingast, 1994: 155). The particular form of the chosen institutional solutions depends strongly on existing constitutional rules of the collective decision process; among others, on the type of voting system (plurality rules or proportional representation), the number of legislative chambers and on the legislative role of the executive. These rules influence the severity of the enforcement problem and shape the adequate institutional responses.

In the following section, four different institutional devices are discussed that cope with enforcement problem of legislators, namely committees, parties, coalition governments in parliamentary systems and multicameral legislatures.[2] As will become clear, these institutions are to some extent substitutable solutions but to some degree also complementary. Most legislative systems are characterized by a combination of these (and other) institutions.

4.1.1   Committee System

Committees play a key role in the organization of the US Congress and it is not surprising that this institution has attracted much attention by US scholars (classical studies are Fenno, 1973, Shepsle, 1978 and Krehbiel, 1991). According to Weingast and Moran (1983: 771–2), the committee system mitigates the enforcement problem that plagues vote trading in the following way:

> Each legislator gives up some influence over many areas of policy in return for much greater influence over the one, that for him, counts the most. Thus, we find that representatives from farming districts dominate agriculture committees and oversee the provision of benefits to their farm constituents. Members from urban districts dominate banking, urban, and welfare committees overseeing an array of programs that provide benefits to a host of urban constituents.

For committees to potentially institutionalize a swap of influence across jurisdictions they must possess the following properties:

1. Each committee has jurisdiction over a specific subset of policy issues.
2. Within their jurisdictions, committees must retain extraordinary influence
   in their respective policy areas. An important aspect is the committees'
   gatekeeping power (Denzau and Mackay, 1983); the right to initiate
   proposals and the right to prevent proposals made by others from arising for
   a vote. Other procedural advantages can be restrictive amendment rules
   that are beneficial for committees (Weingast, 1989c), and *ex post* veto
   powers due to the involvement of committees in the conference procedure,
   in which bicameral differences are resolved (see Shepsle and Weingast,
   1987a and 1987b).
3. There must be a mechanism enabling legislators to be assigned to a
   committee whose jurisdiction they care for intensively, and these positions
   must be regarded as secure, subject only to successful reelection. Both
   features seem to be partially realized in the US Congress with its bidding
   mechanism for the committee assignment (Shepsle, 1978) and the strong
   seniority system.

Illustration of the point that the committee system allows exchange of votes to
become durable is given with the help of Figure 4.1. Assume that legislator A
and B agreed to replace q with y_1. To make their exchange durable, they further
agree to the following committee assignment: A is appointed to the committee
that has jurisdiction over x_1, and B is assigned to the committee that has jurisdiction over x_2. Suppose that both committees have veto powers such that they
can prevent a harmful policy change in their jurisdictions. Consider the case that
B wants to enter a coalition with C and to replace y_1 with y_2, a policy inside
$W_{BC}(y_1)$. This requires a change of the policy issue x_1 over which legislator A
has a veto right. Since any increase in x_1 is harmful to A, she will invoke her
authority and veto the proposal. On the other hand, if A wants to renege and to
form a coalition with C, B will use his veto right over changes in policy
dimension x_2 and will prevent a policy change. Consequently, committee jurisdiction rights can contribute to the long-term durability of legislative exchange
by preventing reneging and, in the example, allow policy y_1 to become durable.
A committee system with these properties influences the structure of committee
membership, the distribution of policy benefits among the legislators and the
timing of policy changes.

Most debated in the literature is the first point, whether committees are
composed of members with different preferences than the entire parliament
('preference outliers'), as the distributional argument implies (Shepsle and
Weingast, 1987a; Weingast and Marshall, 1988), or whether they are repre-

sentative of the entire Congress (Krehbiel, 1990). Hall and Grofman (1990) pointed out correctly that the self-selection process is a maximization within constraints (size of the committee, each legislator receives no more than two seats, observance of party and regional proportions). Consequently, committees with a narrow jurisdiction whose issues tend to have concentrated benefits and dispersed costs are likely to be composed of preference outliers or high-demanders (for example, the Agriculture Committee). In contrast, broad committees, such as the Appropriations and Budget Committee, are likely to be more representative of the entire legislature.[3]

There is nonetheless substantial evidence that committee members in the US Congress receive a disproportional share of the benefits from their committees (Weingast and Marshall, 1988: 152–5). Among others, committee membership influences the geographical allocation of pork-barrel projects, the distribution of antitrust suits and also the pattern of campaign donations by firms. The classical study is Ferejohn (1974) which documents the number of new projects started in each state as a function of committee membership. In addition, since committees retain a veto right over policy change, policies are partially insulated from small changes in legislators' preferences. A sufficient condition for policy change is that there is a substantial turnover in committee membership so that the new members of the committee have preferences which differ from those of their predecessors.

Referring again to Figure 4.1, suppose legislator A is replaced by legislator C on the committee that has jurisdiction over x_1. After such a turnover in the committee, policy y_1 is no longer stable but will be replaced by a policy inside $W_{BC}(y_1)$, for example by y_2. Several studies have confirmed this argument, and have shown that a large swing in committee preferences leads to large swings in policy. For example, Weingast and Moran (1983) argue that the abandonment of the aggressive consumer activist policies by the Federal Trade Commission in 1980 was due to turnover in the membership of the responsible committee. A similar explanation is put forward by Weingast (1981) to explain airline deregulation, and by Weingast (1984) to explain the deregulation of the New York Stock Exchange. On the same theme Moser (1990, chapter 8), shows that the substantial change in US trade policy with the delegation of trade policy making to the President in the Reciprocal Trade Agreement Act in 1934 was preceded by a substantial turnover in the Senate Finance Committee.

Finally, the knowledge regarding which interests are represented in the relevant committees enhances the predictive power of the economic theory of regulation, particularly if there are more than two interest groups. Gilligan, Moran and Weingast (1989) use such information in their study on the inception of the Interstate Commerce Commission. They argue that because the railroads dominated the committee with jurisdiction in the Senate and the short-haul shippers dominated the corresponding committee in the House of Representatives, these two groups benefited from the regulation at the expense of the long-haul shippers which were not represented in these committees. Ferejohn (1986) shows in his study of food stamp legislation how two interest groups (farmers and those interested in welfare programs) can institutionalize logrolling relationships via the control of the relevant committees.

The politics of exchange approach to committees focuses on preference-based or demand-side rationales for increasing the utility of legislators, but neglects the issue whether committees can increase the efficiency of collective decisions by revealing information and thereby improving the quality of legislative policy deliberation. The latter argument is developed convincingly by Gilligan and Krehbiel (1989) and Krehbiel (1991) (see also Gilligan, 1993 and Gersbach, 1992). If legislators do not know the precise relationship between the selected instruments and the outcome subsequently produced, there is a demand for information and expertise. Granting committees extraordinary influence in their respective policy area gives their members incentives to acquire such information. This argument provides an *additional* reason for why committees are influential; not only because of agenda privileges but also because of informational advantages. Gilligian and Krehbiel insisted that according to the informational argument, committee membership will reflect more a median position – because more representative committees are more credible in providing information to the legislature – and are not composed of preference outliers as claimed by the distributional view. Hence, the two approaches lead (partially) to different predictions.

However, as Shepsle and Weingast (1994: 168) emphasized, since the informational approach is limited to a single policy dimension it assumes away the possibility of legislative exchanges across issues. In a multidimensional space, there exists in general no median position to which the members of a committee could be representative. Nevertheless, the informational approach draws attention to the important point that the efficiency gains based on acquiring and disseminating new information constrain the exchange of influence via committee assignments.

In conclusion, the research on the committee system in the US Congress is an outstanding example of a productive interaction between theoretical and empirical work. The debate among scholars revealed how important institutional details can be for policy choices, and thereby advanced the theoretical understanding of legislative institutions substantially.

4.1.2 Parties

Starting with the path-breaking work by Downs (1957), the focus of the public choice literature on parties has been on the behavior of parties and their platforms, the behavior of voters in choosing representatives and on the characteristics of the outcomes (for surveys see Mueller, 1989, chapters 10–12; Ordeshook, 1986, chapter 4; Bernholz and Breyer, 1994, chapter 14, and the contributions in Enelow and Hinich, 1990 and Ursprung, 1990). Until recently, less attention was paid to the contribution of parties to improve vote trading among legislators. Although the model of Weingast and Marshall (1988) is concentrated on committees, the authors conjectured in their conclusions that strong parties and strong committees are substitutes as institutional underpinnings of legislative exchange. Parties like firms can build reputations different from those of their individual members (on this point, see also Demsetz, 1990). To the extent that they can influence the behavior of their members, parties provide an alternative means of enforcing agreements. Referring again to Figure 4.1, suppose legislators A and B are members of the same party, a strong party leadership may be sufficient to enforce policy y_1, which is a mutually beneficial policy compared to q for both party members.

Cox and McCubbins (1993) develop a theory of party formation (see also Rohde, 1991 and, on the function of leadership in general, Calvert, 1992). First, Cox and McCubbins emphasized that a component of every legislator's election prospect is his or her party label. The attractiveness of the party label is a public good for the members that must be developed, maintained and protected. Since the party reputation is a public good for all legislators in the party, it is likely to receive less attention than it deserves, because of the free-riding incentives of each member. Party members must, therefore, create collective mechanisms to resolve disputes over reputation and to prevent shirking that would undermine reputation.

To improve party reputation and to mitigate enforcement problems, Cox and McCubbins argue that, first, the party members select a party leadership whose renewal depends on the party success in the next election. Therefore, party leaders have an incentive to internalize the collective electoral fate of the party. Second, party members grant their leaders extraordinary influence. For the US Congress, Cox and McCubbins claimed that committee jurisdiction, assignments to committees and floor deliberations are under party control. In more European-style parliamentary governments, it is widespread that party control extends to the allocation of resources for reelection or to the distribution of the seats on the party lists in systems with proportional representation.

Cox and McCubbins provided a large body of empirical evidence. For example, they showed that the party leaders use their appointment power to advance those members in the committees that are more loyal to the party leadership, that is, whose votes are more in accordance with the party leadership (Cox and McCubbins, 1993: 173; see also Crain, 1990). As a consequence, their empirical test based on roll-call votes shows that committees which affect all members tend be representative of the party median (or leadership), while in those committees with a narrow jurisdiction, party considerations are less constraining on self-selection, and preference outliers are possible.[4] Crain, Leavens and Tollison (1990) report that parties control the allocation of political benefits to their members such that less electorally vulnerable members are more successful in having passed bills sponsored by them. There are only a few empirical studies that analyse the impact of party dominance on policy choices. An important exception are Kiewiet and McCubbins (1991) who show that the partisan composition of the US Congress is a key determinant of how funds are allocated to the countless programs and agencies of the federal government.

Parties and committee systems are complementary enforcement mechanisms which may support each other. The argument of Cox and McCubbins adds important insights into the role of parties in organizing coalitions to support legislation and to keep deals intact in the deliberations on the floor, and on the potential damage to parties' reputation from uncoordinated individual optimizing. This approach is particularly successful in countries with a strong party system. Ramseyer and Rosenbluth's (1993) investigation of the Japanese political system is a good illustration as to how a majority party can control the behavior of its members, of the bureaucracy and even of the courts. As Shepsle and Weingast (1994: 170–2) highlighted, what is not addressed satisfactorily by Cox and McCubbins is how the different preferences of members are aggregated into a collective partisan view. The same problem that plagues the legislature as a whole also affects collective decisions within parties, although probably to a smaller extent because parties tend to be more homogeneous than the legislature.

4.1.3 Coalition Governments

Many parliamentary systems, in which the parliament elects the executive, are characterized by coalition governments. This is often the case in those countries that use a system of proportional representation. Formal coalition theory focuses on the formation of coalitions, their size and whether the coalition is stable *at the stage of formation*, that is, whether competing coalitions cannot overturn the proposed policy outcome or the proposed allocation of cabinet positions (the classical studies are Riker, 1962 and Axelrod, 1970; see Laver and Schofield, 1990 and Schofield, 1993 for a survey and extensions and Laver and Budge, 1992 for recent applications). These models devote little attention to what happens *after* a government has been formed. The formation of a government after an election raises several compliance problems, very much analogous to those of individual legislator's trading votes. First, the government might pursue a different policy on an issue than that promised to a coalition member in the coalition agreement. Second, some coalition members might renege by holding up legislation promised to another member.

Austen-Smith and Banks (1990) and Laver and Shepsle (1990, 1996) propose that one way to mitigate these compliance problems is the ministry system. Ministries have the jurisdiction over a well defined set of policies and usually have the right to initiate legislation in their areas. An important variable in the coalition agreement is the assignment of ministers. Delegating initiation and implementing power to the ministries limits the ability of coalition members to pursue a different policy than was promised because the relevant ministry holds the right to initiate legislation and thereby can at least block any policy change.

Following Laver and Shepsle (1990: 875), Figure 4.2 illustrates the ideal points (black dots) of three parties, A, B and C, in a two-dimensional policy space. Suppose, in an extreme case, that ministers can implement their own or their party's most preferred policy within their jurisdiction. This means that only those policy proposals are *credible* that enact the policy preferred by the party that receives the relevant ministry. Figure 4.2 shows the nine credible policy proposals. The first letter identifies the party controlling the cabinet position with jurisdiction over x_1, the second letter identifies the party

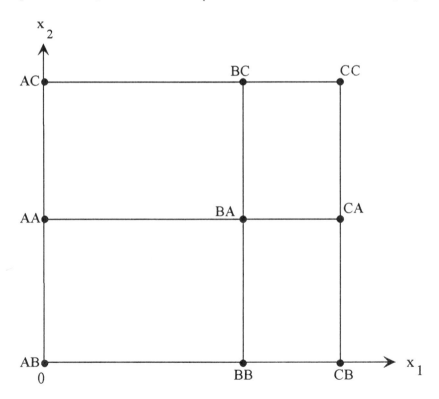

Figure 4.2   Credible policies in coalition governments

controlling the ministry with jurisdiction over x_2. Notice that *AB* and *BA* represent different coalition governments, although they involve precisely the same partners. However, in the former coalition, party *A* controls issue x_1 and party *B* x_2, and in the latter the allocation is the opposite.

This approach to the ministry system has several interesting implications:

1. All policy proposals in the policy space are no longer feasible policy outcomes but only those that are credible, that is, which are policed by an allocation of cabinet positions. The number of credible positions may be quite small if the number of policy dimensions is low, the number of parties small and internal party discipline high.
2. The concept of credible proposals reduces the problem of instability drastically. An alternative coalition can only replace the incumbent government if the alternative is a credible policy and if this is preferred by a legislative majority.
3. This approach explains the existence of minority as well as oversized majority governments. The policy position of a minority government may be preferred by a majority to the incumbent government and itself be invulnerable to other coalitions or minority governments. It is also possible that a party may be needed for the credibility of a proposals even if it is 'surplus' to the legislative majority.

But the ministry system alone seems insufficient to initiate new legislation, and the assumption of policy dictatorship by ministers, underlying the argument illustrated in Figure 4.2, is too strong. However, a main feature of parliamentary systems is that a government proposal has to be approved by each party of the coalition (Tsebelis, 1995a) and that governments can be forced to resign by a 'no confidence' vote. This possibility allows coalition partners to threaten the government if it is not fulfilling the coalition agreement (Baron, 1993). While certainly an imperfect mechanism, the fact that party leaders wish to remain in power places some limits on the degree to which they can deviate from the original exchange without consent of the coalition members.

Empirical research in this area is only beginning and many aspects are not yet fully understood. The contributions in Laver and Shepsle (1994) find substantial support of the central assumptions of the model. These studies also highlight the special role of the prime minister, who sets the agenda and has veto rights in all policy dimensions. Still missing are studies which address the question of the extent to which different portfolio allocation influence policy choices.[5]

4.1.4 Multicameral Legislature

In contrast to the three institutional mechanisms discussed so far, the number of legislative decision-making bodies is determined by the constitution and cannot be chosen by the legislators themselves. For example, bicameral legislature are widespread. Money and Tsebelis (1992, 31) reported that out of 187 territories surveyed by the 1989 *Europa World Yearbook*, 54 have bicameral legislatures. Federal states have almost always and unitary states have sometimes two chambers (Herman, 1976: 4). Furthermore, not only parliamentary chambers act as legislative decision-makers but such a function can also be allocated to voters (as in the case of a popular referendum), to the executive (as in the case of an executive veto that may be overridden only by a qualified majority or not at all) or even to the constitutional court (if the court has the right to review the constitutionality of a legislative act). In addition, parties in a government coalition can act as veto players. The importance of bicameralism in creating checks and balances has long been recognized, starting with Montesquieu (1748) and the Federalist Papers (Madison, Hamilton and Jay, 1788, particularly in number 51) to more recent contributions (Buchanan and Tullock, 1962, chapter 16; Hayeck, 1979; Hammond and Miller, 1987; Riker 1992; survey by Money and Tsebelis, 1992; Krehbiel, 1996 and Tsebelis and Money, 1997, chapter 1).

Multicameral legislatures contribute to the stability of policy choices if the several decision-making bodies have unconditional or at least conditional veto rights.[6] In this case, the results discussed in Section 3.4 on veto rights apply directly. Policy stability increases with the number of veto players or legislative bodies, the more different their policy positions are, and the smaller the differences within the decision-making group is. The impact of the veto rights in the US legislative decision making on the size of the SIE have been analysed in two dimensions by Carter and Schap (1987), Hammond and Miller (1987), extended by Hammond and Knott (1996), and for one-dimensional choices by Ferejohn and Shipan (1990). The relative impact of these institutional actors is shaped by subtle procedural rules (Dearden and Schap, 1994), by the use of commitment devices (Ingberman and Yao, 1991), by partial transmission of information by presidential rhetoric (Matthews, 1989) to reap advantages in these bargaining situations, and by presidential proposals serving as a focal point for legislative activity (Miller, 1993).

The few systematic empirical studies which attempt to measure the extent of the presidential influence find a surprising small impact of the president. Kiewiet and McCubbins (1988) report that from 1948 to 1985 only 6 per cent of the appropriations requested by the president for agency budgets were approved by Congress in an unaltered form. Furthermore, as expected from the logic of the veto right, the president has much greater influence on congressional appropriations when he or she prefers to spend less than Congress rather than more. Surprisingly, the president still has some influence when he or she prefers more than the congressional choice. In contrast, the study by McCarty and Poole (1995) indicates that Congress accommodates less than the agenda control models predict, and that public commitments are ineffective while partisan support of the president in Congress is favorable for the president.

Finally, the distribution of power in multicameral legislatures influences policy choices. Important examples of the relevance of the interaction of various institutions are Alt and Lowry's (1994) investigation of fiscal policy by US state governments and Lohmann and O'Halloran's (1994) study of US trade policy. Alt and Lowry report that fiscal policy (expenditures, budget deficit) is influenced by constitutional constraints (balanced budget requirements), and by the majority party, and that it matters whether both legislative chambers are controlled by the same party or whether party control is divided.

4.1.5 Direct Democracy

A survey on the impact of legislative institutions on policy choices would be incomplete without considering direct majority rule decision by voters. The formal research was initiated by Romer and Rosenthal (1978) and extended by Steunenberg (1992) who analysed the impact of referenda and initiatives on public expenditure. Policy choice is however one-dimensional in this literature, and the agenda setter is usually a single player (for example, an executive or a unicameral legislature). With the emergence of the global cycling theorem, direct democracy has been identified as a pure majority rule and, therefore, regarded as being unable to generate stable outcomes (see particularly Riker's, 1982, critique of populism). However, in many countries, direct democratic decision making combined with representative forms in fact induce policy stability. An example is Switzerland, which is the country with the most intensive use of direct democracy at the federal level. Legislative decisions require the approval of both chambers in parliament and the support of a majority of voters if 50 000 citizens ask for a referendum. Consequently, the Swiss political system consists of three veto players. This creates substantial stability (see Blankart, 1992 and Chapter 5 in the present volume).

In contrast to many previously discussed legislative institutions, there is considerable empirical research on the impact of direct democracy on policy choices. The classical study is by Pommerehne (1978) who analysed the expenditures of the 110 largest towns in Switzerland. Classifying the towns according to their degree of direct democratic participation, Pommerehne reported first that the median voter theorem is important only in those towns with direct democratic participation and, second, that the growth of the expenditures is lower in towns with direct democracy than in towns with representative forms of government. Schneider and Pommerehne (1983) estimated for the communities with representative democracy that their growth of expenditure between 1965 and 1975 would have been 6.8 per cent instead of 9.6 per cent if they had been organized as direct democracies. Similar results are found by

Matsusaka (1995) with regard to the US states. In those states with referenda with respect to expenditures, the expenditures are $60 lower per capita than in those states with pure representative decision making. Direct democracy also tends to reduce public debt, a result reported again for Swiss communities (Feld and Kirchgässner, 1999) and US states (Kiewiet and Szakaly, 1996). The right to participate directly also seems to improve the tax moral. Pommerehne and Weck-Hannemann (1996) show that tax evasion is lower in those Swiss cantons in which the citizens can more directly influence the budget. Finally, Feld and Savioz (1997) reveal an important relation between direct democracy and economic performance in Swiss cantons, measured as the gross domestic product (GDP) per capita. In 1990, the GDP per capita was 15 per cent higher in those cantons with a high degree of direct democracy compared to purely representatively organized cantons. For the average of the period 1984–90, the difference was still 5 per cent.

These results indicate that the choice between representative and direct democracy, or more precisely the degree of representation, has a substantial impact on policy choices. The empirical research has focused on the behavior of lower level governments in federal systems characterized by an intensive competition among jurisdictions. The open issue is to what extent and in which direction does a higher degree of direct democracy influence decisions of large central governments?

To summarize, the literature on legislative institutions highlights the important role of these institutions in mitigating the exchange problem of legislators on the one hand, which allows legislators to improve the enforcement of their policy choices. On the other hand, recent contributions pointed out that legislative institutions are also important in creating incentives for providing information and for improving the quality of policy choices. What is missing in the literature is a unification of these two approaches that would allow the assessment of the relative importance of the distributional and informational impact. A step toward the integration of distributional and informational approaches is the work by Persson, Roland and Tabellini (1996) who show that separation of power induces the revelation of information privately held by the policy makers. The important consequence that follows for applied research is that it is necessary to consider in detail the particular institutions that influence legislative choices, a point analysed in detail with regard to the choice of central bank institutions in Chapter 10.

4.2   BUREAUCRATIC INFLUENCE

A large part of policy choices are not made by the legislators themselves. Rather the legislators often delegate authority to an agent, such as to ministers in cabinet governments, commissions or to bureaus. Such delegation from principals to agents allows the realization of gains from specialization based on training and situation-specific knowledge. A conflict of interest arises between principals and agents whenever they have different preferences or face different constraints *and* the principals cannot observe the efforts of the agents directly (Jensen and Meckling, 1976; Holmstrom, 1979; the survey by Hart and Holmstrom, 1987 and the application to economic policy by Dixit, 1996). This allows agents to follow their own preferences to some degree. Two sources of agency discretion can be distinguished: informational advantages and advantages resulting from the structure of the legislative process.

4.2.1 Information-induced Discretion

It is usually argued that agents possess superior information, for example, they know the costs of providing services which legislators do not know (Niskanan, 1971), or that they are better informed about the consequences of policy choices (Gilligan and Krehbiel, 1987). Agents can use this informational advantage strategically in consciously failing to pursue the policy objective that legislators would desire. The literature on bureaucratic and regulatory behavior has focused mainly on information-induced advantage (Noll, 1989). According to one view, bureaucracies operate with considerable independence from legislators, and the behavior depends significantly on what they maximize: the budget (Niskanan, 1971); the surplus (Migue and Belanger, 1974); a combination of both (Frey and Kirchgässner, 1994: 182–5); or employment (Bernholz and Breyer, 1994, chapter 15) or their own policy agenda. On the other hand, a host of studies on US agencies argue that bureaucrats' decisions directly reflect the wishes of their principals such that there is not much deviation.

The dispute in this literature concerns whose wishes are followed, those of a representative politician (Stigler, 1971; Peltzman, 1976); of Congressional committees (Fenno, 1973, Weingast, 1981, 1984; Weingast and Moran, 1983; Gilligan, Moran and Weingast, 1989); the majority party (Kiewiet and McCubbins, 1991); or the president (Moe, 1985). According to the latter view, elected officials induce agent compliance by using such tools as decentralized information gathering, for example, by particularly affected interest groups (McCubbins and Schwartz, 1984; Banks and Weingast, 1992; Epstein and O'Halloran, 1995). The same purpose is served by organizational structures (Shughart, Tollison and Goff, 1986; Macey, 1992), budgetary control (Carpenter, 1996) and by administrative procedures which ensure that benefits flow to the relevant legislative constituents (McCubbins, Noll and Weingast, 1987, 1989; the limits of this hypothesis are pointed out by Hill and Brazier, 1991).[7] Furthermore, principals can use appointments in order to commit to a certain policy (Rogoff, 1985; Calvert, McCubbins and Weingast, 1989; Spulber and Besanko, 1992; Havrilesky, 1995) and employ promotions as a means to compensate loyal behavior. In any case, politicians can make themselves better off by shifting some resources to monitoring bureaus that are absorbing revenues in ways that do not benefit their constituencies (Bendor, Taylor and van Gaalen, 1985, 1987; Banks, 1989).

4.2.2   Structure-induced Discretion

Besides the informational advantage of agencies or bureaus, agency discretion results from the structure of the legislative process. The idea is straightforward. When legislators delegate authority to an agency, they permit the agency to make the first move; to establish a policy or a course of actions which will be the policy that prevails, unless preempted by legislative action. If legislative decision making were completely unstructured, any policy chosen by an agency could be replaced, whenever several dimensions are involved. This is a direct consequence of the global instability of pure majority rules. However, since most legislatures have structures that constrain majority rule comparisons – of the types discussed in section 4.1 – legislative equilibria exist. Whenever legislative equilibria are created because several veto institutions exist, then, the agency faces multiple principals with different preferences, and can take advantage of this.

This idea is illustrated with the help of Figure 4.3, following McCubbins, Noll and Weingast (1989: 438).[8] There are two chambers (A and B) with equal legislative rights. For simplicity, these are treated as single players with ideal points at x_A and x_B respectively. Since the status quo q is off their contract line $x_A x_B$, both chambers can improve their utility by agreeing to policy y_1 which an agency is asked to implement. If the agency implements a policy off the contract line, the two chambers can reverse the agency's policy. However, if the agency chooses another policy *on* the contract line, say y_2, the legislators cannot reverse the decision because of conflicting interest: chamber B favors the policy by the agency and does not agree to reverse policy back to y_1. Consequently, the agency can potentially choose any point on the contract line $x_A x_B$, with the two chambers unable or unwilling to reverse the policy. Agency discretion is even larger if there are three veto institutions, for example, an executive with legislative veto power. If the executive has preferences different from the two chambers, as illustrated in Figure 4.3 with x_C being the executive's ideal point, no legislative correction or punishment is possible as long as the agency stays within the triangle $x_A x_B x_C$.

The magnitude of agency discretion depends on legislative institutions, including decision rules and party organizations. Models in this line of research accordingly have to include a reasonable set of institutional actors (on US legislative institutions, see Calvert, McCubbins and Weingast, 1989; Ferejohn

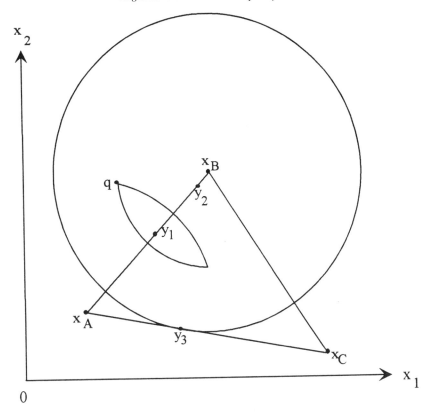

Figure 4.3   Legislative structure and agency discretion

and Shipan, 1989, 1990; Eskridge and Ferejohn, 1992; Epstein and O'Halloran, 1994 and Hammond and Knott, 1996; for parliamentary systems, see Steunenberg, 1994a and Tsebelis, 1995a). One result merits emphasis: the introduction of a gatekeeping institution (for example a committee or a cabinet) without an *ex post* veto power increases the set of policies from which the agency can choose. Under these rules, once the gatekeeping institution has introduced legislation, it no longer has control over the legislative decision. Therefore, a committee or a cabinet with such powers will be reluctant to start a legislative process in the first place that can be exploited by the regulatory agency.

To illustrate this point, suppose now that B in Figure 4.3 is the only player that can introduce a legislative proposal, but has no veto right. B has to predict the legislative outcome when deciding whether to introduce a proposal. The legislative equilibrium will be on the contract line $x_A x_C$, but which point on this line will be chosen depends on the relative bargaining strength and on the precise location of the agency's policy. The most preferred point for B on the contract line $x_A x_C$ is y_3, which corresponds to the most optimistic prediction of the legislative choice. The agency can not only choose a policy inside the Pareto set (triangle $x_A x_B x_C$) but also a point outside this set as long as it is inside the preferred-to set of y_3, the area inside the indifference circle through y_3. Then, the agency can be certain that B will not introduce a legislative proposal. Consequently, gatekeeping rights without *ex post* veto substantially increase agency discretion.

The argument that legislative structure determines the range of agency discretion creates additional reasons for protection against agency noncompliance. Specifically, this is the case in those legislative systems that have several heterogeneous veto and gatekeeping institutions (McCubbins, Noll and Weingast, 1989: 439). First, if political actors are risk-averse, all prefer greater certainty in policy implementation as compared to random noncompliance. Second, they have an incentive to avoid the following negative sum game: after passing the legislation, each political actor has an incentive to spend resources persuading the agency to move policy toward his or her most preferred policy.

Structure-induced agency discretion has interesting consequences for regulatory oversight, as pointed out by McCubbins, Noll and Weingast (1989). Since it is often impossible for legislators to correct agency's decisions, *ex post* rewards are not an effective means for achieving compliance. Rather cumbersome decision-making processes, such as hearings, that warn the principals of noncomplying decisions before they are taken, can be in the interest of political actors. The ineffectiveness of *ex post* sanctions provides an additional argument why politicians have an incentive to set up decision-making environments which compel the agency to be responsive to the constituency interests that were represented in the enacting coalition. In this way, it is difficult for the agency to deviate from the agreed policy which is in the interest of the enacting coalition. Examples of such constraints are the allocation of the burden of proof and the granting of rights to take legal actions against agency decisions affecting particular interest groups.

The implementation process of common policies in the EU is a good example of structure-induced discretion. The Commission is an important player in the legislative process (as discussed in detail in Chapter 8), and is also allowed to implement common policies. Because of the qualified majority (and sometimes even unanimity) requirement in the Council, the veto rights of the EP and because of the Commission's agenda rights, the size of the legislative SIE can be quite large, particularly if the players have heterogeneous preferences. This set of points represents the feasible Commission policies, defined as those policies that the Commission can implement without being reversed by the legislators. In addition, the implementation decisions of the Commission are made conditional on specific procedural requirements, the so-called 'comitology procedures' (analysed in detail by Steunenberg, Koboldt and Schmidtchen, 1996, 1997 and Steunenberg, 1997). A common element in these procedures is that a committee of national governmental officials from the various member states reviews the Commission's implementation proposal. While such procedures may reduce the informational advantage of the Commission, it is possible that structure-induced discretion increases. The reason is that additional gatekeeping players are created: the committee might accept or not disagree with a proposal by the Commission because otherwise the Council can choose a policy which might be worse to the decisive committee member than the Commission's proposal. Then, the Commission can take advantage of this behavior (Steunenberg, 1997). Notice that the comitology procedure may reduce the informational source of the Commission's discretion while the structure-induced discretion rises, leaving the net effect ambiguous.

This approach is not limited to regulatory and executive behavior but can be and has been extended to explaining the behavior of courts.[9] The logic of the argument is the same as for a regulatory agency. A court interprets a statute or a regulatory action but its interpretation can be corrected by the legislators in case of a statutory interpretation or by the constitutional decision makers in case of a constitutional interpretation. Since such corrections are often impossible, particularly if a change in the constitution is required, courts enjoy a large degree of discretion. In this case, appointments and promotions as well as accepted legal reasoning serve as important constraints for courts.

4.2.3 Summary

This chapter, has reviewed major applications of spatial models to existing legislative processes. First, various institutions, such as committees, parties, cabinet systems and multicameral legislatures are not only important in improving the quality of the discussion, but also, by creating veto institutions, they make it more likely that an equilibrium of collective choices exists in multidimensional issues. A second result is that the design of legislative procedures, particularly the allocation of agenda rights, influences the outcome of policy choices which, once chosen, cannot be readily modified. As a result, this literature contributes to an institutionally enriched theory of public choice and provides a theoretical basis for comparative empirical research. A third point is that the existence of political institutions has implications for legislative delegation to agencies. A regulatory agency can take advantage of structure-enhancing legislative institutions and choose the most preferred policy within the set of stable outcomes. Legislators may wish to constrain such agency discretion by regulatory oversight, particularly because *ex post* sanctions are often an ineffective means. The structure of an agency, process requirements and appointments become important means of regulatory oversight.

NOTES

1. The same argument is the starting point for the work by Milgrom, North and Weingast (1990) who argued that institutions facilitate exchange by providing information on the behavior of others in a large group. North and Weingast (1989) and Greif, Milgrom and Weingast (1994) extended this argument by emphasizing that institutions play an important role in coordinating the punishment against transgressors. A related argument is used by Root (1989, 1994) to explain commitment problems of the French monarchy.
2. For excellent in-depth studies of the impact of parliamentary structures on legislative outcomes in West European countries, see the contributions in Döring (1995).
3. Both sides of the debate provide empirical evidence supporting their views. The most comprehensive test is by Krehbiel (1990) who found no committee bias. His test is criticized by Hall and Grofman (1990) because Krehbiel's test is based on roll-call votes which tend to underestimate differences in the presence of logrolling. Using constituency characteristics, Hall and Grofman found evidence that the Agriculture Committee and several subcommittees are biased compared to the entire Congress. On this issue, see also Londregan and Snyder (1994).
4. In contrast, Krehbiel (1993) could not find a significant influence of parties after controlling for preferences. However, there is a problem of causality: representatives with substantially different preferences usually belong to different parties. For a more general critique of the use of roll-call votes, see Hall and Grofman (1990) and Snyder (1992).
5. An interesting extension is to combine theories of election with theories of coalition formation (Austen-Smith and Banks, 1988; Baron 1991, 1993). If voters are interested in policy outcomes, they have to take into account the subsequent coalition formation already at the election stage.
6. Conditional veto rights can be defined as the veto rights of one chamber that can be overridden by the other chamber(s) but only by a decision rule that requires a larger majority than is otherwise used.
7. Of course, the courts' interpretation of procedural rights constrains politicians in designing procedures to endure a particular policy outcome (McCubbins, Noll and Weingast, 1990). However, legislators can also influence statutory interpretation by courts. As Rodriguez (1992) argued, since courts pay attention to legislative history, legislators have an incentive to shape legislative history such that it constrains judicial interpretation.
8. For a one-dimensional representation see Ferejohn and Shipan (1990) and Steunenberg (1996).
9. For constitutional interpretation, see Marks (1988); Gely and Spiller (1990 and 1992); for statutory interpretation, see Ferejohn and Weingast (1992) and Ferejohn (1993); for the choice between judicial doctrines, see Spiller and Spitzer (1992); for an empirical test with respect to the Supreme Court, see Segal (1997); for a related explanation of the behavior of the European Court of Justice, see Garrett (1995a).

PART II

Institutions and stability:
Checks and balances in the Swiss political
system

Introduction to Part II

As discussed in Part I, political stability depends on the structure within which political decisions are taken. Since the overwhelming part of the literature focuses on the political system of the United States, most analyses are concentrated on forms of representative democracy. Direct democracy has not drawn much attention until recently because it may be regarded as a pure majority rule and, therefore, would seem unable to generate stable outcomes (see Riker's, 1982, critique of populism). An exception is the literature initiated by Romer and Rosenthal (1978), and also the work by Steunenberg (1992) who analysed the impact of referendum and initiative on public expenditure. However, in this work policy choice is one-dimensional and the agenda setter is usually a single player (for example an executive or a unicameral legislature).

However, the arguments presented in the following Chapters 5 and 6 point out that direct democratic decision making combined with representative forms can, in fact, induce policy stability.[1] Switzerland is the prototype of such a combination of direct democratic decision making with representative forms of democracy and has long been admired for its political stability. Swiss politics is predictable in the sense that major policy changes are regarded as very unlikely to occur. This characteristic proved to be a major advantage because it provided stable property rights. In recent years, however, Swiss economic policy has been criticized for its lack of action in face of worldwide deregulation which has eroded traditional advantages of Switzerland (Borner, Brunetti and Straubhaar, 1990). The same groups that benefited from the political stability now seem to be harmed by its immobility. Not surprisingly, a number of proposals have been advanced that aim at changing the political process (Borner, Brunetti and Straubhaar, 1990, 1994; Germann, 1990, 1994; Kolz and Müller, 1990; Borner et al. 1991; Moser, 1991; Wittmann, 1992; Linder, 1994; Kleinewofers, 1995) and some of these proposals have been included in the recent proposition for a new Constitution by the Federal Government (Bundesrat, 1995).[2] However, all these proposals are ad hoc in the sense that they are not based on a comprehensive and theoretically rigorous analysis of the political system. Part II of this study takes a first step in this direction by applying spatial models or positive political theory that allows the analysis of major aspects of the Swiss political system.

The organization of Part II is as follows: first, the characteristics of the Swiss political system are summarized below. In Chapter 5, the legislative decision making process is analysed. Chapter 6 focuses on the constitutional decision rules, and assesses the impact of two prominent reform proposals, namely the modification to the optional referendum and the introduction of a constitutional review of statutes by the Federal Court. Chapter 7 extends the model to include uncertainty of legislators about the location of the median voter and analyses the impact of interest groups.

THE POLITICAL SYSTEM OF SWITZERLAND

In 1848, the previous loose confederation of states in Switzerland was replaced by a soundly structured federal state, and the Swiss Federal Constitution was drawn up. This reserved some limited powers to the federal authorities but gave all the rest to the 26 cantons. In the course of time further obligations were allotted to the central authorities and a number of popular rights were guaranteed federally.

The senior executive body at the federal level is the Federal Council, which consists of seven ministers of equal rank. They are elected individually for a four-year term by Parliament, and each year one of them is elected to the post of President of the Confederation. This does not give the holder any additional power except to chair meetings of the Federal Council and to carry out certain representative duties. Since 1959 the Federal Council has been composed of two Radicals, two Christian Democrats, two Social Democrats, and one representative of the Democratic Union of the Centre, which is oriented toward farmers and businesspeople. Parliament consists of two chambers: the National Council represents the population as a whole. Its 200 members are elected for a term of four years, the distribution of seats being calculated according to the strength of the political parties. The Council of States, with 46 members, represents the cantons. Each canton, regardless of size, elects two members according to its own electoral system. The Federal Court reviews legislation by cantons and communities whether these are in accordance with the Federal Constitution. However, the Court does not have the right to review federal statutes.

The voters in Switzerland always have the last word. In constitutional decisions, any amendment must be approved by the majority of the voters nationwide and by majorities in a majority of the cantons (qualified majority rule). In addition, changes to the Federal Constitution can be requested by means of a petition signed by at least 100000 voters. In legislative decisions, voters cannot put forward a proposal, but if a minimum of 50000 voters challenge a proposed federal law, the proposal is submitted to a simple majority vote (optional referendum).

NOTES

1. Less formally developed but related to the arguments presented here is the research by Blankart (1992).
2. The two recent volumes by Hug and Sciarini (1996) and by Borner and Rentsch (1997) comprise a large number of interesting contributions that discuss the need and possible directions of institutional reforms in Switzerland.

5.   A model of legislative decisions

The details of the legislative decision rule in Switzerland are as follows: proposals can be initiated by members of both chambers of the parliament and by the executive. For a legislative proposal to become law it has to be approved by the Council of States and the National Council by a simple majority vote. If 50 000 people sign up for a referendum, the proposal is submitted to a simple majority vote. Otherwise, the legislative proposal becomes law without a formal approval by the voters.

The impact of this rule is analysed on the degree of stability; first, for single issue decisions and second, for decisions that include simultaneously two different issues. For simplicity, assume that the costs to collect 50 000 signatures are trivial because it requires only the support of about 1 per cent of all voters. Therefore, suppose for the moment that a referendum takes place whenever the median voter prefers the status quo to the proposal. Chapter 7 includes the costs of collecting signatures and uncertainty into the model which allows the analysis of the strategic interaction between the parliament, interest groups and the median voter.

5.1   ONE-DIMENSIONAL CHOICES

An example of a one-dimensional choice is given in Figure 5.1. The ideal points of the medians in both chambers (S and N) will generally not be identical because the regional composition in the two Councils differs and their members are elected under different rules (two member districts with majority rule for the Council of States versus list system with proportional representation for the National Council).[1] In a pure bicameral system, the equilibrium includes all points in the interval [S, N]. If the status quo is inside this interval no proposal will be forthcoming because a move to the right would be vetoed by the Council of States and a move to the left by the National Council. With the introduction of the optional referendum a third player exists, namely the people. If the median voter's ideal point (P) is between S and N (as in Figure 5.1(a)), the referendum does not change the set of equilibrium points. If P is outside this interval (as in Figure 5.1(b)) the equilibrium of the bicameral referendum game comprises a larger interval than in the bicameral game and includes the set of

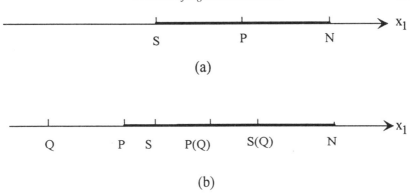

Figure 5.1   Equilibrium in one-dimensional legislative choices

points between P and N.[2] The larger the set of equilibrium points the more likely it is that the status quo is an equilibrium point and no policy change possible. Therefore, the following proposition follows:

Proposition 5.1   In one-dimensional decisions, the set of equilibrium points in the bicameral-referendum game is at least as large as in the bicameral game

How much does the optional referendum constrain the two Councils if the status quo is outside the equilibrium? This depends on the position of P. In the case of Figure 5.1(b), P is constraining the bicameral choice, because policy cannot be moved to the right of $P(Q)$, the point that leaves the median voter indifferent to Q. Otherwise, the proposal is vetoed by the people. Hence, the choice of the Council of States and the National Council is restricted to a policy between S and $P(Q)$. Assuming that their bargaining position is equally strong, it is supposed that the two chambers agree on a policy that corresponds to the middle of the feasible equilibrium interval $[S, P(Q)]$, that is to $(P(Q) + S)/2$. For the ordering in Figure 5.1(b) (with $Q < S < S(Q) < N$), the solid line in Figure 5.2 characterizes the relationship between the position of P and the outcome. There are four different cases depending on the location of P:

(i) $P \le Q : x = Q$

(ii) $Q < P \le \dfrac{Q+S}{2} : x = P(Q)$

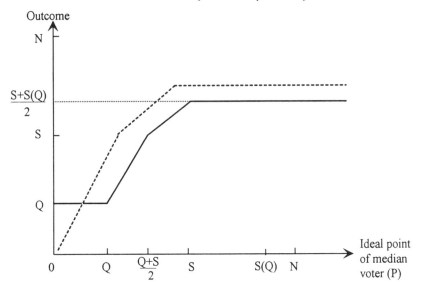

Figure 5.2   Location of median voter and legislative choices

(iii) $\dfrac{Q+S}{2} < P < S : x = \dfrac{S+P(Q)}{2}$

(iv) $P \geq S : x = \dfrac{S(Q)+S}{2}$

In the first case, where P is at the status quo or to the left, Q is an equilibrium point and no change occurs. If P is between Q and $(Q + S)/2$ both Councils want to move policy as far as possible, that is to $P(Q)$. In the third case, which corresponds to the situation drawn in Figure 5.1(b), the Council of States and the National Council split the distance between S and $P(Q)$. Finally, if P is at S or to the right, the referendum does not restrain the bicameral game and the point in the middle of S and $S(Q)$ is chosen. In the absence of the referenda, the parliament always chooses $(S(Q) + S)/2$ as in the fourth case. Consequently, the referendum has a status quo preserving bias inasmuch as it reduces policy changes in certain conditions and has no impact otherwise.[3] This is precisely stated in the following proposition:

Proposition 5.2   In one-dimensional decisions, the threat of a referendum prevents or reduces a policy change if and only if P *is on the same side outside the equilibrium of the bicameral game (interval* [S, N]) *as* Q

In addition, as Romer and Rosenthal (1978) established, the impact of the referendum is smaller the further away the status quo or reversion point from the ideal points of the three players. The dashed line in Figure 5.2 represents the outcome if the status quo is equal to zero. For most possible locations of P, the shift of the status quo from Q to zero reduces the impact of the people. The reason is that (for $P > Q$) the median voter dislikes a status quo at zero more than at Q which allows the agenda setters (N and S) to realize a policy closer to their preferences. As a consequence, sunset clauses which set the reversion point to zero can reduce the impact of the referendum.

Concluding this section, some comparative static results are pointed out. First of all, many changes in the ideal points P, S, N do not translate into policy changes. Assume that P and Q are between S and N. If N and P move to the right but S does not shift, no policy change occurs. The status quo will only be replaced if the ideal points of the players move in such a way that Q shifts outside the set of points included between P, S and N. This is the case, for example, if P, S and N all shift enough in the same direction. Second, the induced policy modification typically will not be marginal but rather substantial. Since once the status quo is outside the equilibrium range, the win set is typically large in the sense that a substantial policy change can be realized. Hence, as long as Q is an equilibrium point, nothing happens. If the range of equilibrium outcomes moves such that Q is outside, a discontinuous policy change occurs. This result corresponds with an observed pattern in politics in which a policy is stable for a long time but, at some point in time, a substantial reform takes place.[4]

5.2   TWO-DIMENSIONAL CHOICES

The introduction of a second issue changes the nature of the results for majority-based voting systems fundamentally, inasmuch as no equilibrium exists in general. In the following, an investigation is carried out on whether the results found for one-dimensional decisions are valid in two-dimensional choices as well. First, I look at the bicameral game and then add the referendum.

Hammond and Miller (1987) demonstrated that, in the case of two dimensions, bicameral games have an equilibrium in certain conditions.[5] To describe these conditions the concept of bisectors is introduced. For an odd number of members, a *chamber bisector* is a line through two ideal points of members of the same chamber such that the number of ideal points lying on this line plus the number of ideal points to one side constitute a majority and the number of ideal points on the line plus the ones on the other side constitute a majority. A *bicameral bisector* is a line through the ideal points of two members from different chambers such that the ideal points on the line plus the ideal points on either side of the line constitute a joint majority in both chambers. For an odd number of members in both chambers, the bisectors are attractive both ways, that is, for any point not on the bisector there is a point on the bisector that is preferred by a majority. These definitions are illustrated in Figures 5.3 and 5.4 with the two chambers each having three members (S_1, S_2, S_3 and N_1, N_2, N_3). The chamber bisectors are drawn in Figure 5.3. Since there are only three members in each chamber, the chamber bisectors are the lines between the ideal points of each member. In Figure 5.3, there is just one bicameral bisector, namely the line through N_3S_2 while three bicameral bisectors exist in Figure 5.4.

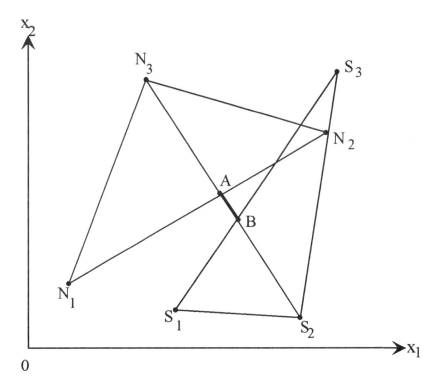

Figure 5.3   Chamber and bicameral bisectors with equilibrium

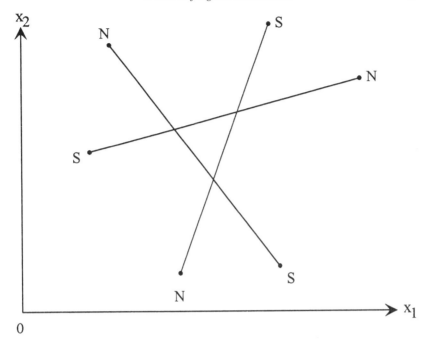

Figure 5.4   Bicameral bisectors without equilibrium

For an odd number of members, an equilibrium exists only if:

1. in the case of three or more bicameral bisectors they intersect all at the same point; or if
2. in the case of one bicameral bisector there is a point *x* on the bicameral bisector such that chamber bisectors from only one chamber intersect at the bicameral bisector in each direction from *x* (Theorems 2 and 3 in Hammond and Miller, 1987).

Condition (2) is illustrated in Figure 5.3. The set of points between *A* and *B* on the bicameral bisector $N_3 S_2$ is the equilibrium because majorities in both chambers want to move in opposite directions. Condition (2) requires that the two chambers are substantially heterogeneous. Otherwise, an equilibrium exists only if condition (1) is met, a case that is unlikely to occur (see Figure 5.4 where no equilibrium exists). However, if there is an even number of members in one or both chambers, Hammond and Miller conjectured that there is usually an equilibrium.

To introduce the referendum into the bicameral game, voters are regarded as a third player which can veto any changes. The following proposition is easily proved:

Proposition 5.3   An equilibrium in the bicameral referendum game exists if an equilibrium exists between at least one pair of the three players

By definition of the bicameral referendum game, any change has to be approved by all three players (both chambers and the people). If a point is an equilibrium in the interaction between two of these players, a change would make at least one of the two players worse off and she would, therefore, veto it. With the introduction of a third veto player, a point inside the two-player equilibrium remains an equilibrium point. Hence, if an equilibrium exists between a pair of the three players, this point is also an equilibrium in the bicameral referendum game.

To keep the illustration tractable, only three voters (P_1, P_2, P_3) are depicted which could stand for three homogeneous groups of voters of equal number. Figure 5.5 shows a situation in which an equilibrium in the bicameral

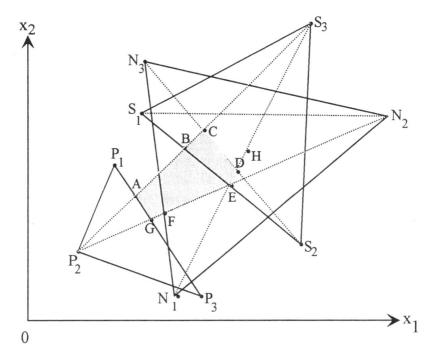

Figure 5.5   Equilibrium in the bicameral referendum game

referendum game exists although there is no bicameral equilibrium. The voters have an equilibrium with each of the chambers (line AB on the bicameral bisector P_2S_3 with the Council of States and line GF on the bicameral bisector P_2N_2 with the National Council). However, the equilibrium of the bicameral referendum game is much larger than the sum of the two-player equilibria and comprises the area $ACDEG$. A point inside this area cannot be replaced by another point. For example, a point that the two chambers prefer C lies on the bicameral bisector N_1S_3, as for instance point H. However such a change would be vetoed by the people. In contrast, H is outside of the equilibrium because majorities in both chambers and the people would prefer a point on N_3S_2.

Obviously, an equilibrium in the bicameral referendum game does not always exist. If the ideal points of both chambers and the people are identically distributed, the bicameral referendum game is the same as a unicameral system and no equilibrium exists. The more heterogeneous the distribution of ideal points among the three players, the more likely is an equilibrium.[6]

5.5.1 Summary

In a bicameral system with referendum, an equilibrium is more likely to exist and if it exists the set of undominated points is often larger than in a bicameral system without referendum. The larger the equilibrium, the more likely it is that the status quo is inside the equilibrium and no policy change can occur. Consequently, the introduction of the referendum tends to increase policy stability for legislative choices not only in decisions involving one-dimensional but also in two-dimensional choices.

NOTES

1. This is supported by the fact that the party composition in both chambers differs considerably. In the legislative period 1995–99, the two largest conservative parties (FDP and CVP) have together 40 per cent of the seats in the National Council but a solid majority of 72 per cent in the Council of States. In contrast, the Social Democrats have 27 per cent in the National Council but only 11 per cent of the seats in the Council of States.
2. It might be wondered whether P can lie outside the interval $[S, N]$. Since the small cantons have the same weight as the populous ones in the Council of States, the median member of the Council of States and the median voter do not have the same policy position in general. Less obvious is the deviation between N and P because the National Council's membership is according to the population share of each canton elected by a list system with proportional representation. Nonetheless, the link between voters and representatives is indirect, because a vote first counts for the party list which determines the number of seats for the party and only afterwards decides which candidate receives one of the party seats. How often P is outside the interval $[S, N]$ is, of course, an empirical question.
3. This conclusion is well accepted in political science (Möckli, 1993), however not as a theoretically derived conclusion but rather as a stylized fact. A different explanation for the status quo bias is given by Ursprung (1994), who argued that the status quo preserving function of the

referendum is due to a status quo bias in individual decisions in an environment of incomplete information. In the model in this study, the bias is a consequence of the decision rules and occurs even if all actors are completely informed. See Chapter 7 for a discussion of the impact of uncertainty.

4. The executive which applies the statutes has not been mentioned here. Obviously, the larger the set of equilibrium points in the bicameral referendum game, the larger the set of politically viable interpretations by the executive or the larger their discretion (see Chapter 4, section 4.2).

5. With more than two dimensions, an equilibrium does not exist in general, but an uncovered set is likely to exist (Tsebelis, 1993).

6. Furthermore, it is possible to find situations in which no equilibrium exists between any two players but there is an equilibrium in the interaction between all three. However, it is not possible to state the necessary conditions for this case.

6. A model of constitutional decisions

The Swiss Constitution can be changed either completely or partially. A proposal can be put forward either by the parliament (that is by a majority in both houses) or by any group of people that has support for their proposal from 100 000 citizens (popular initiative). A proposal is only allowed to include a single issue otherwise it can be invalidated by the parliament.[1] For a proposed amendment to be accepted, it has to be approved by the majority of the voters nationwide and by majorities in a majority of the cantons (qualified majority rule). Since the existence of the constitution in 1848, the Constitution has been amended more than 130 times, and complete revisions took place in 1974 and 1999. The following analysis examines the impact of the decision rules on stability; in section 6.1, for choices about one issue and; in section 6.2, for choices involving two issues. Finally, in section 6.3, the consequences of recently suggested reform proposals are discussed.

6.1   ONE-DIMENSIONAL CHOICES

Because of the existence of the popular initiative, the parliament no longer possesses its monopoly for proposals as it does in the legislative process. Consequently, in constitutional decisions only two players are decisive, the median voter nationwide and the median voter in the median canton. The following proposition identifies the equilibrium of the qualified majority rule for one-dimensional choices:

Proposition 6.1   For one-dimensional decisions, the qualified majority requirement generally expands the set of equilibrium points in comparison with simple majority rule

Since cantons differ in their economic structure and are of unequal size, the ideal point of the median voter in the nationwide electorate (P) and the ideal point of the median voter in the median canton (C) are different in general, as depicted in Figure 6.1. While with simple majority rule the equilibrium is the ideal point of the median voter (P), the qualified majority rule increases the range of the equilibrium which includes all points in the interval $[C, P]$. These points are stable because the majority of the cantons and the majority of the people want

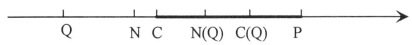

Figure 6.1   Equilibrium in one-dimensional constitutional choices

to move in opposite directions and, therefore, no constitutional change can take place. The size of the equilibrium increases the larger the distance between C and P which expands with diverging economic and demographic development among others.[2]

The magnitude of a possible policy change is determined by the location of the status quo (Q). In Figure 6.1, not all points of the interval $[C, P]$ can defeat Q but only those in the win set ($W(Q) = (Q, C(Q))$). If the parliament had the exclusive right to make constitutional proposals, it could choose a point inside the win set or, if the ideal point of one chamber is in Q or to the left of Q, not make any proposal at all. However, because the support of only about 2 per cent of the voters is sufficient to put a popular initiative on the ballot, the agenda-setting process is quite competitive. Consequently, the player who is first in making a proposal, which is inside the win set of the status quo and inside the equilibrium, has an important *first mover advantage*. Since her proposal is inside the win set, it defeats the status quo and because it is inside the equilibrium, no future proposition can successfully challenge it. Consequently, the parliament has an incentive to change the status quo if it is outside the equilibrium. In fact, since 1891 (the year in which the popular initiative for a partial revision of the constitution was introduced), 77 per cent of all partial revisions of the constitution (102 out of 132) have been initiated by the parliament (as of 31 May 1995).

A particular procedure allows the parliament to make a counter-proposal to a popular initiative.[3] Unless the organizing group withdraws the initiative, both proposals are put on the ballot at the same time. The citizens can vote in favor of one or both proposals and have to decide which proposal they prefer in case both proposals are approved. A proposal is approved if it receives the support of a majority of the people and the cantons. If both proposals are accepted by a qualified majority, the separate question becomes decisive. If a qualified majority prefers one to the other, the preferred one becomes law. If the majority of the canton favors one proposal and the majority of the people favors the other, the status quo prevails. This procedure has the following effect:

Proposition 6.2   The right of the parliament to make a counter-proposal strengthens the influence of the parliament if the ideal points of both chambers and the status quo are on the same side outside the equilibrium range

Consider again Figure 6.1 where the exposition is simplified by assuming that the ideal points of the median members in both chambers of the parliament are identical and at point N. A group with an ideal point to the right of P wants to move the constitutional issue as much to the right as possible. Without the threat of a counter-proposal, the largest change the group can achieve is from Q to $C(Q)$ because a policy to the right of $C(Q)$ would not find the support of a majority of the cantons. In Figure 6.1, a policy reform to $C(Q)$ leaves the parliament worse off than at Q. However, with the right to make counter-proposals, the parliament can avoid such a change by making a counter-proposal at point C, its most preferred policy inside the equilibrium. Subsequently, both proposals receive support by a qualified majority against Q. Assuming sincere voting, a majority of the cantons prefer the counter-proposal while a majority of the people favor the original proposal.[4] According to the rules, Q prevails which leaves the parliament better off than at $C(Q)$. To avoid a counter-proposal, the group has to pick the point C. If the group chooses a point to the right of C the parliament can always counter by proposing C. This leaves the group with the choice either to withdraw their proposal and thereby realizing C or to leave the proposal on the ballot and both proposals failing. Since the group prefers C to Q it withdraws.[5] In conclusion, the right to make counter-proposals constrains the feasible set of successful popular initiatives as long as the parliament has an incentive to defend the status quo.

6.2   TWO-DIMENSIONAL CHOICES

Simple majority rule does not have an equilibrium in two-dimensional choices and the same is true in general for the qualified majority rule in the Swiss Constitution. Although no equilibrium exists, the qualified majority rule can decrease the win set and thereby excludes some policy changes which could occur under a simple majority rule. Figure 6.2 illustrates this conclusion for the simplest case of five voters each belonging to one of three cantons. With a simple majority rule the win set of the status quo is the shaded area. If the voters are divided into three cantons such that voter *1* and voter *2* are one canton each and voters *3, 4* and *5* constitute the third canton, the win set is reduced to include only the heavily drawn part of the shaded area. For example, the ideal point of voter *4*, which is preferred by a majority of the voters (*3, 4* and *5*) against the status quo, is opposed by cantons 1 and 2 and, therefore, is outside the win set of the qualified majority rule. However, if the voters are divided differently, for example voter *2* and voter *4* are one canton each and voters *1, 3* and *5* are the third canton, the win set of the simple and qualified majority rule are identical.

Besides the qualified majority rule, the Constitution requires that a proposed amendment has to include one issue only. This condition transforms a two-dimensional choice into two one-dimensional decisions. Not surprisingly, an equilibrium exists in an issue-by-issue majority rule (see Chapter 3, section 3.2).

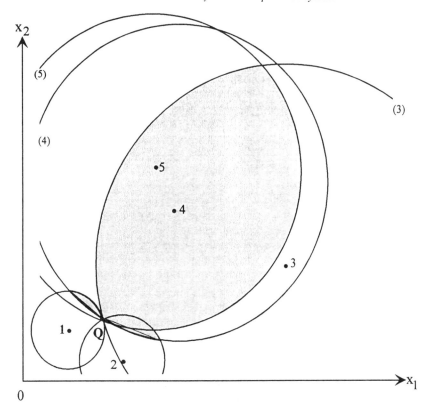

Figure 6.2   Win set with simple and qualified majority rule

Consider Figure 6.3 with the same ideal points of five voters as in Figure 6.2. If voting is restricted to issue 1, voter 5 is in the median position and therefore x_{E1} cannot be beaten. In an independent vote on the second issues, x_{E2} is the undominated position with person 3 being the median voter. Consequently, point E is the *issue-by-issue median* which is stable as long as only motions along one issue at a time are considered. E is the equilibrium of a simple majority rule with a single issue requirement. With this observation, the following proposition is presented:

Proposition 6.3   With a single issue requirement for constitutional amendments an equilibrium exists and the qualified majority rule increases the size of the set of equilibrium points compared to the simple majority rule if the preferences of the median voter nationwide and the median voter in the median cantons diverge

In Figure 6.3, assume again that voters are divided in the following way: voters *1* and *2* represent cantons 1 and 2 respectively and voters *3, 4* and *5* constitute the third canton. Fixing the second issue at x_{E2}, the line between *F* and *E* represents the equilibrium for choices about the first issue because a movement from *F* toward *E* would be vetoed by cantons 1 and 2 and the reverse movement would be rejected by a majority of the voters (*3, 4* and *5*). If the status quo is between *E* and *H*, no change of the second issue is possible because of the opposing interests of median voter *3* and median canton 1. As a result, the equilibrium comprises all points inside the rectangle *EFGH*. The size of the equilibrium increases the larger the divergence between the median voter nationwide and the median voter in the median canton on each issue.

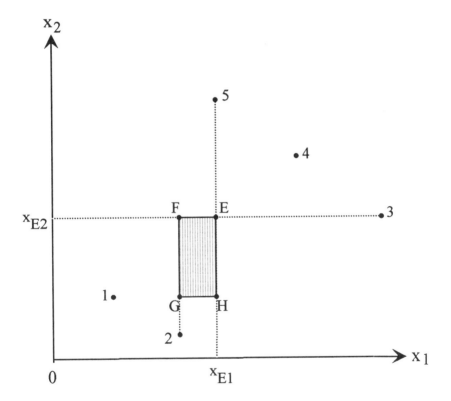

Figure 6.3   Equilibrium with single issue requirement and qualified majority rule

6.3   REFORM PROPOSALS

The models on legislative and constitutional decisions can be used to assess the impact of reform proposals on political stability. Of course, stability is usually not the goal of reform proposals. However, the degree of stability is decisive for the political outcome and, therefore, reformers should know what the consequences of their proposals are. Notice that in a stable system a change of the status quo is less likely to occur but once a policy change takes place it is more durable than in a less stable political process. The following section concentrates on two issues, namely on modifications in the optional referendum for legislative decisions and on the introduction of a constitutional review of statutes by the Federal Court.[6] On both issues, modifications are suggested in the constitutional proposal by the Federal executive (Bundesrat, 1995).

6.3.1   Optional Referendum for Legislative Decisions

The extent of and the requirements for the optional referendum are controversial. On the one hand, some scholars advocate reducing its impact as, for example, Germann (1990). He recommends giving the parliament the right to decide whether a referendum can take place. His proposal would replace the optional referendum with a decisive plebiscite, but also an integration into the EU would reduce (although not eliminate) the range of statutes that could be challenged by a referendum (Schindler, 1990). On the other hand, Kölz and Müller (1990), among others, would like to extend the optional referendum to financial expenditures above a certain limit, as is common in many cantons.

The consequences of modifying the optional referendum for political stability are straightforward and follow from propositions 5.1 and 5.2 (see Chapter 5). The smaller (larger) the impact of the optional referendum, the smaller (larger) the set of equilibrium points that implies a less (more) stable political system. The proposed plebiscite by Germann, for instance, would, in fact, transform the political structure into a pure bicameral system.

6.3.2   Constitutional Review of Federal Statutes

Since the Federal Court lacks the power to review the constitutionality of federal statutes, a large number of scholars favors the introduction of such a review.[7] Also the constitutional proposal by the Federal Government (Bundesrat, 1995) suggests granting the Federal Court the right to review federal statutes. The model is modified so as to assess the impact of a judicial review of statutes on policy stability. For simplicity, only one-dimensional choices are considered here.

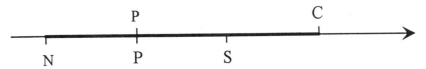

Figure 6.4   Comparison of the equilibrium in legislative and constitutional decisions

Using the results of the previous analysis, Figure 6.4 depicts an example of a structure-induced equilibrium for constitutional decisions (the interval $[P, C]$) and for legislative decisions (the interval $[N, S]$). These equilibria are in general not identical. Since the median voter (P) is relevant in both decision processes, both equilibria have at least one common point. In the case of no constitutional review of statutes, the legislators are not bound formally by the constitution and any point inside the legislative equilibrium is feasible.

By introducing a judicial review of statutes the Federal Court becomes a decisive player. Following Ferejohn and Weingast (1992), two interpretive stances that a court might adopt are distinguished:

1. *Naive textualist*   The court interprets the constitution as close as possible to that desired by the enacting majorities, or literally if the constitution is precise.
2. *Constrained policy advocate*   The court has well defined preferences over policy outcomes and attempts to impose its own preferences. However, the court dislikes it if its interpretation is modified by a formal constitutional revision. The court is sophisticated (as opposed to naive) and takes into account whether its interpretations are politically viable.[8]

If the court acts as a naive textualist, any statutes that do not correspond to the constitutional status quo (Q) will be modified such that they conform to the constitution.[9] Even if Q is outside the equilibrium for constitutional decisions, a naive court tries to maintain Q. In this case, the constitutional decision makers become active and replace Q by a policy located in the interval $[P, C]$ which then will be enforced again by the court. Constitutional review by a court behaving as a textualist strongly constrains the legislative process to the constitutional choice. Whether such a judicial review increases or decreases policy stability depends on the relative size of the equilibria for constitutional and legislative decisions. Referring to Figure 6.4, if the interval $[P, C]$ is smaller than the interval $[N, S]$, the constitutional process provides less stability than the legislative one, and vice versa. The point is that the introduction of a judicial review of legislation alone does not guarantee more durable policies even if the court follows precisely the instructions of the constitutional decision makers.

A court behaving as a constrained policy advocate can choose any point inside the equilibrium of the constitutional decision making. The interval between P and C becomes the set of *political viable interpretations*, that is, those that would not provoke a response by the constitutional decision makers. What such a court does depends upon its preferences. If its ideal point is located inside the equilibrium, it will hold constitutional only those statutes that correspond to its most preferred interpretation of the constitution. Otherwise, the court will attempt to modify the statute by giving it a constitutional 'correct' interpretation or by requiring the legislators to change the statute such that it is in accordance with the court's ideal point. If the court's ideal point is outside the equilibrium for constitutional decisions the court is constrained and will enforce either C or P.

A constitutional review by a court acting as a policy advocate reduces policy stability compared to the present legislative procedures. While in the latter three veto players exist (both chambers and the people), the durability in the former depends only on the stability of the preferences of one player. If the court's ideal point is inside the equilibrium of the constitutional decision rules, any change in the court's position translates into a policy change. If the court is constrained (because its ideal point is not politically viable), the policy outcome depends on the preference of the constraining player (either P or C).

6.3.3   Summary

This chapter has analysed the constitutional decision rules and discussed the effects of proposed changes in legislative and constitutional decision rules. With regard to constitutional decisions, the single issue requirement causes an equilibrium to exist. The qualified majority rule together with different interests between small and larger cantons enlarges the equilibrium and thereby increases the stability of the constitution. The importance of the single issue requirement stands in contrast to its lax enforcement. The parliament has the right to invalidate popular initiatives that violate the single issue requirement. However, this has happened only three times. Furthermore, most amendments are proposed by the parliament that has to observe the single issue requirement too but, in those cases, the compliance cannot be enforced. In the past, there have been several proposals that violated the single issue requirement.[10]

By reducing the impact of the referendum and by introducing a judicial review of statutes, political stability is likely to be reduced. With regard to the judicial review, this effect will be stronger the more the court acts (or has the freedom to act) as a policy advocate.[11]

NOTES

1. Article 121.3 of the Swiss Constitution states: 'If an initiative proposes to revise or to add to the Constitution several issues, each issue has to be formulated as a separate initiative' (translation by the author). The parliament has used the power to invalidate popular initiatives on this ground only three times, namely in 1955, 1977 and 1995.

2. As Germann (1991, 1994) correctly argued, the regional unequal population growth in Switzerland, with the large cantons growing faster than the small ones, has increased the constitutional stability by raising the distance between C and P. Germann (1994: 135) reported that six out of the seven votes in which the majority of the people preferred a change and the majority of the cantons preferred the status quo occurred after 1970.

3. The described procedure has been in force since 1987. Before, the voters had to choose one out of three possibilities (status quo, initiative and counter-proposal). Only if either the initiative or the counter proposal were supported by a majority of the people and the cantons was the amendment approved. Otherwise, the status quo prevailed.

4. Even with sophisticated voting there exists a coordination problem. The median voter in the median canton and the median voter nationwide are better off by supporting the *same* proposal. However, such a coordination in their voting behavior is unlikely to occur.

5. However, if the interaction between the same players is repeated over time, a group can build a reputation of not withdrawing and thereby becomes able to pick a point between C and $N(Q)$ without provoking a counter-proposal. Notice that if the group does not withdraw its proposal the status quo prevails which is also costly for the parliament which prefers its own proposal at C to the status quo.

6. For a more extensive discussion of these and other reform proposals based on a slightly modified model, see Moser (1996c).

7. See, for example, Auer (1991), Borner *et al.* (1991), Kölz and Müller (1990) and Moser (1991). In contrast, Blankart (1994) argued that initiative and referendum are a preferable substitute for a constitutional court.

8. The assumption of the court acting as a sophisticated policy advocate is often used in models of the interaction between legislator and court (Marks, 1988; Gely and Spiller, 1992). Although this assumption might appear extreme, the relative independence of judges, vague constitutional provisions and the intransparent decision making by the Federal Court give large discretion to the interpreting judges and allows them to follow at least partially their policy preferences (on this point, see also Kirchgässner, 1992).

9. It is assumed that the court can give a constitutionally correct interpretation of a statute or that the court invalidates unconstitutional parts of the statute and replaces them with provisions derived from the constitution. Such behavior seems more likely if the court considers individual cases than if it judges the constitutionality of new statutes.

10. For example, the two popular initiatives in 1899 and 1939 which proposed a popular election of the executive and an increase in the number of executive members at the same time. A more important violation was an approved amendment in 1947 (proposed by the parliament) which granted regulatory power to the federal legislators in many domains including agriculture, small businesses, regional and social as well as antitrust policy.

11. If the Federal Court behaves as a policy advocate, the election of judges would become more important political decisions than they are presently. Since federal judges have to be reelected every four years, the threat of not being reelected would constrain the judges further, which is not considered in this model.

7.   Uncertainty and interest groups

To keep the model simple, two assumptions were made in the previous Chapters 5 and 6. First, the models do not take into account the costs of collecting the signatures necessary for a referendum or a popular initiative. Second, it is assumed that all players have perfect and complete information, that is, each player knows the preferences of the other players and the moves occur in sequence. With these assumptions, the parliament never passes a statute that can be vetoed by the people and, therefore, a referendum never takes place in equilibrium. Furthermore, in such a setting interest groups' activities cannot be addressed.

By introducing uncertainty it becomes possible to take into account the fact that referenda occur (against about 7 per cent of all statutes) and that referenda may fail as well as to model how interest groups' activities influence legislative choices (Hug, 1995). One approach, chosen by Ursprung (1994), is to assume voters are uninformed about the consequences of policy choices and that interest groups can change voters' decisions through propaganda. In such a structure, the outcome depends to a large part on the relative strength of conservative and progressive interest groups. It becomes possible that voters reject a legislative proposal that they would prefer if they were fully informed about its consequences. However, these results are derived by using strong assumptions. First, uninformed voters are presumed to make systematic mistakes by voting for the status quo even if fully informed they would prefer the proposed legislative change.[1] Second, Ursprung implicitly assumed that parliamentary decisions are immune or less likely to be influenced by the same interest groups. A second approach to model uncertainty is to assume that the parliament (agenda setter) has imperfect information about voters' preferences (Denzau and Mackay, 1983; Rosenthal, 1990) and that interest groups are better informed about voters' preferences (Austen-Smith and Wright, 1992). This chapter, outlines some results for legislative decisions using the second approach. In section 7.1, a model is developed which is illustrated with two examples in section 7.2.

7.1   A MODEL OF THE REFERENDUM GAME[2]

Consider a one-dimensional policy space as illustrated in Figure 7.1 with the status quo (Q) at zero. In stage 1, the parliament chooses a proposal (x_N). To

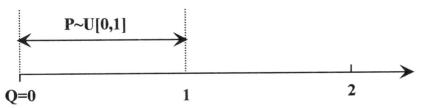

Figure 7.1   Uncertainty of the parliament about the location of the median voter's ideal point

simplify the exposition, bicameral differences are neglected. The parliament knows that the ideal point of the median voter (P) is uniformly distributed on 0 and 1. In stage 2, the interest group with an ideal point at 0 decides whether to launch a referendum. The interest group is assumed to know the median voter's ideal point. In the last stage, voters decide between the proposal and Q if a referendum was initiated, otherwise the proposal becomes effective. The actors' utility functions take the following form:

for the interest group,

$$U_1(x) = -x - \delta c; \tag{7.1}$$

for the median voter,

$$U_P(x) = -\,|\,x - P\,|; \tag{7.2}$$

for the parliament,

$$U_N(x) = -\,|\,x - N\,|. \tag{7.3}$$

The utilities of all actors decrease linearly the further away the policy choice (x) is from their ideal points. The interest group has to incur cost (c) if it uses the referendum ($\delta = 1$).

The game is solved by backward induction. In the last stage, if a referendum takes place, the median voter always favors the policy closer to his or her ideal point. He or she approves the proposal whenever $x_N < 2P$. Consequently, the interest group will only initiate a referendum in the second stage if it knows that it will be successful, $x_N > 2P$, and if it is worth doing, $x_N > c$.[3] In the first stage, the parliament knows these reactions and maximizes its expected utility (or minimizes its loss of utility) with respect to its proposal x_N:

$$EU_N(x_N) = -\mid x_N - N \mid (1 - x_N/2) - \mid 0 - N \mid (x_N/2) \qquad (7.4)$$

The parliament's strategy depends on the existence of positive costs for initiating the referendum.

7.1.1   No Costs ($c = 0$)

There are three strategies for the parliament which can be distinguished: $x_N = N$, $x_N < N$, and $x_N > N$. The last case will never be chosen such that focus is only on the first two cases. If the parliament chooses its ideal point as its proposal ($x_N = N$) then its expected utility is

$$EU_N(x_N = N) = -N^2/2. \qquad (7.5)$$

Maximizing the expected utility (7.4) with respect to x_N and assuming that the proposal x_N is smaller than N leads to $x_N = 1$ as the optimal proposal. The expected utility in this case is

$$EU_N(x_N = 1) = 1/2 - N. \qquad (7.6)$$

The comparison of the expected utilities in (7.5) and (7.6) reveals that the optimal choice (for $c = 0$) is $x_N = N$ if $N \leq 1$ and $x_N = 1$ if $N > 1$.

7.1.2   Positive Costs ($c > 0$)

With positive costs, the interest group will only initiate a referendum if the utility loss of the proposal by the parliament (x_N) is larger than the utility loss of organizing the referendum (c). Again, the two situations $x_N = N$ and $x_N < N$ need to be considered separately. If N is between 0 and 1, it is known that in the absence of costs, the parliament would propose its ideal point and the expected utility is $N^2/2$, as in (7.5). It will be shown that the parliament can increase its utility by proposing c instead of N if $c < N$ but not too small. If it proposes c then the parliament realizes its proposal for sure, that is, its utility becomes

$$EU_N(x_N = c) = -(N - c). \qquad (7.7)$$

(7.6) exceeds (7.5) if $c > N - N^2/2$. Therefore, the optimal proposal for a parliament with N between 0 and 1 is

$$\begin{aligned} x_N &= c \quad \text{if } N - N^2/2 < c < N \\ x_N &= N \quad \text{otherwise.} \end{aligned}$$

In the second case in which $N > 1$ such that the parliament proposes $x_N < N$, the expected utility for $x_N = 1$ is $EU_N(x_N = 1) = 1/2 - N$, as in (7.7). If the parliament chooses c as its proposal, its utility is given by (7.7). Solving for c such that the expected utility is equal in (7.7) and (7.6) yields $c = 1/2$. Therefore, the optimal strategy for the parliament with $N > 1$ is

$$
\begin{aligned}
x_N &= 1 \quad &&\text{if } c < 1/2 \\
x_N &= c \quad &&\text{if } 1/2 \le c < N \\
x_N &= N \quad &&\text{if } c \ge N.
\end{aligned}
$$

7.2 EXAMPLES

This section illustrates the results of this model with two examples. As a first case, consider the situation in which there is no systemic difference between the ideal points of the median voter and the parliament ($N = 0.5$). The optimal proposal (x_N) depends on the cost (c) for the interest group. The optimal strategy for the parliament is to propose its ideal point, $x = 0.5$, whenever $c < 0.375$. A successful referendum is initiated in 25 per cent of all cases and the proposal is defeated. However, if the parliament faces an interest group with $c = 0.4$, the optimal proposal is 0.4. In the latter case, the parliament can increase its utility by accommodating its proposal toward the interest group such that it no longer has an incentive to organize a referendum. Therefore, the parliament can realize its proposal for sure. However, notice that the expected value of the realized policy is 0.375 in the case of $c < 0.375$ while the realized policy is 0.4 if $c = 0.4$. Hence, low cost interest groups have more influence inasmuch as they reduce the expected policy more than interest groups with higher costs. However, while the parliament accommodates its proposals to higher cost groups, low cost interest groups have to use the costly referendum, as long as they cannot credibly inform the parliament on the location of the median voter's ideal point in some other way.

In the second case, assume a systematic divergence between the median voter's preferences and those of the parliament, for example $N = 2$. The optimal proposal is

$$
\begin{aligned}
x_N &= 1 \quad &&\text{if } c < 1/2 \\
x_N &= c \quad &&\text{if } 1/2 \le c < 2 \\
x_N &= 2 \quad &&\text{if } c \ge 2.
\end{aligned}
$$

As shown in Figure 7.2, although the optimal proposal does not rise monotonically with higher c (solid line), the expected policy increases with higher costs (dashed line). Consequently, if institutional reforms increase c (for

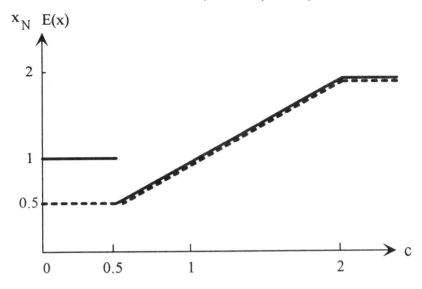

Figure 7.2   Optimal proposal and expected policy if the ideal point of the parliament is at N = 2

example by raising the required number of signatures) the parliament can deviate more from the preferences of the median voter. Furthermore, the number of referenda will decline but the proposals by the parliament might, in fact, become more conservative if c was below 1/2 and is between 1/2 and 1 after the reform.

Two further implications are worth pointing out. First, in single proposals (with no possibility to learn the median ideal point) the uncertainty constrains the parliament such that its proposals sometimes fail, even if the parliament does not have different preferences systematically. If P were at 0.5 for certain, the parliament with $N = 2$ could realize 1 for certain. Because of uncertainty a referendum will take place in 50 per cent of all proposals (for $c < 1/2$) with an expected value of the proposal of 0.5. Second, only conservative interest groups who want to preserve the status quo are active in legislative decision making. Progressive interest groups cannot use the referendum to credibly signal that they have better information about the location of the median voter's ideal point than the parliament. This observation has led scholars of Swiss politics (Borner, Brunetti and Straubhaar, 1990: 170) to attribute the stability in legislative decision making to the existence of well-organized (conservative) interest groups who use the referenda to veto changes in the status quo.

The same observation has a completely different interpretation in the model described here. Conservative interest groups are active participants but they are only successful if the status quo is closer to the median voter's ideal point than the proposal by the parliament. Consequently, the interest groups play a *beneficial role* inasmuch as they can turn down parliamentary proposals that deviate much from voters' preferences. The lower the group's organization cost, the better the group is informed about voters' preferences, the more successful it is in constraining the parliament. The larger the bias between parliament's and voters' preferences and the more uncertain the parliament is about voters' preferences, the more beneficial is the potential use of a referendum by interest groups.

NOTES

1. The public debate in direct democracies is regarded more favorably by Bohnet and Frey (1994), Frey (1994), Frey and Kirchgässner (1993) and Eichenberger and Serna (1996). They argued that a referendum stimulates public discussion and thereby reduces uncertainty and can break cartels of politicians directed against voters and taxpayers. Furthermore, Lupia (1992, 1994) pointed out how voters can use information cues (such as interest group endorsement or the costliness of a initiative) to make more accurate inferences about electoral or policy alternatives. Schneider (1985) provides empirical evidence of the importance of interest group endorsement for voters' choice in Switzerland.
2. Simon Hug provided valuable comments on the model presented in this section.
3. If the group were not perfectly informed about the median voter's ideal point, its referendum would sometimes fail.

Summary of Part II

This part of the study on institutions and stability presented a model of the political system of Switzerland that can explain policy change and policy stability in legislative (Chapter 5) and constitutional decisions (Chapter 6) and is capable of analysing the effects of institutional reforms. It identified two attributes of the Swiss political system that are decisive for stability. With regard to legislative decisions, the combination of the bicameral system with the optional referendum makes it more likely that an equilibrium exists in decisions involving one or two dimensions. If an equilibrium exists, it is larger than without a referendum if the preferences of the two chambers and of the people are sufficiently diverse. Furthermore, a change of the position of one of the three players (Council of States, National Council or the people) in general is not sufficient to induce a policy change. In the case of constitutional decisions, stability is created by the requirement that each proposed amendment has to include one issue only. Stability is enlarged by the qualified majority rule which requires the support of a majority of the people and of a majority of the cantons for a constitutional change. The introduction of uncertainty about voters' preferences (Chapter 7) does not modify these results qualitatively but gives a more accurate description of the equilibrium strategies (with successful referenda taking place) and accounts for the role of interest groups.

Since the Federal Court lacks the right to review federal legislation, there is no mechanism to enforce the Constitution in the legislative process. A rather surprising result is that an introduction of a judicial review of federal statutes is unlikely to induce more durability but rather the opposite. Such a reform would give more weight to the constitutional decision process. However, the legislative process tends to be more stable than the constitutional one because (1) there are three veto players in the legislative process and only two in the constitutional process and (2) because statutory proposals can only be introduced by members of the two chambers and by the executive but not by a group of people, as with the popular initiative for constitutional proposals. Moreover, the durability of a procedure with judicial review depends to a large extent on the interpretative stance a court adopts.

PART III

Institutions and policy choice:
The conditional influence of the European
Parliament

Introduction to Part III

Among scholars studying European decision making, the impact of the European Parliament (EP) is a much disputed issue. The traditional view is that the influence of the EP is rather limited although it has made significant progress since the Single European Act and the Maastricht revision of the Treaty (Jacobs and Corbett, 1990; Wessel, 1991; Westlake, 1994). While these contributions are not based on an explicit analytical model, some applications of public or rational choice-based analysis support this view: Steunenberg (1994b) and Crombez (1996) came to the conclusion that the EP is barely able to affect EU policy choices.[1] In contrast, a growing number of scholars of European decision making now recognize that the EP sometimes has considerable influence on policy choices. Empirical evidence indicates that successful amendments by the EP are not rare and that they *sometimes* involve substantial policy changes. One of the most spectacular cases of the EP's influence is the decision on car emission standards. In this case, the EP succeeded in forcing the Commission and the Council to approve the stricter emission standards preferred by the EP. However, there are numerous cases in which the attempts of the EP failed to influence the final decisions. In their careful study of several decision situations, Judge, Earnshaw and Cowan (1994: 49) recognized the contingency of the EP's influence and concluded that: 'statements about the "influence" of the European Parliament should be specific rather than general and empirical rather than assertive . . . Significant variations across and within policy fields and across and within particular time periods are to be expected'.

In the theoretical literature, several reasons for the contingent influence of the EP are provided. Tsebelis (1994) claims that the effect of the EP is due to conditional agenda rights which is disputed by Moser (1996a) because Tsebelis' result is based on inaccurately constructed decision rules (Tsebelis' reply is in Tsebelis (1996)).

In this part, spatial models or positive political theory are applied to analyse the impact of the EP. Chapter 8 provides a consistent public or rational choice-based explanation of why the EP is sometimes influential. It is argued that if the restrictions that the EP faces change during the decision process unexpectedly, it may become possible for the EP to propose amendments, and thereby to take advantage of these changes. Three sources of changing restrictions are identified that allow the EP to realize a policy choice closer to its policy positions: a change of the policy position of the decisive Council member or of the Commission, and a change of the reversion point.

In Chapter 9, the model is applied to the decision on car emission standards in which the EP succeeded in realizing its most preferred policy against the original opposition of the Commission and a majority in the Council. This case is widely analysed and documented which allows comparison of the argument developed in this part of the study with competing explanations. While Jacobs and Corbett (1990) claimed that the success of the EP was because of its threat of rejection of the common position and Tsebelis (1994) ascribed the success to conditional agenda-setting rights, it is argued here that the main cause for the EP's success was a change of the perceived reversion point.

The Political System of the EU

This section provides information about the political system of the EU. The four most important decision-making groups are the Commission, the Council, the Parliament (EP) and the Court of Justice.

The Commission
The Commission consists of 20 members appointed, after mutual consultation, by the governments of the member states for a four-year period. Each of the five largest countries appoints two members; all other countries appoint one member. The EP needs to approve the composition of the Commission. One member acts as president and is responsible for the consistency of the various policies. Formally, however, decisions within the Commission are made by a simple majority vote. The major tasks of the Commission are the initiation of actions, the execution of policies, the implementation of the budget and, finally, the enforcement of the laws. To perform its task, the Commission has at its disposal an international staff (about 19 000 officials in the mid-1990s).

The Council
The Council consists of one representative minister of the governments of each of the member states who are accountable to their national parliaments. The composition of the Council varies with the matter in hand. On a number of subjects the Council decides with unanimity (on defense and taxes, for example). On most subjects it decides with a qualified majority. Depending on the size of the countries, the representatives have a different number of votes. Germany, France, Italy and the United Kingdom have 10 votes each, Spain 8 votes, the Netherlands, Belgium, Greece and Portugal 5 votes each, Austria and Sweden 4 votes each, Denmark, Ireland and Finland 3 votes each and Luxembourg has 2 votes. A qualified majority requires at least 62 votes of the total number of 87 votes. The major role of the Council is in decision

making. The council has a major say and often the final say in Community legislation. In some cases it has to share this function with the EP. Since 1975, there have been regular meetings of the *European Council*, which is composed of the heads of government and the president of the Commission. The European Council's role is to give general directions, for example, with regard to new stages of integration.

The European Parliament (EP)

The members of the EP are elected directly for a term of five years. There are 626 members, distributed roughly proportional to the population among the member countries with, for example, Germany having 99 seats and Luxembourg 6 seats. However, the EP members are not grouped along national lines but along party groups. The preliminary work is carried on in parliamentary committees. A member of a committee, the rapporteur, reports on subjects to be treated in the full Parliament. The EP usually decides by the simple majority rule. In the past the competence of the EP remained far below those of national parliaments. Originally, the EP had only an advisory capacity. It discussed the proposal of the Commission and drew up a report, which was submitted to the Commission and the Council. This procedure of *consultation* continues to be applied to agriculture, taxation, competition, harmonization of legislation not related to the internal market, industrial policy and aspects of social and environmental policy (subject to unanimity).

The EP has striven successfully to extend its authority. With the Single European Act in 1987, the *cooperation procedure* was introduced in selected policy areas. Here the position is strengthened, as the Council can reject amendments of the EP only unanimously. This procedure will be described and analysed in detail in Chapter 8. With the Maastricht revision, the EP was given the right of *codecision*, which adds a conciliation process in the case of disagreement between the EP and the Council. With the introduction of the Amsterdam Treaty in 1999, a simplified codecision procedure now applies to 39 legal bases in the EC Treaty that allow for the adoption of legislative acts. It may, therefore, be considered a standard legislative procedure. Finally, since 1987 the *assent* of the EP is required among others for the conclusion of treaties and for the extension of the EU.

The Court of Justice

The Court is composed of 15 judges who are appointed by member state governments, by mutual agreement, for a period of six years. They must be entirely independent and cannot be dismissed. The Court has been entrusted with the task of ensuring the proper and consistent interpretation and application of the European law. Access to the Court is not only possible for member states and EU institutions but also for citizens and legal entities. Individuals can request a national judge, who is not sure about the interpretation of European law, to demand a preliminary ruling from the European Court. The number of cases brought before the Court has increased rapidly. The actions of the Court have been very important in advancing European integration. For example, the Court has repudiated many forms of national protection against the free movement of goods and services within the EU.

NOTE

1. A collection of papers that analyse the strategic interaction in EU politics are contained in Moser, Schneider and Kirchgässner (2000). See also Schneider (1997).

8. Strategic interactions in legislative procedures in the European Union

In this chapter a model is presented that addresses the strategic interaction between the Commission, the Council and the EP in legislative procedures (section 8.2), and that identifies the conditions under which the EP influences the equilibrium outcome (section 8.3). Since the cooperation procedure was applied in the decision about emission standards (see the analysis in Chapter 9), the model is focused on the cooperation procedure. However, the technique can easily be adapted to other legislative procedures. Before presenting the model, the details of the cooperation procedure in the EU are described, as stated in Article 252 of the Treaty, evidence of its working is reported, and the differences between the cooperation and the now more widely applied codecision procedure are pointed out.

8.1   DESCRIPTION OF LEGISLATIVE PROCEDURES

The cooperation procedure, introduced with the Single European Act in July 1987, was used until November 1993 for decisions regarding the free movement of workers, the freedom of establishment, the treatment of foreign nationals, the mutual recognition of diplomas, the coordination of national provisions on the activities of self-employed persons, and most important, for decisions about the harmonization or mutual recognition of national measures to achieve the internal market. With the Maastricht revision of the Treaty, the codecision procedure replaced the cooperation procedure in these areas, but the cooperation procedure remained in place for decisions regarding rules against discrimination (Article 6), the improvement in the health and safety of workers, economic and social cohesion and aspects of research and development (R&D) programs. Furthermore, the cooperation procedure was extended with the Maastricht Treaty to decisions regarding transportation, aspects of fiscal and monetary policy, vocational training, the European Social Fund, measures to further the cooperation with developing countries, and of particular significance, to aspects of environmental policy. As previously stated, with the Amsterdam revision of the Treaty, the cooperation procedure has been replaced in most areas by the codecision procedure. It applies now only with respect to the coordination of economic policy (Article 99), the application of access to financial institutions (Article 102), the liability of the Community for financial commitments of lower level governments (Article 103) and with regard to the issue of coins (Article 106).

The cooperation procedure comprises the following stages:

1. The Commission submits a proposal to the Council.
2. After consulting the EP (first reading), the Council determines in its first reading the common position: it can approve the Commission's proposal by a qualified majority or modify it unanimously.
3. The EP can accept, modify or reject the common position in its second reading.
4a. If the EP accepts the common position, the Council can adopt the common position in its second reading by qualified majority rule. Otherwise the status quo prevails.
4b. If the EP rejects the common position, the Council can only approve the common position unanimously. Otherwise, the status quo prevails.
4c. If the EP amends the common position, the Commission decides whether to approve the amendment.
5a. If the Commission approves the amendment of the EP, the Council can accept the amended proposal by a qualified majority or modify it unanimously.
5b. If the Commission does not approve the amendment of the EP, the Council can approve the unamended common position by qualified majority rule, or modify the common position and thereby include the proposal of the EP by unanimity.

One clarification should be made. The Commission does not have the sole right to initiate legislation. A simple majority of the Council members can request the Commission to submit a proposal according to Article 208. The same right is granted to the EP (Article 192) if the request is supported by a majority of all members in the EP. It is disputed in the legal literature whether such a request is binding for the Commission. While Kapteyn and Verloren van Themaat (1989: 252) regarded such requests as not binding – although they admit that the Commission often yielded to the pressure of the Council partic-ularly – von der Groeben, Thiesing and Ehlermann (1991: 4307) and Lenz and Borchardt (1994: 1018, 1059) argued that such requests are binding but that the Commission is free to decide when to make the proposal and what to include in the proposal. In the following, it is assumed that the Commission cannot keep the gates closed against the will of a majority in the Council or in the EP, but that only the Commission can make the proposals.

8.1.1　Cooperation Procedure Statistics

Table 8.1 depicts the statistical impact of the EP in the cooperation procedure. In the period from July 1987 to October 1993, the Commission accepted 55 per cent of the EP's first reading amendments and 44 per cent of the EP's second reading amendments. The Council approved 43 per cent of the EP's first reading amendments and included them in its common position. In its final reading, the Council still approved 23 per cent of the EP's second reading amendments, about half of all second reading amendments that were approved by the Commission.[1]

Table 8.1　Cooperation procedure statistics: July 1987 to October 1993

Number of Commission proposals	316	
Number of 1. Reading amendments by EP	4397	(100%)
Number of acceptance by Commission of 1. Reading amendments	2403	(55%)
Number of acceptance by Council of 1. Reading amendments	1882	(43%)
Number of 2. Reading amendments by EP	1031	(100%)
Number of acceptance by Commission of 2. Reading amendments	452	(44%)
Number of acceptance by Council of 2. Reading amendments	242	(23%)
Number of rejections by the EP (until November 1991)	3	

Source: Westlake (1994: 39).

In the literature, it is disputed whether this quantitative record is a good indicator of the EP's influence. Wessel (1991: 145) argued that 'except for some rare cases, the impact of the EP on crucial issues of the Council's deliberations is rather limited'. In contrast, Tsebelis (1994: 136) insisted that there are various cases in which the EP substantially influenced the policy decision. Also Earnshaw and Judge (1993) and Judge, Earnshaw and Cowan (1994) provided case studies that point out the variability of influence by the EP.

8.1.2　Decision about Car Emission Standards

One of the most spectacular cases of the EP's influence is the decision on car emission standards. In February 1988, the Commission proposed to reduce the emission standards for small cars to 30 g CO (carbon monoxide) and 15 g HC (hydrocarbons) plus NO_x (nitrogen oxides). In the first reading in September

1989, the EP proposed an equivalent of the stricter US-83 standards (20 g $CO/5$ g HC plus NO_x) which require the use of catalytic converters. The Council ignored the opinion of the EP and approved the Commission's proposal as its common position. In the second reading in April 1989, the EP insisted on the stricter US-83 standards. The EP (by its rapporteur Vittinghoff) threatened to reject the common position unless the Commission supported the stricter standards. During the debate in the parliament, the Commissioner responsible for environmental policy, Ripa Di Meana, promised to support the EP's amendment this time around. After this promise, the EP approved the amended common position with the stricter standard. In June 1989, the Council gave in and approved the stricter standard by a qualified majority.

8.1.3   Open Questions

Both the statistics, as well as the decision on emission standards, point out that the EP sometimes has considerable influence on policy choice. Particularly with regard to second reading amendments, two questions arise:

1. Why does the Commission support the EP's amendments and yet did not choose to include these issues in its original proposal?
2. Why does the Commission support EP's amendments that do not receive a qualified majority support in the Council?

The first question will be focused on since in these situations the impact of the EP becomes most visible. To address the second question, it would be necessary to include imperfect information either about each other's preferences (as in Chapter 7; Enelow and Hinich, 1987 and Rosenthal, 1990) or about the implication of policy choices, as discussed in Chapter 4, section 4.1.

8.1.4   Differences between Cooperation and Codecision Procedure

With the Maastricht revision of the Treaty, the codecision procedure (Article 251) replaced cooperation for some matters, most importantly with regard to the completion of the internal market, the free movement of workers and the mutual recognition of diplomas. Furthermore, codecision was introduced in new areas such as consumer protection, and framework programs in environment and research and technology development. With the Amsterdam revision of the Treaty, the codecision procedure became the standard legislative procedure.[2] The codecision procedure provides an additional stage to the cooperation procedure. As with cooperation, the EP can accept, amend or reject the common position. If the EP accepts, the Council can confirm the common position and it becomes EU policy. If the EP rejects it, the status quo prevails.

If the EP amends it and the Council does not approve the amendments, a Conciliation Committee convenes. It consists of the members of the Council and an equal number of members of the Parliament. Its task is to reach an agreement. If the joint text is supported by a qualified majority in the Council and by a simple majority in the EP, the joint text becomes EU policy. If the Conciliation Committee does not reach an agreement, the status quo prevails. Before 1999, it was possible that in the case of a disagreement in the Conciliation Committee, the Council could confirm its common position, possibly by including some of the amendments by the EP. If the EP did not reject this confirmed position by an absolute majority, it became EU policy.

There are at least two major differences between the cooperation and the codecision procedures. First, the EP has an unconditional veto right since its veto cannot be outvoted by a unanimous Council in the codecision procedure. In policy choices, these differences may not matter that much because if the EP vetoes a decision there is usually one member in the Council that supports the veto. However, the EP's position is likely to be strengthened in procedural choices in which Council members and the EP are more likely to have opposing views. Second, the influence of the Commission is reduced in the codecision procedure compared to the cooperation procedure because the Council and the EP reach agreement without the consent of the Commission. Remember that the Council can accept amendments by the EP by a qualified majority rule in the codecision procedure even if the Commission does not support these amendments. In the model presented in the following section, an indication is given where the codecision procedure would lead to different conclusions.

8.2   THE MODEL

To explore how much influence these decision rules give to the EP, a simple model can be developed. First, some necessary technical preliminaries are outlined, and second, the interaction between the Commission and the Council is analysed. Subsequently, the impact of the EP is explored and conditions for successful second reading amendments by the EP are identified.

8.2.1   Assumptions

The same assumptions as discussed in section 2.1 are used here. Each player has to choose over an n-dimensional issue space $X = R^m$, and is endowed with a strictly quasi-concave utility function over X, $U^i(x)$. Two kinds of win set are relevant in EU decisions; the *unanimity win set* of x, defined as $UW(x) = \{y \in X \mid y \: P_i x \: \forall i\}$, and the *qualified majority win set* of x, $QW(x) = \{y \in X \mid y \: P_i x$

$| \geq Q \}$ where $| y \, P_i x |$ is the number of agents who prefer y to x. $QW(x)$ is the set of alternatives that are supported by at least a qualified majority of votes (Q) against x, and points in $UW(x)$ are preferred by all agents against x. Finally, there is an informational requirement that all players have complete and perfect information and that none of the players prefer their decisions to be overturned. To derive the equilibrium outcomes, the concept of subgame perfectness is used which provides unique Nash equilibrium strategies for the game discussed in this study.

To keep the exposition as simple as possible, two further assumptions are made. First, it is assumed that the Council is composed of five members (instead of fifteen) and that a qualified majority requires the support of four members (80 per cent instead of 71 per cent).[3] Second, it is supposed that not only the Commission but also the EP is a unitary actor, such that both have a single ideal point.[4]

8.2.2   Interaction between Commission and Council

A possible preference configuration of the five Council members is depicted in Figure 8.1. Depending on the location of the status quo (q), three cases can be distinguished (Steunenberg, 1994b):

1. *A unanimous Council*   In this case, Pareto-efficient policy changes are possible because q is outside the pentagon 1–5, that represents the *Pareto set*, as in Figure 8.1. The Pareto set includes all alternatives in X from which the utility of all members cannot be improved simultaneously. Since the Commission makes the first proposal, it can choose its most preferred point that is inside $QW(q)$ – the shaded area in Figure 8.1 – and inside the Pareto set. If the Commission chose a point that was outside the Pareto set (but preferred to q by a qualified majority), the Council would unanimously modify the Commission's proposal. Suppose that the Commission's ideal point (C) is at 5, in which case it proposes a_1, which is approved by Council members 1, 3, 4 and 5, and becomes the common position. Notice that in the case of a unanimous Council, the Commission cannot defend the status quo if it wishes to do so. Since the Council can demand a proposal from the Commission, and can unanimously modify it, as long as it is outside the Pareto set, the Commission may be forced to initiate a proposal against its will.[5]

2. *A supportive Council*   In this case, q is inside the Pareto set but a qualified majority win set of q, $QW(q)$, exists (see Figure 8.2). A policy change is preferred by a qualified majority in the Council, but not by all members. The Commission can propose a policy inside $QW(q)$ and the Council is not able

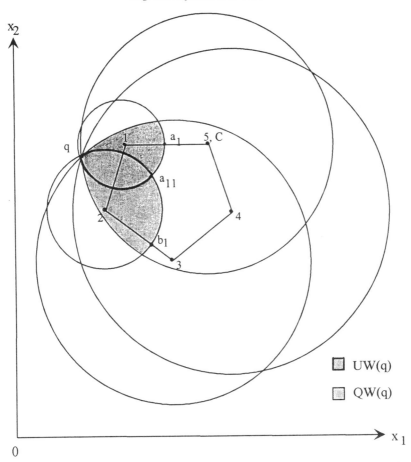

Figure 8.1   Unanimous Council

to amend such a proposal. Assuming again that the ideal point of the Commission is at 5, it proposes a_2 which the Council approves by a qualified majority (against the vote of Council member 2). a_2 becomes the common position. In contrast to the case of a unanimous Council, the Commission can, in fact, keep the gates closed. If the Council demands a proposal, the Commission can make a proposal that corresponds to the status quo. The Council cannot modify this proposal because unanimity is required to do so.

3. *A divided Council*   In this case the status quo is more 'centrally' located such that both $UW(q)$ and $QW(q)$ are empty. Consequently, no policy change is possible.

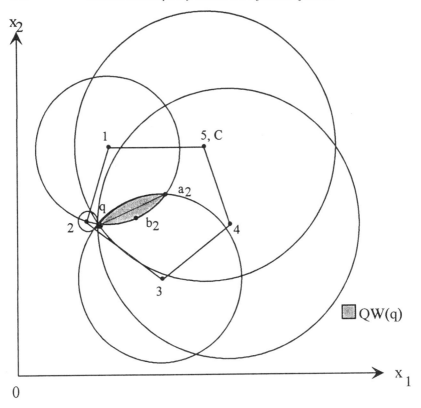

Figure 8.2   Supportive Council

8.2.3   The Limited Impact of the EP

To analyse the impact of the EP, attention is restricted to the case of a unanimous and supportive Council in which new policies can arise. Depending on the preferences of the EP compared to those of the Commission, the EP may prefer the same policy change as the Commission, a different policy change or no change at all. Of interest are those situations in which there is some conflict between the EP and the Commission.

First, suppose that the EP prefers a different policy change than the Commission. For example, the ideal point of the EP is at 3. In the case of a unanimous Council (Figure 8.1), consider that the EP proposes b_1, its most preferred policy in $QW(q)$. Since the Commission does not support such an amendment, the Council has to prefer b_1 to the common position a_1 unanimously in order for the amendment to be successful. This is not the case.

Since the common position is already in the Pareto set, a change of the common position against the will of the Commission, which requires consent in the Council, is impossible. Therefore, any proposed amendment of the EP will fail, even if this amendment is inside the unanimity win set of q, $UW(q)$. Consequently, the subgame perfect strategy of the EP is not to make an amendment; and the Commission is not constrained by the EP in making its proposal. The same conclusion holds for a supportive Council (Figure 8.2): b_2 will not defeat the common position a_2 unanimously. Consequently, in the cooperation procedure, the right of the EP to make amendments does not seem to give the EP any impact in EU decision making if it prefers a different policy change than the Commission.[6]

If the codecision procedure applies, the Commission has to take the policy positions of the EP more into account. In the case of a unanimous Council, a_1 is no longer an equilibrium choice for the Commission because, in the conciliation stage, a qualified majority of the Council and the EP can replace a_1. Consequently, the Commission will propose a more centrally located point, such that the qualified majority win set of this proposal is empty or has no intersection with the preferred-to set of the EP. However, in the situation depicted in Figure 8.2, a_2 is the optimal choice in both procedures, because $QW(a_2)$ is empty.

Second, assume that the EP is conservative such that the status quo is its most preferred policy in $QW(q)$. With the codecision procedure, no change is possible. However, with the cooperation procedure, changes are rare since a rejection of the common position by the EP forces the Council to support the common position unanimously. This reduces the agenda influence of the Commission. In the case of a supportive Council, the EP also has effective veto power in cooperation because its veto cannot be outvoted unanimously. In the case of a unanimous Council, the EP cannot defend q successfully because its rejection can be outvoted by a unanimous Council.[7] Nevertheless, the EP has an impact on the policy choice. The Commission's subgame perfect strategy is no longer to propose a_1 because the Council does not unanimously prefer a_1 to q. Rather, the Commission is forced to choose its most preferred point in the unanimity win set, $UW(q)$, which is a_{11} and thereby to accommodate partially to the wishes of the EP (see Figure 8.1). Therefore, a conservative EP, in the sense defined above, also has effective veto powers in the cooperation procedure if the status quo is inside the Pareto set but its impact becomes smaller, the further away q is from this set.

There is a third case in which the EP's most preferred point in $QW(q)$ is not the status quo but such that it prefers q to the common position. This situation is represented in Figure 8.3 which depicts the status quo (q), $QW(q)$, the ideal points of the Commission (C) and the EP, and the most preferred point in

$QW(q)$ by the Commission (a_2) and by the EP (b_3). If the Commission proposed a_2, and the Council approved a_2 as the common position, the EP could credibly threaten to reject the proposal in the second reading since it prefers the status quo to a_2. This holds for both procedures. Such a credible veto threat forces the Commission to accommodate partially to the preferences of the EP. It proposes its most preferred point that is in $QW(q)$ and in the preferred-to set of the EP: $QW(q) \cap P_{Ep}(q)$. In Figure 8.3, a_3 is the Commission's optimal proposal that will not be vetoed by the EP and will be approved by the Council.

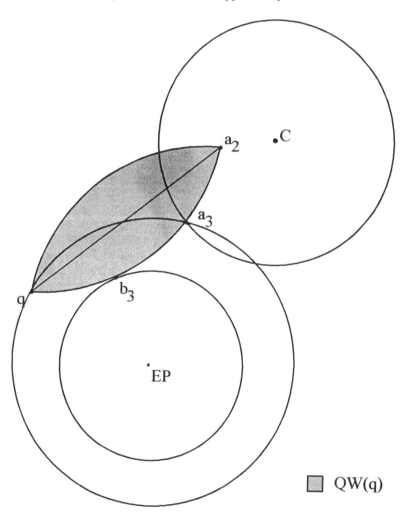

Figure 8.3   Credible veto threat by the EP

Consequently, if the preferences and status quo remain constant during the decision process, the EP's right to propose amendments is without impact in the cooperation procedure and has some but limited consequences in the case of codecision. Only its right to reject is an effective instrument under the condition that the EP prefers the status quo to the common position as it was chosen without the participation of the EP. In accordance with Steunenberg (1994b), Tsebelis's (1994) phrasing could be adopted and it could be concluded that the EP is a *conditional veto player*.

8.3   CONDITIONS FOR SUCCESSFUL AMENDMENTS BY THE EP

In contrast to the preceding theoretical conclusions, the evidence summarized in Section 8.1 indicates that the EP can sometimes make amendments in the second reading that are supported by the Commission and approved in the Council by a qualified majority. This holds for decisions under codecision as well as under cooperation. The previously mentioned decision about car emission standards is such a case. It is important to realize that the theoretical conclusions were derived under the assumption that the policy positions or preferences of the players and the status quo or reversion point remain constant between the adoption of the common position and the second reading in the Council. However, whenever some restrictions for the decision makers change after the adoption of the common position and these changes have not been anticipated, successful amendments of the EP can become possible.

Two institutional details are important in this respect. First, after the adoption of the common position, the Commission can no longer substantially change its proposal. Therefore, if the possibility of successful amendments arises, it is the EP that moves first and the Commission can approve or reject these amendments. Second, modification in the preferences or in the reversion point are possible because some time elapses between the adoption of the common position and the final decision. The Treaty in Article 189c requires that the Council's final decision must be within seven months after the adoption of the common position. Usually, the maximum allowed time period is not used: Wessel (1991: 143) reports that in 1988 and 1989 the time lag was on average 125 days. In the case of the decision about emission standards, however, the maximum time limit was used: the second reading in the Council was in June 1989, almost seven months after the formal adoption of the common position in December 1988, and almost a year after the compromise was reached in principle in June 1988.

Theoretically, the EP can make a successful second reading amendment in the cooperation procedure if the restrictions change in such a way that:

1. the Commission prefers the amendment to the common position;
2. at least one member of the Council prefers it to the common position;
3. the amendment is preferred to the reversion point by a qualified majority in the Council.

In the codecision procedure, successful EP amendments are also possible against the support of the Commission if these amendments are sustained by a qualified majority in the Council in the conciliation stage. In the following, the cooperation procedure is focused on because this was applied in the decision on car emission standards.

The set of points that fulfill these three conditions must be in the preferred-to set of the Commission with regard to the common position, $P_C(CP)$, inside the *Pareto set (PA)*, and inside the qualified majority win set with regard to the status quo, $QW(q)$. Here, the set of successful second reading amendments is called 'amendment win set', $AW(q, CP) = \{y \in X \mid y \in P_C(CP) \cap QW(q) \cap$ *Pareto set*\}. Three hypotheses that lead to a nonempty amendment win set can be identified:

Hypothesis 1   Change of the policy position by the decisive Council member

Assume that the decisive Council member is the binding restriction, that is, the Commission is constrained in its proposal by the requirement to be supported by a qualified majority in the Council in its first reading. Suppose that after the adoption of the common position, the decisive member changes position. Such a modification can be due to a change of the party (or party coalition) in government or be induced by a changed perception of the particular issue in public opinion which induces the decisive Council member to revise its position. Both the Commission and the EP would like to take advantage of this change but only the EP can propose amendments to the common position after the first reading in the Council. Consequently, the EP can make an amendment which is supported by the Commission (and which the Commission could not make in the first stage), and which is supported by a qualified majority in the Council.

An example of such a situation is illustrated in Figure 8.4. The common position (CP) reflects the best achievable policy for the Commission (C) that is approved by a qualified majority with Council member 1 being the constraining member. Suppose that the ideal point of member 1 moves toward the ideal point of the Commission (from 1 to 1') which increases the qualified majority win set, $QW(q)$. The EP can now choose a point in the $AW(q, CP)$, reflected by the shaded area in Figure 8.4. The optimal amendment for the EP

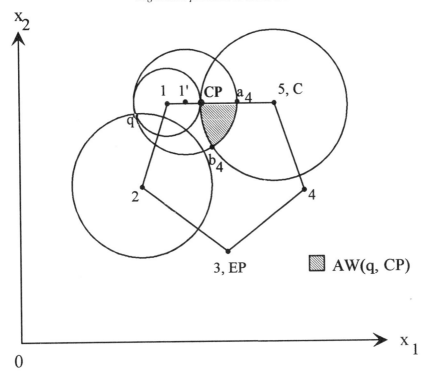

Figure 8.4   Change of the policy position by the decisive Council member

is b_4, which is weakly preferred by the Commission to the *CP*, cannot be modified by the Council and defeats q. Notice that there is some conflict between the Commission and the EP, because the Commission's optimal policy choice is now at a_4. However at that stage, only the EP can make substantial amendments which the Commission can only accept or reject.

Hypothesis 2   Change of the policy position by the Commission

Consider a situation in which the Commission can realize a common position at its ideal point and is not constrained by the preferences of the decisive Council member. If the policy position of the Commission changes, for example because the responsible Commissioner is replaced, then it may become possible for the EP to take advantage of this preference change in its second reading. This is the case whenever the EP can make a proposal such that the Commission is marginally better off than with the common position, and which is also supported by the decisive Council member.

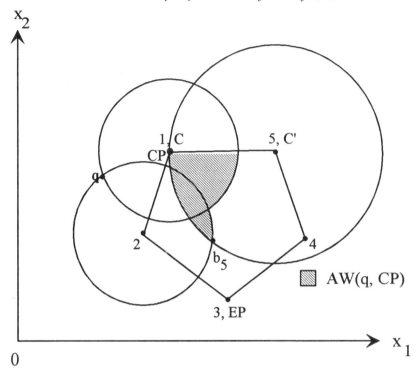

Figure 8.5   Change of the policy position by the Commission

In Figure 8.5, assume that the ideal point of the Commission is originally at 1 such that it can realize its optimal policy as the common position. Suppose that the Commission's ideal point moves from $C = 1$ to $C' = 5$. This creates an amendment win set for the EP corresponding to the shaded area in Figure 8.5. The EP proposes b_5 which the 'new' Commission accepts, which cannot be modified in the Council and is preferred to q by the Council (against the vote of member 1).

Hypothesis 3   Change of the reversion point

The perceptions of what happens if no decision is taken can change. Quite often in EU politics, the member states that advocate a major policy change by the EU threaten to enact these policy changes unilaterally if no satisfying decision is forthcoming in the Union. However, the possibilities for unilateral policies by the member states is severely limited by the Treaty, as it is interpreted by the European Court of Justice. If the perceived possibility of unilateral actions changes in the course of the decision process, the reversion point moves such that it may become possible that now the Commission and a qualified majority in the Council are prepared to accept an amendment by the EP (that they were not before). With such a decision unilateral policies by some member states can be avoided.

A change in the status quo or reversion point can have different implications. First, it can become possible that the Commission can achieve a better policy choice than the common position. Second, the common position can no longer be realized, because it is no longer in the qualified majority win set of the new reversion point. Figure 8.6 depicts an example of the first situation in which the reversion point moves from q to q'. This creates an amendment win set, with b_5 being the optimal amendment of the EP.

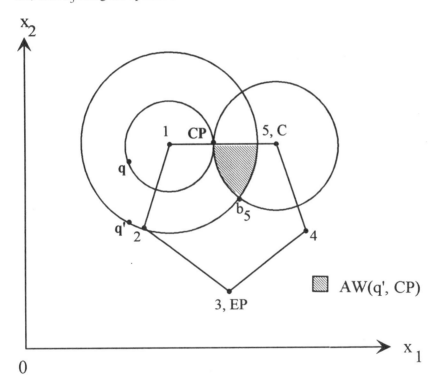

Figure 8.6   Change of the reversion point

8.3.1   Summary

Concluding Chapter 8, the EP is more than a (conditional) veto player in legislative decisions. Rather, it can take advantage of unanticipated changes of restrictions during the decision process. Modifications of the policy positions of the decisive Council member or the Commission, or changes of the reversion point can provide the EP with such opportunities. Consequently, the impact of the EP in EU decisions depends on: (1) which decision rule applies; and (2) whether restrictions change during the decision process in such a way that the EP can take advantage of these changes.

With respect to condition (1), it is not surprising that the influence of the EP is small or absent in those policy issues that are decided by the consultation procedure in which the EP is only consulted but has no other procedural rights. The EP can at best influence the decision by threatening to delay it. An important case in this respect was the decision about the first phase of Economic and Monetary Union. Since the Commission was anxious to avoid delay, it made an important concession to the EP (Jacobs and Corbett, 1990: 166). However, more influence by the EP can be expected on policy issues that are decided by the cooperation procedure or by the codecision procedure.

If the cooperation or the codecision procedure applies, the EP can only successfully influence policy choices – other than blocking them – if condition (2) is met. Whether one or several of the derived hypotheses are capable of explaining successful amendments by the EP requires careful analyses of individual cases. The relevant policy dimensions, the location of the reversion point and the induced preferences of the relevant players need to be determined, and it is necessary to analyse whether reversion point, preferences or maybe even the policy dimensions changed during the decision process. This is the research strategy used in Chapter 9.

NOTES

1. The data do not distinguish whether the Council only approves amendments of the EP that are supported by the Commission or whether the Council also accepts the EP's amendments that are not supported by the Commission.
2. For a detailed analysis from a legal point of view, see Fitzmaurice (1988) and Dashwood (1994); for a comparison of the various procedures, see Garrett (1995b); for a theoretical analysis of the codecision procedure, see Crombez (1997); for the conciliation procedure see Moser (1997a) and Tsebelis (1977); and for an empirical evaluation, see Earnshaw and Judge (1996).
3. Since 1995 the qualified majority requires 62 out of the 87 votes in the Council.
4. Most controversial is probably the assumption that the EP is a unitary actor although since 1995 it has been composed of 626 members. Tsebelis (1995b) argued that the committee structure with the institution of a rapporteur enables the EP to make cooperative decisions. Technically, this replaces the ideal point with an ideal area. As Tsebelis showed, the size of this area is reduced the further away it is from the status quo. On the committee system in the EP, see Bowler and Farrell (1995).
5. Here, this study differs with Steunenberg (1994b, Figure 2b) who assumed that the Council cannot force the Commission to open the gates.

6. This result differs substantially from Tsebelis's conclusion (1994) that the EP has conditional agenda power. He assumed that the EP can make the first proposal. This would allow the Parliament to choose its most preferred policy in QW, say b_2 in Figure 8.2. The Commission is then forced to support b_2 because it prefers b_2 to q. However, the sequence of decision rules in Tsebelis's model does not correspond accurately to the cooperation procedure. For a detailed critique of Tsebelis's argument, see Moser (1996a).
7. The Council is obliged to consult the EP before taking the decision. Although there is no time limit for the first reading of the EP, most observers deny that the EP can block a decision by not holding its first reading. However, the EP can substantially delay a decision by postponing the vote on the Commission's proposal, as pointed out by Jacobs and Corbett (1990: 165).

9. Case study on car emission standards

This chapter analyses the decision about car emission standards in the EU. Not only was this case an important policy decision but also a landmark case with regard to the influence of the EP. From a theoretical point of view, it is interesting to investigate whether one or several of the hypotheses derived in the previous chapter are capable of explaining successful amendments by the EP in this case. After describing the information relevant for the decision structure, the developed hypotheses are evaluated.[1]

9.1   CAR EMISSION POLICY IN THE EU

To apply the model, the relevant policy dimensions have to be determined first. Consider two dimensions: the degree of environmental protection as reflected by the choice of the emission standards, and the degree of market integration. The latter was also a central issue in this case because countries that sought stricter standards threatened to introduce them on their own, thereby creating markets with different regulations.

Second, it is necessary to know the location of the reversion point, that is the policy that is exercised if no decision is forthcoming. In the beginning, the reversion point was perceived as being the status quo. It was defined by the regulation (88/76/EC) formally approved by the Council on 3 December 1987 based on Article 95 (previously 100a) by a qualified majority and with Denmark and Greece voting against.[2] Among others, the regulation included three aspects:

1. Emission standards were differentiated according to the size of car, defined by motor capacity (see Table 9.1). This had different implications for the car producing countries of Germany, France, Italy, the United Kingdom and Spain. German car manufacturers, whose production concentrates on medium and large cars, had to follow stricter standards than the producers in the other member states who specialize more in the production of small cars. Above all, the standards were lower than the US-83 standards favored by environmental groups and by Denmark and Greece.[3] At least for small- and medium-sized cars, the standards could be achieved without using costly catalytic converters.

2. Different standards were tolerated because the regulation was based on the concept of optional harmonization. Cars that met the EU standard had to be permitted in all member countries. However, countries could also accept cars that met a less demanding national standard. For example, this allowed the British producers (who in 1985 exported only about 12 per cent to other EU-countries) to produce cars for the domestic market according to the less demanding UK emission standards.

3. Tax incentives were allowed but only for cars that fulfilled the EU standards in advance. Owners of small cars could be given a maximum tax deduction of DM750 if their cars emitted 15 per cent less than the EU standards. In this way, member countries could not use tax incentives to promote cars with catalytic converters.

Table 9.1   Car emission standards (approved on 3 December 1987)

Motor capacity	Time of introduction		Emission standards		
Liters	New models	New cars	CO	HC + NO_x	NO_x
Above 2 liters	1.10.88	1.10.89	25	6.5	3.5
1.4 – 2 liters	1.10.91	1.10.93	30	8	–
Below 1.4 liters 1. Stage	1.10.90	1.10.91	45	15	6
Below 1.4 liters 2. Stage	1.10.92	1.10.93	To be determined by 1987		

Source: Holzinger (1994: 247).

To complete the structure of the model, it is necessary to obtain information about the preferences of the decisive players over the two-dimensional issue space (degree of environmental protection and market integration). These preferences are (partially) revealed in the negotiations over the standards for small cars for the second stage. On 15 February 1988, the Commission proposed the same emission standards for small cars as for medium-sized cars, namely 30 g CO and 8g HC plus NO_x (30/8) to be introduced in October 1992. These standards could be met without using catalytic converters. The Commission's proposal was supported by Belgium, Luxembourg and Ireland. Italy, the United Kingdom, Spain, Portugal and most vigorously France opposed the proposal because they considered these standards as too strict. They were against any substantial tightening of the standards for small cars and favored a standard of 35/12 (35 g CO, 12 g HC plus NO_x). Germany, the Netherlands, and Greece preferred the US-83 standards of 20/5 which required catalytic converters. Denmark preferred the slightly stricter US-87 standards.[4] The position of the

EP was revealed in its first reading in September 1988. It proposed substantial amendments, supporting the US-83 standards (20/5) for all cars (not only the small cars), and allowing member states to grant tax incentives for the early fulfillment. In addition, the EP wanted to exempt car producers that could not meet the standards for a maximum of two years.[5]

With regard to market integration, assume that a single standard for the common market (total harmonization) is favored by the Commission and the EP, because of their general support for a single market. It is also reasonable to suppose that Germany preferred total harmonization as political pressure in Germany for strict standards was very strong. The German car industry, however, wanted their European competitors to follow the same standards. Italy, France and Spain have substantial export shares to other EU countries: France 39 per cent, Italy 24 per cent and Spain 57 per cent, as of 1985. Consequently, they supported a uniform European standard so as to exploit scale economies for export production, but wanted to keep the option to lower the standard for their own markets which still constituted the main market for most producers in these countries. Therefore, assume that these countries' favored policy was optional harmonization. The same position seemed politically optimal for the United Kingdom, although with its much lower export share of only 12 per cent, the United Kingdom was less worried about market integration. However, since it preferred less demanding standards it could realize these by optional harmonization. Those countries with less or no car production, Denmark and the Netherlands among others, were likely not to be concerned about the establishment of a single standard. Rather, they preferred national autonomy, that is the possibility to set different national standards.

In Figure 9.1, a plausible configuration is drawn of ideal points of some players and the status quo that reflects the above arguments. Of course, there always remains some uncertainty that, because of inherent strategic considerations, the revealed preferences may be different from the true preferences. This is a particular problem with the location of the Commission's most preferred policy (C).[6]

The negotiations in the Council continued until the common position was reached on 24 November 1988 and formally passed on 21 December, with the Netherlands, Denmark and Greece voting against. However, a first compromise had already been reached in June 1988, before the EP had held its first reading. Consequently, the suggested amendments by the EP did not influence the debate in the Council very much. In the common position, the Council supported the standards as proposed by the Commission (30/8) with two modifications. First, a third stage with stricter standards should be introduced five years at the earliest after the introduction of the second stage. Second, the Commission promised to use its power to prevent unilateral action by member states. This was considered necessary (particularly by France) because the Netherlands,

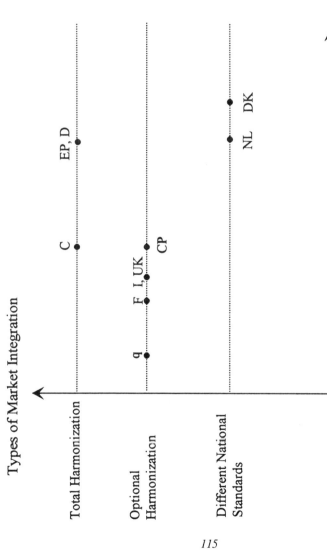

Figure 9.1   *Ideal points with regard to car emission standards*

Denmark and Germany planned tax incentives for cars meeting the US-83 standards (20/5).[7]

Plans for tax incentives were most advanced by the Netherlands. In July 1988, they informed the Commission of their plan to grant a tax reduction of 1700 Dutch guilders for cars of all sizes that met the US-83 standards. The revenue loss would be compensated by an increase in the sales tax for new cars. On 18 October 1988, the Commission opened a procedure based on Article 93 to examine whether this measure was a subsidy and whether it impeded the common market. The Netherlands could not bring their tax incentives into force until the Commission had reached a decision.

In summary, the common position brought about a tightening of the emission standards compared to the status quo, still based on the concept of optional harmonization. Countries preferring less demanding standards were allowed to keep such standards for their national market. In contrast, stricter standards were considered to be prohibited particularly by France (who pushed the Commission to act against the Netherlands and Denmark) and probably also by the Commission at that time. They argued that such tax incentives treated cars from different countries differently and, therefore, restricted trade in the common market. Therefore, the common position (*CP*) is depicted in Figure 9.1 as implying optional harmonization with a European standard of 30/8, that is with no possibility for stricter national standards.

9.2   EVALUATION OF THE HYPOTHESES

A check in now made on whether one or several of the hypotheses derived in Chapter 8 (Section 8.3) are supported by the available information. Since the relevant data are incomplete, the judgment is conditional on the information available at the time of the analysis.

Hypothesis 1   Change of the policy position by the decisive Council member

To evaluate the first hypothesis, it has to be determined who is the decisive Council member. The decisive Council member is characterized by having the possibility of blocking the decision and by the fact that this member is almost indifferent between the status quo and the proposal. The common position was approved by 63 votes with the Netherlands, Greece and Denmark voting against. Since 54 votes are required for the qualified majority, each of the large countries (France, Germany, Italy and the United Kingdom) each with their 10 votes could have blocked the decision. While Germany wanted stricter standards, the other three large members preferred less demanding standards. It was France that used its veto position most intensively: in July 1988, France revoked its support of the compromise agreed on in June. Only after its demands had been met did France support the common position in November 1988. In particular, France wanted to make sure that the second stage would last at least five years and that member countries could not use tax incentives to promote cars meeting stricter standards.[8] Referring again to Figure 9.1, France's ideal point was to the left of those of Italy and the United Kingdom. Hence, it is plausible that the common position reflected the best policy for the Commission that France would still accept.

There is no systematic information that would support the hypothesis that the French ideal point moved to the right after the adoption of the common position. Such a claim is made by Arp (1992: 35) who argued that the resistance of French and Italian car manufacturers weakened. It is correct that Renault and Fiat no longer opposed the introduction of catalytic converters, but they had already changed their position before the common position was adopted. In contrast, the very influential opposition of Peugeot-Citroën continued. Therefore, this hypothesis is regarded as unlikely to explain the EP's successful second reading amendment.

Hypothesis 2   Change of the policy position by the Commission

Given the situation in Figure 9.1, three conditions have to be fulfilled for the support of hypothesis 2. First, the common position must be identical with the ideal point of the Commission. Second, the Commission was not constrained by the decisive Council member when choosing its proposal. Third, the position of the Commission must change toward the position of the EP after the adoption of the common position.

In contrast to the assumptions in Figure 9.1, the first condition could be met. It is not impossible that the Commission preferred optional harmonization because it was the EP and not the Commission that first embraced total harmonization.

With regard to the third condition, there is insufficient information to conclude with certainty whether the position of the Commission changed after the adoption of the common position. According to Article 219, the position of the Commission is determined by the absolute majority rule. Nevertheless, each Commissioner has a considerable degree of freedom of action in his or her own policy field (Donnelly and Ritchie, 1994: 38). Therefore, if a Commissioner is replaced by a person with different policy preferences, a change in the Commission's position in this policy area would be expected.[9] Two directorates general were mainly involved in the policy decision on car emission standards. The main responsibility was at the directorate for the internal market (DG III) because the decision involved a harmonization of technical standards which are typically assigned to this directorate. Nevertheless, the Commissioner for the environment, nuclear safety and civil protection (DG XI) represented the Commission in the Council. Interestingly, on 6 January 1989 the Commissioners responsible for these two directorates were replaced.

The Commissioner responsible for the environment, Harold Clinton Davis (UK), was replaced by Carlo Ripa di Meana (I), former Commissioner for culture and former member of the EP, and Martin Bangemann (D) succeeded Lord Cockfield (UK), as the head of the directorate for the internal market. Since personal voting records of the Commissioners are not public, it is difficult to determine the policy preferences of individual Commissioners. With regard to the change of the Commissioner for the environment, Holzinger (1994: 323) reported in her careful study that already Clinton Davis was known as a supporter of environmental protection and Ripa di Meana proved to be of similar stance (to the surprise of many observers). With regard to the environmental policy stance of the Commissioner for the internal market, there is no information available about Lord Cockfield's position. In contrast, Bangemann was a minister in the German government before becoming Commissioner and supported actively the German position that member states should be allowed to use national measures if no acceptable agreement was forthcoming in the EU (van den Bos, 1994: 36).

Although it is possible that the common position was the Commission's ideal point and that the Commission's position moved toward stricter standards due to replacements of these Commissioners, the second condition is considered as not being met. The Commission was, in fact, constrained when choosing its proposal. The behavior of France indicates that it was constraining the proposal of the Commission, or at least that a modification of the Commission's position alone would not be sufficient to make a successful proposal by the EP feasible.

Hypothesis 3   Change of the reversion point

Two conditions are necessary for the support of hypothesis 3. First, there must be new information about the consequences of a disagreement such that the reversion point changes. Second, given the new reversion policy, the Commission and a qualified majority in the Council must prefer the amendment by the EP to the new reversion policy. This hypothesis is the most convincing in explaining the successful amendment in the decision on emission standards.

The new information was about the possibility of unilateral action by member states and was provided by the European Court of Justice in the *Danish bottle case*, decided on 20 September 1988 (Case 302/86, *Commission v. Denmark*, (1988) ECR 4607). In this decision, the Court regarded the Danish deposit-and-return system for drink containers as conforming with the Treaty, but rejected the requirement to use only bottles approved by the Danish bureau for the environment. This decision is regarded as the leading case with regard to the trade-off between the national environmental policy and the requirement of the free movement of goods in the common market. For the first time, the Court recognized explicitly that environmental protection is a mandatory requirement that can justify restrictions of the free movements of goods and services in the common market.[10]

9.2.1 The Importance of the *Danish Bottle Case*

To clarify the importance of this decision, it is necessary to describe briefly the legal test, as developed by the Court, to determine whether a national restriction of the free movement of goods is permitted or prohibited by the treaty.[11] If the European Union has harmonized an issue based on Article 95 (as in the case of the emission standards) then unilateral actions remain possible according to Article 95(4).[12] An essential requirement is that the national measure passes the test based on Article 28 and 30.[13] In a first step, the Court determines whether a measure can potentially restrict trade between member states. Since the *Dassonville case* in 1974, the Court's interpretation of such potential effects has been very broad and was further extended to different national regulation in the *Cassis de Dijon case* in 1979. If such potential trade effects are present, the Court determines in a second step whether a different national regulation is justified by Article 30 which allows trade restriction among others in order to protect the health and life of humans, animals or plants. The Court interprets Article 30 restrictively and considers the enumeration of justifications as exhaustive. Therefore, the majority of environmental measures cannot be based on Article 30 (Krämer, 1993: 117). However, since the *Cassis de Dijon case*, the Court has accepted national measures if they are justified by mandatory requirements.

Before the *Danish bottle case*, the Court recognized as mandatory requirements among others the necessity of fiscal control, fair trading practices and consumer protection (Krämer, 1993: 120). In addition, any national regulation that is justified by a mandatory requirement must finally pass a test of proportionality: it must be the least trade restrictive regulation that is suitable to achieve a mandatory requirement. Since the protection of the environment was not recognized as a mandatory requirement before the *Danish bottle case* nor could be based on Article 30, there was at least considerable dispute whether national environmental regulation that restricts the free movement of goods was permitted by the Court. Illustrative for this dispute is the fact that not only the Commission attacked the Danish bottle regulation but that it was followed in its assessment by the Advocate General who prepares the cases for the Court.[14]

9.2.2 Consequences for Unilateral Action

Recognition of environmental protection as a mandatory requirement by the Court has implications for the consideration of tax incentives plans for cars using catalytic converters. If these tax incentive plans are not considered as subsidies – and there are many arguments against regarding them as subsidies (Sevenster, 1989: 558; Becker, 1991: 66) – then they can potentially restrict trade. The reason is that they shift demand toward cars using catalytic converters and thereby potentially change the structure of trade in the common market. With the *Danish bottle case*, such an impediment to the free movement of goods has become acceptable because it serves the legitimate interest to protect the environment in a way that intervenes only modestly in the freedom of trade.

The change in the Court's case law influenced the controversy between the Netherlands and the Commission. Since the Commission had not reached its final decision about the Dutch tax incentives plan, the Netherlands took legal action at the Court against the Commission on 31 January 1989. The Netherlands demanded that they be allowed to bring their tax incentives into force. Before the Court ruled on this issue, the Commission decided on 8 March 1989 to end the examination procedure on the Dutch tax incentive plan, which allowed the Netherlands to withdraw their complaint at the Court and to bring the tax incentives into force immediately. Soon after this decision, Denmark went even further in passing a bill that required the US-87 standards for all cars after October 1990, and granted a tax reduction for cars meeting this standard before October 1990. The Commission took no legal action against Denmark.

Referring back to Figure 9.1, the jurisprudence of the Court implied that the expected reversion point was no longer the status quo, q, that is, the situation defined by the Luxembourg compromise. Rather, if no decision were forthcoming, different national standards could be introduced and the strictest standards would be the US-83 standards (as favored by the Netherlands, Germany and the EP) or even the US-87 standards, as endorsed by Denmark. For many member countries (particularly France and Italy) and for the Commission, the new reversion point was worse than the status quo because of the disintegration effect. In particular, France who formerly blocked decisions and thereby defended the status quo had an interest in a decision being reached which would avoid unilateral action. The EP could exploit this situation because it is the only player that can propose substantial amendments after the common position is approved.

In the second reading, the responsible committee of the EP insisted among others on a standard of 20/5 for all cars and on the concept of total harmonization; that is, member states are allowed to require neither stricter nor less demanding standards. The committee proposed to reject the common position if the Commission did not support these amendments. The EP knew that with its rejection the common position would definitely fail, since no unanimity could be reached in the Council on the common position. In this case, the new reversion point would prevail. It is likely that the EP preferred this reversion point to the common position, because the benefit of more environmental protection in a substantial part of the Union outweighed the loss due to the disintegration effect. Consequently, the threat by the EP was credible and was recognized as such by the Commission. In the parliamentary debate on 11 April 1989, the Commissioner, Ripa di Meana, followed the general practice and took a position on each of the suggested amendments. The Commissioner promised to support the standards of 20/5 for cars of all sizes and the concept of total harmonization. After this statement, the EP amended the common position accordingly with 311 votes in favor of the amendments, exceeding the then required absolute majority of 260 votes.

Subsequently, the Council faced the following situation at its second reading. First, it was not possible to substantially change the amended common position with its stricter standards (the Commission proposed 19/5) because this would have required consent which was not feasible. Second, if the Council did not support the amended common position, some member countries would introduce stricter standards unilaterally. In addition to the Netherlands and Denmark, Germany announced such an intention on 27 April 1989. Therefore, the discussion was mainly about the time of the introduction. Finally, on 9 June 1989, the Council approved a compromise by a qualified majority (with Denmark and Greece voting against) that the standards of 19/5 be introduced on 31 December 1992 for new cars based on the concept of total harmonization. However, member states were allowed to grant tax deductions for cars that met these standards before December 1992, and thereby they could, in fact, introduce these standards earlier.

Summarizing the evidence for the third hypothesis, the changed perception by the member states and by the Commission of the likelihood of stricter national standards allowed the EP to realize its optimal policy. The reversion point changed such that the Commission and a qualified majority in the Council supported stricter standards in order to avoid a disintegration of the market.

NOTES

1. A detailed description of the decision process on car emission standards is provided by Holzinger (1994). Furthermore, Bueno de Mesquita and Stokman (1994) analysed the bargaining process inside the Council but do not take into account the impact of the EP.
2. Informally, the compromise was already reached in June 1985 in Luxembourg but the decision was blocked because of the Danish veto which became ineffective after the Single European Act replaced the unanimity rule by the qualified majority rule in July 1987.

A question remains why Denmark voted against the compromise which it clearly preferred to the status quo. One explanation could be that at that time it was not clear whether a country could choose unilaterally stricter regulations based on Article 95(4) if it had supported the decision. Since Denmark knew that the necessary qualified majority existed to pass the regulation, it could vote against the proposal so as to preserve its option of unilateral action.

3. The US standards are measured by a different technique. Consequently, there are different numbers depending on the rules used to convert the US standards into the European measure. 20 g CO, and 5 g HC plus NO_x are used as an approximation of the US 83 standards.

4. With regard to the emission standards, this study reaches the same conclusions as van den Bos (1994: 58) who determined the policy positions of the member countries on emission standards based on data published in *Agence Europe*, the leading press agency in this field.

5. In the EP, 243 votes were in favor of the amendments and 63 against it. Hence, the EP did not support the amendments by the absolute majority of 260 votes which was necessary to make the amendments in the second reading.

6. Figure 9.1 suggests that both dimensions are continuous. However, market integration is a discontinuous variable because three types are distinguished. Therefore, indifference curves cannot be drawn.

7. Furthermore, some German Länder introduced regulations that allowed only the use of cars with catalytic converters in case of smog alert.

8. The French Government was lobbied by the Peugeot-Citroën Company (PSA) which was most committed to the concept of a 'lean burn engine' and, therefore, opposed the introduction of catalytic converters vigorously (Holzinger, 1994: 277).

9. This argument is developed in general for coalition governments by Laver and Shepsle (1990), and discussed in Chapter 4 (section 4.1).

10. In an earlier case (Case 240/83, *ADBHU*, (1985) ECR 531) the Court recognized the protection of the environment as an objective for the EU and, therefore, to provide a competence for the Union to regulate the use of the environment. However, this decision did not necessarily imply that the member states could interfere with the free movement of goods in order to protect the environment. It was with the Danish bottle case that 'the Court recognized that the protection of the environment was such a mandatory requirement which could justify restrictions to the free circulation of goods' (Kramer, 1993: 121; Rengling and Heinz, 1990: 616; see also the Court's decision, case 302/86, ECR 4630, para 8).

11. There is a large legal literature on this subject; examples are Pernice (1990), Becker (1991), Krämer (1993) and Ziegler (1996).

12. It is disputed in the legal literature whether unilateral actions are also possible for countries that voted in favor of the harmonization in the Council or if the decision was unanimous (see the discussion in Pernice, 1990: 207).

13. If national measures regulate issues that have not been dealt with by the EU (as the Danish bottle regulation), they have to pass the same test.

14. An indication that the *Danish bottle case* changed the perception of the allowed policy autonomy with regard to environmental policy is the discussion about the smog regulation introduced in some German Länder. While Moench (1989) argued that the prohibition to drive cars without catalytic converters during smog alarms is not permitted by the treaty, Heinz (1989) claimed that they are permitted and refers explicitly to the modified jurisprudence due to the *Danish bottle case*.

Summary of Part III

This part of the study provided a rational choice-based explanation of why the EP is sometimes influential in the legislative procedures. A conservative EP can use its right of rejection to block a decision in the codecision procedure and, whenever there is no consent in the Council, also in the cooperation procedure. A progressive EP can successfully use its amendment right in the second reading whenever the constraints have been changed unexpectedly since the adoption of the common position such as to create an amendment win set. Then, the EP can choose its most preferred policy in this set which is supported by the Commission, cannot be changed by the Council and is preferred against the status quo by a qualified majority in the Council. The case study illustrates the argument and reveals that the perceived modification in the reversion point due to the changed or clarified case law of the Court was the primary reason for allowing the EP to use successfully its amendment right.

The analysis and results have two implications for further research. First, detailed case studies are necessary to determine whether the EP has a considerable effect in EU decision making, not only in the cooperation but also in the codecision procedure. General statistics are of limited value. To analyse the extent of the parliamentary influence, it is necessary to determine the relevant constraints for the EP and whether such constraints have changed during the decision process. Such an approach requires case studies. Second, the case study points out the crucial role of the European Court of Justice which was treated as exogenous in the model. Clearly, a next step must involve the inclusion of the Court to improve the understanding about decision making in the EU.

PART IV

Institutions and regulatory behavior:
Checks and balances as a prerequisite for
independent central banks

Introduction to Part IV

The relation between the central bank and legislators is one particular form of delegated policy making. In many countries, the central bank can choose the growth of money supply by setting interest rates, exchange rates or by adjusting the monetary base by other instruments. Legislators in a large number of countries have granted the central bank some degree of independence, for example by appointing the governors of the central bank for a few years without the possibility of recalling them before their term ends. Nevertheless, central banks as other regulatory agents do not have the last word in politics (see Chapter 4, section 4.2). Rather, the legislators can modify statutes and change delegated authorities and grant independence in response to the agents' actions. However, in a political system with two or more veto players, the central bank has discretion in the sense that it can change the policy to some extent without provoking a legislative override. While such discretion is typically a concern for legislators, and they use structures, processes and appointments to mitigate this problem, agency discretion is a prerequisite for central bank independence. Consequently, checks and balances are a necessary institutional condition which allows policy makers to credibly commit to an independent central bank and thereby mitigate the well-known time-consistency problem in monetary policy.

In this part, the argument is developed in detail and tested empirically. Chapter 10 begins by first reporting the discussion in the literature on central bank independence. The model developed by Lohmann (1992) is adapted to analyse the interaction between a central bank and two policy makers with both having veto powers in legislation. It points out that the central bank can choose monetary policy to some extent at its discretion only if the preferences of the policy makers are heterogeneous. Comparing delegated with discretionary policy making, conditions are derived under which both policy makers prefer to delegate monetary policy. In Chapter 11, all the Organization for Economic Cooperation and Development (OECD) countries are classified according to the criteria whether the legislative function is shared equally between at least two decision bodies and whether they have different preferences. Regression analysis reveals that countries whose legislative processes are characterized by extensive checks and balances are associated with significantly more legally independent central banks and with a stronger negative relation between legal independence and inflation than countries without checks and balances.

10. Legislative choice of the monetary institution

10.1 THE DISCUSSION IN THE LITERATURE

Kydland and Prescott (1977) and Barro and Gordon (1983) initiated a large theoretical literature on time-inconsistency in monetary policy.[1] Usually it is assumed that policy makers care about both inflation and unemployment. According to the Phillips curve, the trade-off between inflation and unemployment depends on expected inflation. The policy makers would prefer everyone to expect low inflation. To reduce expected inflation, politicians often announce that low inflation is the principal goal of monetary policy. Low expected inflation would allow policy makers to expand money supply in order to increase the rate of economic growth and thereby reduce unemployment. However, such a policy would also cause higher inflation. Since households and firms know that policy makers have an incentive to renege by expanding money supply it would be foolish for households and firms to believe the announcement of low inflation. Therefore, the attempt of policy makers to stimulate output above the long-term growth rate is futile and results in inflation only.[2]

The surprising outcome of this analysis is that policy makers can sometimes better achieve their goals by having their discretion taken away from them. Rogoff (1985) suggests the creation of an independent central bank and the appointment of a conservative central banker. Allowing for stochastic shocks in the economy and assuming that wages are set before and monetary policy is chosen after the realization of the shock, a central banker who puts more weight on inflation than the government's true objective improves the outcome relative to government setting policy itself. Furthermore, in a democracy with competing parties, the independence of the central bank also serves to reduce election-induced uncertainty about the future course of policy (Alesina and Gatti, 1995). However, Lohmann (1992) points out that central bank independence not only provides a beneficial reduction of inflation expectation but that independence comes at the cost of less flexibility. The forgone flexibility could be used to lower unemployment (or to inflate part of the national debt). Therefore, the politically optimal commitment is not to a completely independent central bank but it is optimal for the government to keep the option to override the central bank's decision at some positive costs. Hence, the central bank applies a nonlinear rule: in time of small output shocks, it determines inflation independently and, in times of large output disturbances, it accommodates the government's demand.[3]

The creation of a (partially) independent central bank is regarded as the main solution to the credibility problem. In fact, it is well documented by empirical research that a higher degree of central bank independence is associated with lower inflation in developed countries (Cukierman, 1992; Alesina and Summers, 1993; Cukierman *et al.*, 1993; Schiemann and Alshuth, 1994; Al-Marhubi and Willett, 1995; Cukierman and Webb, 1995; Eijffinger and Schaling, 1997). Obviously, the question arises; if central bank independence is rather beneficial, why do not all countries grant independence to their central banks?

Only a few studies address this question (Eijffinger and de Haan, 1996, chapter 5). In Cukierman (1994), a government that is uncertain whether it is reelected chooses the degree of central bank independence. He conjectures that the independence will be higher the larger the employment-motivated inflationary bias, the higher political instability and the larger the government debt. However, these predictions are tested and rejected by Cukierman and Webb (1995) and de Haan and van't Hag (1995). Milesi-Ferretti (1995) argues that the inflation-averse party has an incentive to keep a relative low degree of independence because it does not want to solve the incentive problem of its more inflationary opponent. Eijffinger and Schaling (1997) claim in their study that the ultimate determinants of the degree of conservativeness are the natural rate of employment, the benefits of unanticipated inflation, the inflation aversion and the variance of the productivity shock. With one exception, these 'ultimate' determinants are insignificant in their own test.

What almost the whole literature neglects is that the benefits of central bank independence depend on the existence of some costs of withdrawing the independence. These costs are assumed to be exogenous (either explicitly as in Rogoff, 1985, Cukierman, 1994 and Jensen, 1997, or implicitly as in Alesina and Gatti, 1995 and Eijffinger and Schaling, 1998) or supposed to be somehow chosen by the policy maker (Lohmann, 1992). However, as Jensen (1997) points out, if these costs are not indefinitely high and are one argument in the utility function of the government, then, in equilibrium, the government will redefine the degree of central bank independence after labor market contracts have been chosen so as to realize surprise inflation. Consequently, some inflation bias remains even with costly redefinition of delegation.

In the literature, the reasons for these costs are never specified. Since in most countries central bank independence is not a constitutional requirement but rather determined by a legislative statute, the legal independence of the central bank is granted by a majority vote of the legislators and can be removed by the same decision rule. With the exception of some kind of opportunity costs of the legislators, the legally independent central bank is, in fact, dependent on the legislators who can change the law. Why should the wage setters regard a statute that creates an independent central bank as durable and credible?

There are countries which have checks and balances in their legislative decision making. As a consequence, once a statute is in force it cannot be modified by a simple majority rule. An example is a bicameral legislature with both chambers having equal power: assuming that the statute grants independence to the central bank, if one chamber wants to modify the independence but the second chamber prefers the status quo, no change occurs. As long as there are at least two veto players with different preferences, an independent central bank has some discretion in its actions without provoking an override by the legislators. In contrast, a unicameral legislature cannot provide this kind of discretion to a central bank. If the bank does not choose the policy preferred by the median legislator (or by the majority party if there is a strong party discipline), the legislators can always override the central bank's policy. The point of this argument is that those countries with a legislative system that comprises at least two veto players with different preferences have higher costs of withdrawing the independence and thereby are more credible in supplying a legally independent central bank that, in fact, can choose its policy partially independently. For all other countries, central bank independence is a less credible solution to the time-consistency problem in monetary policy. These countries have little incentive to write a statute that grants legal independence to the central bank (if they do so such a central bank would not be behaviorally independent). Rather, these countries must search for other mechanisms to mitigate the consistency problem.

In the following sections, a model is presented that analyses the interaction between legislators and the central bank. First, in section 10.2, the model is described and the outcome of discretionary and delegated policy making is derived. Section 10.3 characterizes the conditions under which policy makers find it to their advantage to delegate monetary policy to the central bank.

10.2   THE MODEL

The following simple macroeconomic model captures the essential features (Lohmann, 1992). The economy is characterized by the supply function

$$y = \pi - w + z \qquad (10.1)$$

where y is output, π is the inflation rate, w is the growth rate of nominal wages, and z is the output shock which is assumed to be normally distributed with zero mean and positive variance (σ_z^2). The model is formulated in logarithms.

The wage setters negotiate nominal wage growth based on their expectation before z and π are observed:

$$w = E\pi. \tag{10.2}$$

π is determined by politics. The political side comprises two policy makers with equal powers, representing, for example, two chambers of a bicameral parliament or reflecting the interaction between the legislative and an executive branch with mutual veto powers. The policy makers are assumed to minimize the loss function

$$L_i = (y - \hat{y}_i)^2 + \chi_i \pi^2 \qquad i = 1,2 \tag{10.3}$$

where $\hat{y}_i$ are the policy makers' output bliss points, $\hat{y}_i > 0$, and χ_i are the relative weights placed on the inflation and output goals, $0 < \chi_i < \infty$. It is assumed that policy maker 1 is more expansionist than policy maker 2 in two ways: he has a higher output bliss point and places less weight on the inflation goal; $\hat{y}_1 > \hat{y}_2$ and $\chi_1 < \chi_2$.

The time-consistency problem arises because the policy makers' output bliss points $\hat{y}_i$ are larger than zero, the normalized logarithm of the natural level of output. This bias is traditionally ascribed to imperfections in the labor markets (Barro and Gordon, 1983, Cukierman, 1992, chapter 3) but could as well reflect incentives caused by the political business cycle.[4] The wage setters determine nominal wages before z is realized and before policy makers set π. The wage setters know that the policy makers have an incentive to stimulate employment and output above the natural level by inflating. Therefore, they include an inflationary markup in their wage contracts so that the policy makers fail to stimulate output above the natural level of output on average while the inflation rate exhibits a positive bias.[5]

10.2.1 Discretionary Policy Making

If the two policy makers determine π at their discretion, it is assumed that the bilateral bargaining among them results in minimizing the sum of the two loss functions:

$$L = L_1 + L_2 = (y - \hat{y}_1)^2 + (y - \hat{y}_2)^2 + (\chi_1 + \chi_2)\pi^2. \tag{10.4}$$

With this description of political preferences, the inflation rate in the equilibrium is

$$\pi_D = -\frac{2z}{(1+\chi_1)+(1+\chi_2)} + \frac{\hat{y}_1 + \hat{y}_2}{\chi_1 + \chi_2} \qquad (10.5)$$

where the subscript D stands for discretion.[6] The first term in (10.5) stands for the inflation caused by the policy response to the exogenous shock z, while the second term represents the inflationary bias. If policy makers could legislate the rule described by the first term in (10.5) and commit to it, they could flexibly respond to shocks but still achieve zero inflation on average. However, such a state-contingent rule would not only require that the policy makers foresee all possible contingencies but that they prefer to follow the rule – and not to change it – in all circumstances. The informational need and the requirement that the policy makers ought not to reconsider their earlier decisions both make this policy rule incredible.

10.2.2   Delegated Policy Making

If monetary policy is delegated to the central banker she sets π but has to observe the threat that the policy makers can withdraw the delegated authority. Since this study is not interested in the choice of the person to serve as central banker it is assumed that the banker is extremely inflation-averse and only concerned about π and that the policy makers have no influence on the banker's preference. She minimizes the loss function

$$L_C = \pi^2 + \delta c \qquad (10.6)$$

where δ is a dummy variable that takes on a value of 1 when the policy makers become active and reverse the bank's decision, and c is the cost to the bank if her policy is actively reversed. This cost includes reputation damages and losses in power in monetary and regulatory policies. It is supposed that this cost is large enough such that the bank dislikes to be overruled by the legislators in all circumstances.[7] If the central bank could act completely independently, the inflation rate would be always zero at the political cost of a higher variance in real output. However, such an independence is not feasible in general which the following model clarifies.

The model of delegated policy making consists of six stages:

Stage 1   The policy makers decide whether to delegate monetary policy to the central bank or to determine π at their discretion.

Stage 2   The wage setters set nominal wage growth w.

Stage 3   The output shock z is realized.

Stage 4   The central bank sets the inflation rate (π_c) if delegated to do so, otherwise policymakers set π_D.

Stage 5   If inflation rate has been set by central bank it is accepted if at least one policy maker does not reject the policy, otherwise, if both policy makers override the central bank's decision they reset π.

Stage 6   Inflation π and output y are realized.

A brief discussion follows regarding some assumptions on which the model is based. First, the policy makers are restricted to a binary choice whether or not to delegate monetary policy to an independent and inflation-averse central bank. Specifically, the policy makers do not choose the preferences of the central banker. This is difficult in practice and of minor importance for the purpose of this study because here the interest is in political control via the threat of a legislative override. Second, it is assumed that laws can be changed in reaction to the observed monetary policy by the central bank before wage setters adapt their expectations. In reality, it is enough to threaten the central bank with changing the law, since the bank does not want its policy to be changed (or its formal independence to be reduced). Such a threat can be quite informal, for example, by the chairperson of the responsible committee or by the leadership of the majority party. Third, it is supposed that there are no costs of override except to find an agreement among the policy makers. Of course, there are additional costs but these are independent of the degree of checks and balances, and thereby can be neglected in this comparative analysis. Finally, this study follows the literature and neglects the transmission mechanism.

The model is solved by backward induction. In proposition 1 in the Appendix to this chapter, the equilibrium of the noncooperative subgame starting at stage 2 is characterized precisely. Figure 10.1 illustrates the interaction between the policy makers and the central banker. In the fifth stage of the game, the policy makers have to decide whether or not to override the central banker's decision. An override is only possible if both policy makers prefer it. The realization of z determines which policy maker is decisive. If $z \in A_2$ the more conservative policy maker 2 would like to set π_{D2} which is always less than policy maker 1's most preferred inflation π_{D1}. If an override were to take place, the decisive policy maker (in this case policy maker 2) would have a strong bargaining position in resetting the inflation rate because he makes an override feasible. Hence, it is assumed that the decisive policy maker could realize his most preferred inflation rate.[8]

Facing this overriding and inflation-resetting response, the central banker sets π_C so as to keep the decisive policy maker indifferent between accepting π_C and overriding the central banker's decision and resetting the inflation rate: $L_i(\pi_C) = L_i(\pi_{Di})$. Since it is assumed that the policy makers face no opportunity cost if they override the decision of the central banker and determine π by

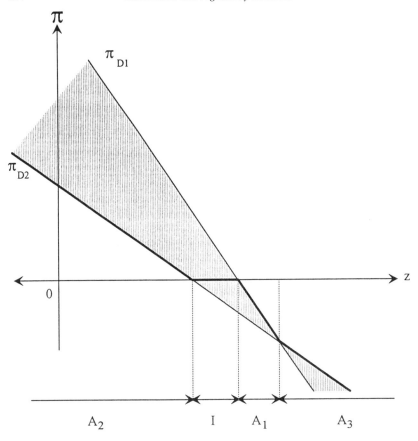

Figure 10.1   Degree of central bank discretion

direct legislation, the central banker is forced to choose the most preferred π of the decisive policy maker. If $z \in A_2$ or $z \in A_3$ the central banker accommodates the preferences of the more conservative policy maker 2: the banker's marginal reaction to z is identical to the one preferred by policy maker 2. If $z \in A_1$ the central bank accommodates the preferences of policy maker 1, who favors an inflation rate that is closer to zero than the preferred inflation rate of policy maker 2 in the range A_1.

Only if $z \in I$ does the central banker have complete discretion to choose her most preferred policy, $\pi = 0$. In this situation, there is a conflict between the two policy makers: the first prefers an expansionist monetary policy and the second favors a restrictive policy. This gives the central banker complete behavioral independence to set her most preferred zero-inflation policy. The range of z in which the behavioral independence of the central banker is largest rises the larger the difference between the policy makers' bliss points. With equal bliss points, I is empty, and the central bank always follows the preferences of the more conservative policy maker. Notice that also for z outside I, the central banker has some discretion in her choice of π: she can pick a π that is at or between the most preferred inflation rates of the policy makers (a point inside the shaded area in Figure 10.1). However, only if z is in I, can the banker realize her preferred zero-inflation policy. Finally, in stage 2, the wage setters set the growth rate of nominal wages equal to their inflationary expectations which they form by taking into account the central banker's reaction function and by taking into account the probabilities with which z is in the range A_1, A_2, A_3 or I.

10.3 INSTITUTIONAL CHOICE

So far, this discussion has presented the equilibrium strategies if the policy makers determine monetary policy at their discretion and if they delegate monetary policy to a conservative central banker who aims at a zero-inflation rate but is constrained by the threat of a legislative override. The following proposition characterizes the conditions under which the policy makers find it to their advantage to delegate monetary policy, that is under which conditions their expected loss is smaller with delegation than with discretion (stage 1 of the model).

Proposition 2   Delegation of monetary policy to an inflation-averse central banker is preferred by both policy makers to discretionary policy making

1.   *if there is some divergence between the policy makers' inflation-output weights, or*
2.   *if the output bliss points of the policy makers are unequal: $\hat{y}_1 \neq \hat{y}_2$, and*
3.   *if the divergence between policy makers' inflation-output weights is limited.*

(See Appendix to this chapter for the proof.)

The two policy makers will only agree to delegate monetary policy to a conservative central banker if they have different preferences either with respect to their inflation-output weights or with respect to their output bliss points, and if their disagreement with regard to inflation-output weights is not too large. The intuition underlying proposition 2 is as follows.

The explanation of part (1) of the proposition is the following. In the case of identical output bliss points $\hat{y}_1 = \hat{y}_2$ but different inflation-output weights, the central banker reacts to output shock z according to the preferences of the conservative politician 2 (χ_2) Any deviation from the preferences of policy maker 2 would trigger an override. This behavior of the bank reduces the time-consistent average inflation rate more than if the policy makers set π at their discretion in which cases they react to z according to their average preferences ($\frac{1}{2}(\chi_1 + \chi_2)$). Delegation is beneficial for policy maker 1 as long as the divergence in the inflation-output weights between the two politicians is not too large (part (3) of the proposition). Notice that this result is similar to the one reported by Rogoff (1985). However, in his model, the decisive difference is between the politician and the central bank while in the model in this study it is the difference between the two politicians. Since in this study the central bank has to accommodate the more conservative policy maker (for identical output bliss points), delegation to the central bank is behaviorally equivalent to delegation to the more conservative policy maker.

As stated in part (2) of proposition 2, different output bliss points create an additional incentive for delegation. In contrast to divergence with respect to χ, divergence with respect to $\hat{y}$ need not be limited as long as $\hat{y}_2 > 0$. The reason is that differences in output bliss points do not generate conflicts of interest over how much to respond to output shock, whereas differences in the relative weight on inflation do. In the case of differences in $\hat{y}$, the central bank follows the preferences of the more conservative policy maker only if z is in the range A_2, sets zero-inflation in the range of I and follows the preferences (of lower inflation) of politician 1 if z is in A_1 (A_3 does not exist because with equal inflation weights the $\pi - z$ reaction lines are parallel). Even if divergence is limited to output bliss points, delegation to the central banker reduces the time-consistent average inflation rate compared to policy discretion for significantly positive output bliss points.[9]

10.3.1 Conclusion

By relating political institutions to commitment ability this model claims to explain why certain countries are successful in coping with the time-inconsistency problem by creating an independent central bank, and why others are not. There are two necessary conditions for delegation by legislators to be credible:

1. The legislative function must be shared equally between at least two decision bodies (parliamentary chambers, executive or the people if a referendum exists) such that the decision bodies possess veto powers.
2. The decision bodies must have different preferences with regard to monetary policy, that is, to some degree, different inflation-output weights (χ) or different perceptions of politically acceptable output or unemployment ($\hat{y}$).

Only countries with legislative decision rules that fulfill these two conditions are expected to carry out legal efforts to create a partially independent central bank.

10.4 APPENDIX: PROPOSITION 1 AND PROOF OF PROPOSITION 2

Proposition 1

The subgame perfect equilibrium is defined by the following set of strategies:

1. The policy makers' overriding and inflation-resetting best response is given by

$$\delta(z) = \begin{cases} 0 & \text{if } L_2(\pi_C) - L_2(\pi_{Di}) \leq 0 \quad \text{or} \\ & \text{if } L_1(\pi_C) - L_1(\pi_{Di}) \leq 0 \\ 1 & \text{otherwise} \end{cases} \tag{A1}$$

$$\text{if } \delta(z) = 1 \text{ then } \begin{aligned} \pi_{Di} &= \pi_{D2} = \frac{w - z + \hat{y}_2}{1 + \chi_2} & \text{if } z \in A_2 \text{ or } z \in A_3 \\ \pi_{Di} &= 0 & \text{if } z \in I \\ \pi_{Di} &= \pi_{D1} = \frac{w - z + \hat{y}_1}{1 + \chi_1} & \text{if } z \in A_1 \end{aligned} \tag{A2}$$

2. The central bank's inflation setting best response is given by

$$\pi_C(z, w) = \begin{cases} \pi_{D2} & \text{if } z \in A_2 \quad \text{or} \quad z \in A_3 \\ 0 & \text{if } z \in I \\ \pi_{D1} & \text{if } z \in A_1 \end{cases} \tag{A3}$$

3. The wage-setters' best response is given by

$$w = \frac{q_2(1+\chi_1)(\hat{y}_2 - z_{A2}^e) + q_1(1+\chi_2)(\hat{y}_1 - z_{A1}^e) + q_3(1+\chi_1)(\hat{y}_2 - z_{A3}^e)}{(1+\chi_1)(1+\chi_2 - q_2 - q_3) - q_1(1+\chi_2)} \tag{A4}$$

where

$$A_2 = \{z \mid z < w + \hat{y}_2\}$$
$$I = \{z \mid w + \hat{y}_2 \le z \le w + \hat{y}_1\}$$

$$A_1 = \left\{ z \mid w + \hat{y}_1 < z \le w + \frac{(1 + \chi_2)\hat{y}_1 - (1 + \chi_1)\hat{y}_2}{\chi_2 - \chi_1} \right\}$$

$$A_3 = \left\{ z \mid z > w + \frac{(1 + \chi_2)\hat{y}_1 - (1 + \chi_1)\hat{y}_2}{\chi_2 - \chi_1} \right\}$$

$$q_1 = Pr\{z \mid z \in A_1\}$$
$$q_2 = Pr\{z \mid z \in A_2\}$$
$$q_3 = Pr\{z \mid z \in A_3\}$$
$$z^e_{A1} = E[z \mid z \in A_1]$$
$$z^e_{A2} = E[z \mid z \in A_2]$$
$$z^e_{A3} = E[z \mid z \in A_3]$$

Proof of Proposition 2

The proof deals only with policy maker 1. The conservative policy maker 2 always favors delegation to discretion because the central bank either chooses a π that corresponds to his ideal policy or that is almost always closer to it than the policy that would result from the bargain between the two policy makers. In equilibrium, the expected loss of policy maker 1 with discretionary policy making is

$$EL^1_D = \frac{(\chi_1 + \chi_2)^2 + 4\chi_1}{(2 + \chi_1 + \chi_2)^2}\sigma^2_z + \hat{y}^2_1 + \frac{\chi_1(\hat{y}_1 + \hat{y}_2)^2}{(\chi_1 + \chi_2)^2}. \tag{A5}$$

If monetary policy is delegated to the central banker, the expected loss can be written as

$$EL^1_C = \frac{1}{(1 + \chi_2)^2(1 + \chi_1)^2}$$
$$\times \{[((1 + \chi_1)(1 + \chi_2 - q_2 - q_3) - q_1(1 + \chi_2))^2 + \chi_1((q_2 + q_3)(1 + \chi_1)$$
$$+ q_1(1 + \chi_2))^2]\sigma^2_z$$
$$+ [((1 + \chi_1)(q_2 + q_3 - 1 - \chi_2) + q_1(1 + \chi_2))^2 + \chi_1((q_2 + q_3)(1 + \chi_1)$$
$$+ q_1(1 + \chi_2))^2]w^2$$
$$+ (q_2 + q_3)^2(1 + \chi_1)^3\hat{y}^2_2 + (1 + \chi_2)^2[(q_1 - 1 - \chi_1)^2 + q^2_1\chi_1]\hat{y}^2_1$$

$$+ 2(q_2 + q_3)(1 + \chi_1)^2[(q_2 + q_3)(1 + \chi_1) - 1 - \chi_2 + q_1(1 + \chi_2)]w\hat{y}_2$$
$$+ 2(1 + \chi_1)(1 + \chi_2)[(q_1 - 1 - \chi_1)(q_2 + q_3 - 1 - \chi_2) + q_1\chi_1(q_2 + q_3) + q_1(1 + \chi_2)$$
$$(q_1 - 1)]w\hat{y}_1$$
$$+ 2(q_2 + q_3)(1 + \chi_1)(1 + \chi_2)[q_1(1 + \chi_1) - 1 - \chi_1]\hat{y}_1\hat{y}_2\}. \tag{A6}$$

To prove that policy maker 1 prefers delegation of monetary policy to discretionary policy making (1) if there is some but not unlimited divergence between the policy makers' inflation-output weights, or (2) if the output bliss points of the policy makers are unequal: $\hat{y}_1 \neq \hat{y}_2$, it is sufficient to show that Lemma 1–4 holds:

Lemma 1: $EL_D^1\big|_{\chi_1 = \chi_2 ; \hat{y}_1 = \hat{y}_2} = EL_C^1\big|_{\chi_1 = \chi_2 ; \hat{y}_1 = \hat{y}_2}$

Lemma 2: $\left|\dfrac{\partial EL_D^1}{\partial \chi_2}\right|_{\chi_1 = \chi_2 ; \hat{y}_1 = \hat{y}_2} < \left|\dfrac{\partial EL_C^1}{\partial \chi_2}\right|_{\chi_1 = \chi_2 ; \hat{y}_1 = \hat{y}_2}$

Lemma 3: $\dfrac{\partial EL_D^1}{\partial \hat{y}_2}\bigg|_{\chi_1 = \chi_2 ; \hat{y}_1 = \hat{y}_2} < \dfrac{\partial EL_C^1}{\partial \hat{y}_2}\bigg|_{\chi_1 = \chi_2 ; \hat{y}_1 = \hat{y}_2}$

Lemma 4: $EL_D^1\big|_{\chi_1 = 0, \chi_2 > 0} < EL_C^1\big|_{\chi_1 = 0, \chi_2 > 0}.$

Under $\chi_1 = \chi_2$ and $\hat{y}_1 = \hat{y}_2$ the policy makers have identical preferences and, therefore, the expected loss with discretionary policy making is identical to the loss with delegation to the central bank (Lemma 1). Lemma 2 implies that, beginning with a situation of identical preferences, if the weight that policy maker 2 ascribes to π increases, the expected loss for policy maker 1 declines more in the case of delegation to the central banker than with legislative discretion. Lemma 3 states that the same effect as in Lemma 2 occurs if the output bliss point of policy maker 2 ($\hat{y}_2$) declines. Hence, Lemmas 2 and 3 imply that policy maker 1 prefers delegation to the central banker if policy maker 2 becomes slightly more conservative than policy maker 1, either by weighting the inflation rate slightly more or by having a somewhat lower output bliss point. Lemma 4 claims that if policy maker 1 places no weight on π at all, he favors legislative discretion, independent of the difference in the output bliss points. This implies that policy maker 1 supports delegation only if the disagreement in χ is limited.

For the evaluation of the expected loss with delegation as expressed in (A6) in the case of identical preferences, it is necessary to determine first q_1, q_2, q_3 and w. With identical preferences, the central banker has to consider only one policy maker, say policy maker 2. In this case, she always accommodates the preferences of policy maker 2: $q_2 = 1$, $q_2 = q_3 = 0$ and according to (A3)

$w = \hat{y}_2 / \chi_2$ because $z_{A2}^e = Ez = 0$. With this, $\chi_1 = \chi_2 = \chi$ and $\hat{y}_1 = \hat{y}_2 = \hat{y}$, (A5) and (A6) become identical and simplify to

$$EL_C^1\big|_{\chi_1=\chi_2;\hat{y}_1=\hat{y}_2} = \frac{\chi}{1+\chi}\sigma_z^2 + \frac{\chi+1}{\chi}\hat{y}^2 = EL_D^1\big|_{\chi_1=\chi_2;\hat{y}_1=\hat{y}_2}.$$

This establishes that Lemma 1 holds.

The partial derivatives of (A5) and (A6) with respect to χ_2 evaluated for identical χ and $\hat{y}$ are

$$\frac{\partial EL_D^1}{\partial \chi_2}\bigg|_{\chi_1=\chi_2;\hat{y}_1=\hat{y}_2} = -\frac{1}{\chi^2}\hat{y}^2$$

$$\frac{\partial EL_C^1}{\partial \chi_2}\bigg|_{\chi_1=\chi_2;\hat{y}_1=\hat{y}_2} = -\frac{2}{\chi^2}\hat{y}^2.$$

This establishes that Lemma 2 holds.

The total differentials of (A5) and (A6) with respect to $\hat{y}_2$, q_1, q_2, q_3, z_{A1}^e, z_{A2}^e, and z_{A3}^e evaluated for identical preferences are

$$dEL_D^1\big|_{\chi_1=\chi_2;\hat{y}_1=\hat{y}_2} = \frac{\hat{y}}{\chi}d\hat{y}_2 \qquad\qquad (A7)$$

$$dEL_C^1\big|_{\chi_1=\chi_2;\hat{y}_1=\hat{y}_2} = \frac{2\hat{y}}{\chi}d\hat{y}_2 + \frac{2(1+\chi)\hat{y}^2}{\chi^2}dq_1 + \frac{2(1+\chi)\hat{y}^2}{\chi^2}dq_2 - \frac{2\hat{y}}{\chi}dz_{A2}^e.$$

$$\qquad\qquad (A8)$$

The case of interest is a reduction of $\hat{y}_2$ which directly reduces the expected loss by $2\hat{y}/\chi$ in (A8) which is twice as much as in (A7). However, a reduction of $\hat{y}_2$ increases q_1 and decreases q_2 ($q_3 = 0$ because of identical χ) but the change in q_1 is smaller than the change in q_2 because the range of independence (I) rises. Hence, these two effects slightly increase the benefit of a lower $\hat{y}_2$. In contrast, z_{A2}^e declines with lower $\hat{y}$ which reduces the benefit. However, $dz_{A2}^e < \frac{1}{2}d\hat{y}_2$ for $\hat{y}_2 > 0.55\sigma_z$.[10] If $\hat{y}_2$ is larger than $0.55\sigma_z$, (A7) is smaller than (A8) which establishes Lemma 3.

Evaluation of (A5) and (A6) at $\chi_1 = 0$ (which implies $q_1 = 0$) gives

$$EL_D^1\big|_{\chi_1=0} = \frac{\chi_2^2}{(2+\chi_2)^2}\sigma_z^2 + \hat{y}_1^2 \qquad (A9)$$

$$EL_C^1\big|_{\chi_1=0} = \frac{(1+\chi_2-q_2-q_3)^2}{(1+\chi_2)^2}\sigma_z^2 + \frac{(q_2-q_3-1-\chi_2)^2}{(1+\chi_2)^2}w^2$$

$$+\frac{(q_2+q_3)^2}{(1+\chi_2)^2}\hat{y}_2^2 + \hat{y}_1^2 + \frac{2(q_2+q_3)(q_2+q_3-1-\chi_2)}{(1+\chi_2)^2}w\hat{y}_2$$

$$-\frac{2(q_2+q_3-1-\chi_2)}{(1+\chi_2)}w\hat{y}_1 - \frac{2(q_2+q_3)}{(1+\chi_2)}\hat{y}_1\hat{y}_2. \qquad (A10)$$

To show that (A9) is smaller than (A10), compare these two equations at the two extreme states of $\hat{y}$. First, assume that $\hat{y}_1 = \hat{y}_2$ (and therefore $q_2 = 1$ and $q_3 = 0$) in which case (A10) simplifies to

$$EL_C^1\big|_{\chi_1=0;\hat{y}_1=\hat{y}_2} = \frac{\chi_2^2}{(1+\chi_2)^2}\sigma_z^2 + \hat{y}_1^2. \qquad (A11)$$

(A11) is always larger than (A9) for positive σ_z. Second, evaluate (A9) and (A10) at the greatest possible divergence of the output bliss points ($\hat{y}_1 = M$ and $\hat{y}_2 = 0$; consequently $q_2 = 0.5$ and $q_3 = 0$). (A9) and (A10) become

$$EL_D^1\big|_{\chi_1=0} = \frac{\chi_2^2}{(2+\chi_2)^2}\sigma_z^2 + M^2 \qquad (A12)$$

$$EL_C^1\big|_{\chi_1=0;\hat{y}_1=\infty,\hat{y}_2=0} = \frac{(\chi_2+0.5)^2}{(1+\chi_2)^2}\sigma_z^2 + M^2 - \frac{1}{1+\chi_2}z_{A2}^e M. \qquad (A13)$$

For sufficiently large M, (A13) is larger than (A12) because the term in front of σ_z^2 is larger in (A13) than in (A12) and the last term in (A13) is positive due to z_{A2}^e always being negative. This comparison establishes that Lemma 4 holds for positive σ_z independent of the difference in the output bliss points.

NOTES

1. For a survey of the literature on central bank behavior, see Kirchgässner (1995) and on central bank independence, see Eijffinger and de Haan (1996).

2. Obviously, if the interaction is repeated (without a certain endpoint) a reputational trade-off is induced into government's *ex post* decision that may lessen the credibility problem. However, as is well known (Folk Theorem) there are a multiplicity of equilibria and it is an open question on which equilibrium all private agents and the government will coordinate. See the discussion by Rogoff (1987) and Lockwood, Miller and Zhang (1996).

3. A second form of delegation is to appoint a central banker subject to a 'performance contract'. The terms of the contract can be set to induce an agent both to avoid inflation and to stabilize as appropriate (Persson and Tabellini, 1993; Walsh 1995a, 1995b; Svensson 1997). The Central Bank of New Zealand has been cited as a case in point. However, the government may not be inclined to punish the central banker in all circumstances, say, for an expansionary monetary surprise before an election (on this point, see also McCallum, 1995).

4. On political business cycles, see the surveys by Hibbs (1992) and Gärtner (1994).

5. The inflation bias would increase substantially if the model were to include output persistence (Grüner, 1996; Gärtner, 1997; Svensson, 1997).

6. Substituting (10.1) and (10.2) into (10.4), taking the first derivative with respect to π, and substituting the expected value of the first-order condition into the first-order condition yields (10.5).

7. This assumption does not affect the equilibrium inflation rate but the equilibrium strategies. With this assumption, an open conflict will never be observed and the bank always avoids a legislative veto. The political control is latent. If c is smaller the policy makers have to use active political control in some conditions (see Calvert, McCubbins and Weingast, 1989, for this distinction).

8. The equilibrium behavior of the central bank would not be modified if it was assumed that the decisive policy maker was forced to partially accommodate the other policy maker's preference, as long as the utility of the decisive policy maker strictly improves by overriding the decision of the central bank. This last condition is certain to hold if the legislative procedure is such that the proposal for change is paired against the status quo in the last vote.

9. For the exact condition, see the proof of Lemma 3 in the Appendix to this chapter.

10. For $\hat{y}_2 = 0.55 \, \sigma_z$, the expected value $E[z \mid z < \hat{y}_2] = 0.4838 \, \sigma_z$ and the partial derivative with respect to $\hat{y}_2$ is equal to 0.4996.

11. Legislative structure and central bank independence

By relating political institutions to commitment ability, the model presented in Chapter 10 claims to explain why certain countries are successful in coping with the time-inconsistency problem by creating a legally independent central bank, and why others are not. There are two necessary conditions for delegation by legislators to be credible:

Condition 1   The legislative function must be shared equally between at least two decision bodies (parliamentary chambers, executive, or the people if a referendum exists), such that the decision bodies possess veto powers.

Condition 2   The decision bodies must have different preferences with regard to monetary policy, that is, to some degree, different inflation-output weights (χ).

Consequently, countries with legislative decision rules that fulfill these two conditions are expected to carry out more legal efforts to create independent central banks than those that do not meet these conditions. In addition, in the former countries, central banks should be more behaviorally independent, as reflected by a strong negative relation between legal independence and average inflation rate. To test this hypothesis, the legislative processes of all OECD countries with a central bank are analysed and classified with regard to the degree of checks and balances.[1] Section 11.2 discusses related empirical work whose results provide additional support for this hypothesis.

11.1   LEGISLATIVE STRUCTURE AND CENTRAL BANK INDEPENDENCE IN OECD COUNTRIES

To categorize the legislative structures of the OECD countries, three groups of political systems are distinguished:

Group 1   Systems with *strong checks and balances*; at least two decision bodies exist which are independent of each other, which have different preferences, and each decision body has veto power. Countries in this group fulfil both conditions.

Group 2   Systems with *weak checks and balances*; at least two decision bodies exist with different preferences, but one decision body is decisive while the other can only delay a decision. Countries in this group meet condition 2 but not condition 1. Although there are two decision bodies, they do not have equal power. Nevertheless, a conflict between the players can substantially delay a policy change which makes an override of the central bank's decision more difficult, and thereby increase the credibility of the legal independence.

Group 3   Systems with *no checks and balances*; there is only one decision body (both conditions are not fulfilled), or if several exist, they have identical preferences (condition 2 is not met).

The classification is reported in Table 11.1 and explained in the Appendix to this chapter. Since the preferences or monetary policy position of different decision bodies cannot be observed directly, this study had to rely on proxies that are likely to induce different policy positions. The following criteria are used: differences in the regional allocation of the seats, in the voting system or in the terms of office, and differences in the party compositions in both chambers. These differences are assumed to induce conflicting preferences about monetary policy. An unequal representation of regions in the two chambers induces different preferences about monetary policy because inflation has differential effects on identifiable constituent groups (Grier, 1991; Waller 1992) and because economic activities tend to be regionally concentrated.[2] Different voting systems yield different electoral constituencies within the same geographic district (Fenno, 1978, chapter 1).

For example, in a plurality system with single member districts the votes for the losing candidate are not represented in the parliament, while with forms of proportional representation minority groups have a better chance of being represented. Finally, differences in the terms of office cause different time horizons. Particularly, a short electoral horizon reduces the weight given to the long-term inflationary consequences of monetary policy. Furthermore, differences in the terms of office can lead to elections at different dates and thereby to conflicting incentives to use monetary policy to stimulate the economy because of reelection considerations. Although these are plausible explanations for the existence of conflicting preferences about monetary policy, the test remains indirect.

Table 11.1   Classification of political systems and measures of central bank independence

Country	LVAU	LVAW	GMTE	GMTP	GMTT	AI
1. Strong checks and balances	*0.52*	*0.52*	*6.80*	*4.60*	*11.40*	*0.62*
Australia	0.31	0.35	6	3	9	0.46
Canada	0.46	0.45	7	4	11	0.57
Germany	0.66	0.69	7	6	13	0.75
Switzerland	0.68	0.64	7	5	12	0.70
United States	0.51	0.48	7	5	12	0.62
2. Weak checks and balances	*0.38*	*0.39*	*4.00*	*2.70*	*6.56*	*0.38*
Austria	0.58	0.61	6	3	9	0.59
Denmark	0.47	0.50	5	3	8	0.50
Finland	0.27	0.28	NA	4	NA	0.28
France	0.28	0.24	5	2	7	0.34
Greece	0.51	0.56	2	2	4	0.41
Iceland	0.36	0.34	NA	NA	NA	0.34
Ireland	0.39	0.44	4	3	7	0.44
Netherlands	0.42	0.42	4	6	10	0.52
Portugal	NA	NA	2	1	3	0.19
Spain	0.21	0.23	3	2	5	0.27
United Kingdom	0.31	0.27	5	1	6	0.32
3. No checks and balances	*0.21*	*0.22*	*3.75*	*1.60*	*5.25*	*0.26*
Belgium	0.19	0.16	6	1	7	0.30
Japan	0.16	0.18	5	1	6	0.28
Italy	0.22	0.25	1	4	5	0.28
New Zealand	0.27	0.24	3	0	3	0.21
Norway	0.14	0.17	NA	2	NA	0.17
Sweden	0.27	0.29	NA	NA	NA	0.29

Notes: LVAU denotes Cukierman's (1992) unweighted legal independence measure; LVAW is the weighted measures of Cukierman (1992); GMTE is the economic independence measure constructed by Grilli, Masciandaro and Tabellini (1991), GMTP is their political independence measure (updated by Eijffinger and van Keulen (1995) for Finland and Norway); and GMTT is the sum of both measures; AI is the average of LVAW and GMTT. GMTT is first divided by 16, so as to convert it to the same zero-one scale as LVAW. In those cases where one index does not report data, the value of the other index is used.

Table 11.1 reports that only five OECD countries qualify as having strong checks and balances (Australia, Canada, Germany, Switzerland and the United States). Most countries' decision rules are characterized by weak checks and balances because one chamber dominates (Austria, France, Ireland, Spain and the United Kingdom) or because in unicameral systems an executive veto exists which can be overridden by the parliament (Finland, Greece, Iceland and Portugal). Finally, in a few countries, legislative decision making lacks checks and balances completely since either their two chambers are equally composed (Belgium, Italy and Japan) or they have a pure unicameral legislature without an executive veto (New Zealand, Norway and Sweden).

11.1.1   Central Bank Independence and Legislative Structure

Table 11.1 depicts several indices for legal central bank independence for individual countries and the average of these indices for the three groups of political systems. The higher the number, the more legally independent is the central bank. Table 11.1 reveals for each index that those countries with strong checks and balances have, on average, the most independent central banks, those countries with no checks and balances have on average, the most dependent central bank, and the central banks of countries with weak checks and balances are more dependent than those of group 1 but less dependent than those of group 3.

To address the relation between central bank independence and legislative decision rules more thoroughly, the indices of legal central bank independence are regressed on a dummy variable which takes the value of one if the country is characterized by strong checks and balances and on a second dummy variable which takes the value of one in the case of weak checks and balances. In addition, a potential effect of external real shocks is controlled because they increase the costs of delegation (Rogoff, 1985). As a proxy for these real shocks, the standard deviation of the growth rate of real GDP (1967–90) is used.

Table 11.2 reports the outcomes of OLS estimations using the different indices of central bank independence as endogenous variables. The coefficients of the dummy variables reflect the differences in the central bank independence indices between the group with strong or weak checks and balances and the group of countries with no checks and balances. Notice that the coefficients of the dummy for strong checks and balances are always significant and positive while the coefficients of the dummy for weak checks and balances are significant and positive in the regression using or including the measure of Cukierman (regressions 1, 2, 3, 8 and 9). The Wald test reports F-statistics, and tests whether the coefficients of the dummy variable for strong and for weak checks and balances are different. With the exception of regression 3, this test indicates that the coefficients for strong checks and balances are significantly larger than the coefficients for weak checks and balances. Consequently, countries with strong checks and balances have more legally independent central banks than countries with weak or no checks and balances; the effect of this is

Table 11.2 Checks and balances and central bank independence

Endogenous variable	LVAU (1)	LVAW (2)	LVAW (3)	GMTE (4)	GMTP (5)	GMTT (6)	AI (7)	AI (8)
Constant	0.233**	0.229*	0.218	7.718***	1.271	9.237***	0.366***	0.311**
	(2.140)	(1.968)	(1.404)	(4.328)	(0.698)	(3.437)	(3.886)	(2.322)
Dummy for strong checks and balances	0.311***	0.304***	0.267***	2.496**	3.081***	5.593***	0.344***	0.313***
	(4.266)	(3.913)	(3.266)	(2.833)	(3.030)	(4.214)	(5.302)	(4.437)
Dummy for weak checks and balances	0.170**	0.173**	0.161*	0.142	1.148	1.197	0.125**	0.140*
	(2.828)	(2.695)	(2.101)	(0.186)	(1.366)	(1.042)	(2.373)	(2.122)
Standard deviation of growth	-0.881	-0.488	-0.770	-149.745**	10.895	-150.458	-3.928	-1.996
	(-0.253)	(-0.131)	(-0.154)	(-2.380)	(0.194)	(-1.587)	(-1.317)	(-0.461)
Price 1900-40			0.004*					0.003
			(2.007)					(1.762)
R² (adjusted)	0.466	0.413	0.551	0.557	0.293	0.623	0.613	0.676
S.E.E.	0.116	0.124	0.116	1.267	1.467	1.909	0.104	0.100
Jarque-Bera	0.40	1.09	1.01	0.49	1.88	0.44	0.80	0.90
Wald test (F-value)	4.637**	3.544*	2.173	10.374***	5.543**	15.935***	14.288***	7.770**
Sample size	21	21	16	18	20	18	22	16

Notes: T-statistics are in parentheses. One, two and three asterisks denote significance at 10 per cent, 5 per cent and 1 per cent level, respectively. Since the inclusion of 'Price 1900–40' reduces the sample size, it is included only in the regression on AI, and if significant. The Wald test reports F-statistics, and tests whether the coefficients of the dummy variable for strong and for weak checks and balances are significantly different.

not trivial. Using regression 7, for example, the index for countries with strong checks and balances is more than double the index for countries with no checks and balances and 50 per cent higher than for countries with weak checks and balances. Table 11.3 reports the summary statistics on the regressors.

Table 11.3   Data summary and sources

Variable	Source	Mean	Standard deviation
LVAU	Table 11.1	0.403	0.174
LVAW	Table 11.1	0.403	0.178
GMTE	Table 11.1	5.462	1.664
GMTP	Table 11.1	3.384	1.805
GMTT	Table 11.1	8.846	2.609
AI	Table 11.1	0.479	0.164
Standard deviation of GDP growth	IMF, International Financial Statistics	0.024	0.004
Price 1900–40	de Haan and van't Hag (1995)	9.100	17.656
Average inflation 1973–89	IMF, International Financial Statistics	7.654	2.967

In addition, the effect of the standard deviation of the growth rate has the expected negative sign but is only significant at standard level in regression 4. Furthermore, a variable reflecting the average level of inflation between 1900 and 1940 (Price 1900–40) has been included. It is often argued that a high rate of inflation is likely to cause popular support for anti-inflationary monetary policy. De Haan and van't Hag (1995) use this variable in their study and find a significant impact. Since the inclusion of this variable reduces the sample size, it is included in the regression on AI, and in regression 3, the only regression where 'Price 1900–40' is significant. The results indicate that past experience with inflation is of minor importance for the choice of the degree of legal central bank independence.[3,4]

According to the argument in this study, the creation of central bank independence is most credible for countries with strong checks and balances, somewhat credible for countries with weak checks and balances and not credible for countries without checks and balances. Therefore, the degree of behavioral independence, as measured by the negative relation between legal central bank independence and inflation, should be largest in countries with strong checks and balances and weakest in countries with no checks and balances.[5] To address this issue, the average inflation rate between 1973 and 1989 is regressed on the three dummy variables, representing the three groups, and on three interaction terms (respective dummy variable times the index of central bank independence, CBI). The coefficients of these interaction terms describe the relationship between central bank independence and inflation for each group of countries. Table 11.4 reports the results of OLS estimations.

The coefficients of the interaction terms *strong checks and balances times CBI* as well as those for *weak checks and balances* are significant and negative (except for regression 4), while the coefficients of the interaction term for *no checks and balances* are only significant and negative in regressions 3 and 5 and even positive at the 10 per cent level of significance in regressions 1 and 2. The Wald test reports F-statistics, and tests whether the coefficients of *no checks and balances times CBI* and of *strong checks and balances times CBI* are significantly different. This is the case for the measures by Cukierman (LVAU, LVAW) and in a weaker form (rejection of equal coefficients for all interaction terms) for GMTE and GMTP. No significant difference is found for regressions 5 and 6. Hence, with regard to Cukierman's measures and the individual measures by Grilli, Masciandaro and Tabellini (GMTE and GMTP), the evidence supports the thesis that the negative relation between legal central bank independence and inflation (degree of behavioral independence) is stronger in countries with strong checks and balances than in countries with no checks and balances. However, there is no difference between those countries with strong and weak forms of checks and balances.

Finally, notice that the coefficients of the shift dummies for strong or weak checks and balances are higher than those for no checks and balances. This is an interesting result. Using, for example, regression 3 (the one with the highest adjusted R^2), the predicted average inflation rates for the three groups are 9.9 (no checks and balances), 12.5 (weak checks and balances) and 6.7 (strong checks and balances). This is not only a reasonable prediction of the average inflation rates of these groups (9.6, 14.2, 6.7) but implies that countries with dependent central banks need not have higher inflation rates. The reason is the different constant term for the three groups. The substantial differences in these shift dummies point out an issue often neglected in the literature: legal central bank independence is not the only reason for different inflation rates. Specifically, countries without checks and balances in their political system are either less exposed to the time-inconsistency in monetary policy or use alternative means to commit to a low inflation monetary policy. However, no systematic evidence of additional causes of inflation could be detected: neither the degree of openness (as suggested by Romer, 1993), nor measures of inequality or the average of government department–GDP ratio (Beetsma and van der Ploog, 1996) are significant in this sample of OECD countries.[6] This indicates that there must be additional mechanisms in place to reduce the inflation bias in monetary policy.

Table 11.4 Checks and balances, and the impact of central bank independence on average inflation (1973–89)

Index of central bank independence (CBI)	LVAU (1)	LVAW (2)	GMTE (3)	GMTP (4)	GMTT (5)	AI (6)
Dummy for no checks and balances	2.513	1.489	16.346***	8.230***	20.020***	14.029**
	(0.640)	(0.333)	(9.013)	(3.286)	(6.035)	(2.343)
Dummy for weak checks and balances	16.391***	14.825***	25.738***	17.645***	26.643***	21.634***
	(6.131)	(5.815)	(14.677)	(7.162)	(13.938)	(7.540)
Dummy for strong checks and balances	16.016***	16.672***	38.150***	16.785**	25.411***	21.368**
	(4.009)	(3.663)	(3.030)	(2.243)	(3.732)	(2.850)
No checks and balances times CBI	33.779*	37.491*	−1.732***	0.893	−1.937***	−17.564
	(1.844)	(1.849)	(−4.024)	(0.748)	(−3.185)	(−0.761)
Weak checks and balances times CBI	−18.951**	−14.382**	−3.306***	−2.272**	−2.283***	−28.639***
	(−2.720)	(−2.233)	(−7.999)	(−2.813)	(−8.245)	(−4.031)
Strong checks and balances times CBI	−17.779**	−19.103**	−4.625**	−2.192	−1.641**	−23.658*
	(−2.409)	(−2.253)	(2.502)	(−1.380)	(−2.767)	(−1.982)
R^2 (adjusted)	0.490	0.430	0.882	0.372	0.861	0.544
S.E.E.	2.249	2.378	1.653	3.622	1.799	2.706
Jarque-Bera	0.35	0.38	1.12	0.43	0.49	1.04
Wald test (F-value)	6.818**	6.628**	2.323[a]	2.411[a]	0.121[b]	0.055[b]
Sample size	19	19	17	20	18	20
(countries excluded)	(Iceland, Greece)	(Iceland, Greece)	(Netherlands)			(Iceland, Greece)

Notes: T-statistics are in parentheses. One, two and three asterisks denote significance at 10 per cent, 5 per cent and 1 per cent level, respectively. The Wald test reports F-statistics, and tests whether the coefficients of 'No checks and balances times CBI' and of 'Strong checks and balances times CBI' are significantly different. Countries that are mentioned as excluded are those for which data were available but which had to be excluded to ensure normality distribution of the residuals.

a Although the null hypothesis of equal coefficients for the first and the third interaction variable cannot be rejected, the hypotheses that all three interaction variables are identical can be rejected at the 2 per cent (regression 3) and at the 8 per cent (regression 4) level of significance.

b The hypotheses that all three interaction variables are identical cannot be rejected.

11.2 DISCUSSION OF RELATED EMPIRICAL STUDIES

An example of a 'technology' has been outlined theoretically and empirically whereby a sovereign, heterogeneous policy-making body characterized by checks and balances can provide a credible commitment to a partially independent central bank: the central banker is able to set the inflation rate independently at her discretion during times with small positive exogenous shocks. Otherwise, the central banker is forced to accommodate the decisive policy maker's preferences in order to avoid being overridden. Notice that the costs of changing central bank autonomy are endogenous in this model and that these costs are neither constant (as usually assumed) nor increasing exponentially (Jensen, 1997). Rather, the overriding costs provided by the checks and balances in the legislative decision rules are indefinitely high during times of small positive shocks and zero in situations of negative or large positive shocks. This shape of the costs can explain the empirical observation that even legally independent central banks accommodate partially to the government in situations of conflicting interests (as reported for the Bundesbank by Frey and Schneider, 1981). This conditional accommodating behavior of a partially independent central bank can explain why empirical research has not succeeded in finding a positive relation between the degree of independence and variability of economic growth as implied by Rogoff's completely independent central bank (Alesina and Summers, 1993; Eijffinger and Schaling, 1998).

Supportive evidence of this hypothesis is provided by Lohmann (1998) in her thorough study of the behavior of the German Bundesbank. Comparing several competing hypotheses, she found that the hypothesis that performs best in explaining the Bundesbank's behavior is the following: the Bundesbank is staffed with nonpartisan technocrats who are partially insulated from political pressure by the federal government. The Bundesbank's independence increases the smaller the number of members in the Bundesrat (second chamber) that support the federal government (which always has a majority support in the Bundestag, the first chamber). Hence, party affiliation provides a reasonably good indicator for differences in preferences in this example. In other words, the larger the support of the dominant party in the Bundestag in the Bundesrat, that is, the more Lander government the majority party of the federal government controls, the more willing the German Bundesbank is to accommodate the federal government's expansionary pressure before elections.[7]

This hypothesis could also clarify the ongoing dispute in the empirical literature about which branch of the US Government influences the decisions of the Federal Open Market Committee. While Grier (1991) found from 1975 to 1984 a link between the monetary growth rate in the United States and the preferences of the leadership of the Senate Banking Committee, and no significant effect of the President once the influence of the committee is controlled for, Beck (1990) could not detect any influence of the US Congress between 1962 and 1987. In contrast, Havrilesky (1995, chapter 4) reports that monetary policy is significantly influenced by the pressure of some (but not all) Administrations. The influence of the Congress on money supply is insignificant (*ibid.*, p. 228) but he found evidence that the Senate Oversight Hearings have an influence on the Federal Fund rate (*ibid.*, p. 239). That there is a complex interaction between the President and the Congress is reported by Havrilesky (1995: 187): 'For example, in 1980–1984 the overwhelming desire of Congress was for monetary ease. Nevertheless, with the Fed's powers in danger from legislative assaults, it chose to respond only to executive branch pressure for tightness.'

While Havrilesky regards this as a paradoxical outcome, this is exactly what the model predicts in this study. If a conservative central banker is forced to accommodate the wishes of the policy makers, almost always she will follow the preferences of the more conservative decision maker. However, who is the most conservative decision maker may change over time, and therefore, the central bank is not always responsive to the same branch of the government.

This model also has implications for the discussion of the optimal design of the structure of the central bank. If the commitment ability of the political institutions is limited, the central bank is controlled by the threat of a legislative override and the decision-making rules inside the bank are of minor importance. If the political process makes an override less likely and thereby the bank has large behavioral independence, then, structure and process (see McCubbins, Noll and Weingast, 1989 and Chapter 4, section 4.2 in this volume) inside the bank and appointments to the bank (Havrilesky, 1995, chapter 9) become important.[8] Illustrative is the case of the planned European Central Bank System: it will be the only central bank whose legal independence is laid down in a constitution, namely in the Treaty of the European Community. Since this Treaty can only be changed by consent, each member country has veto power. Consequently, it will be extremely difficult to modify the legal independence and to override the policy chosen by the European Central Bank. Hence, the political control of the bank has to rely almost completely on the internal decision-making rules.[9] While the decision-making rules are already defined in the Treaty, the appointments to the European Central Bank Council are the only choices left in influencing the future monetary policy. Since membership in the monetary union partially determines who can make appointments to the Council, it does not come as a surprise that the decision about the membership is very controversial: it is a consequence of the weak disciplining possibilities due to the unanimity requirement.

11.3   APPENDIX: CHECKS AND BALANCES IN OECD COUNTRIES

This appendix briefly describes the legislative decision rules in the OECD countries and classifies them as having strong, weak or no checks and balances. First, there is a discussion on whether there are at least two independent decision bodies with equal veto rights. This is the case, for example, in bicameral systems in which both chambers have equal legislative power. Those bicameral parliaments are classified as of equal power if both chambers have to approve the identical text, otherwise the status quo prevails. If a disagreement leads only to a delay but one chamber has the final decision, these systems are evaluated as of unequal power. Decisions can also be delayed if a directly elected president can veto a legislative act by a unicameral parliament and this veto can only be overridden by a qualified majority in the Parliament. If several decision bodies exist, a check is made on whether different voting rules exist that can ensure different policy positions. In bicameral parliaments, a differentiation is made between equally and unequally composed chambers. Differences in the regional allocation of the seats, in the voting system or in the terms of office are used as criteria. In ambiguous cases, a check is made on whether there are differences in the party compositions in both chambers.

Australia: strong checks and balances
Bicameral parliament with equal power and unequal composition of each chamber.

Austria: weak checks and balances
Bicameral parliament with unequal power and unequal composition of each chamber.

Belgium: no checks and balances
Bicameral parliament with equal power and equal composition of each chamber.

Comment   Although the election rules for the two chambers differ somewhat, the seven largest parties have almost identical shares of the seats among the directly elected legislators in both chambers (1981 election). Also the *Europa Year Book* (1985: 326) states: '...as the party complexion of both houses is generally almost the same, measures passed by the Chamber of Representatives are usually passed by the Senate'. Therefore, Belgium is classified as having no checks and balances.

Canada: strong checks and balances
Bicameral parliament with equal power and unequal composition of each chamber.

Denmark: weak checks and balances
Unicameral parliament.

Comment   Weak checks and balances exist because a binding referendum takes place on the request of one-third of the members of the parliament (Folketing). Since the governing coalition almost never has a two-thirds majority in the Folketing, one-third of the members of the Folketing can successfully veto a legislative change if they disapprove it and the median Danish voter rejects it.

Finland: weak checks and balances
Unicameral parliament but the directly elected president can veto a decision by the Parliament. The parliament can override the veto if it passes the bill unchanged after its next election.

France: weak checks and balances
Bicameral parliament with unequal power and unequal composition of each chamber.

Comment In case of a disagreement between the chambers, the final decision is taken by the National Assembly. The president may request a reconsideration of the bill but has no formal veto right.

Germany: strong checks and balances
Bicameral parliament with equal power and unequal composition of each chamber.

Comment   Germany has two different legislative decision rules. For legislation that affects the vital interests of the Länder (*zustimmungsbedürftige Gesetze*), both chambers, the Bundestag and the Bundesrat, have to approve the legislation. For all other legislation (*nicht zustimmungbedürftige Gesetze*) the Bundesrat's decision can be overridden by the Bundestag. If a simple majority in the Bundesrat rejects the legislation, the Bundestag can override this decision by a simple majority. If a two-thirds majority in the Bundesrat supports the veto, a two-thirds majority in the Bundestag is required to overturn it. Whether the law is *zustimmungsbedürftig* is ultimately decided by the German Constitutional Court. Whether the Bundesbank law is a *zustimmungsbedürftiges Gesetz* is a matter of dispute. In 1962, the Constitutional Court found that changes in the Bundesbank law are not *zustimmungsbedürftig*. In 1992, when the Bundesbank law was modified in order to integrate the five East German Länder a dispute arose about the nature of the Bundesbank law (Lohmann, 1998). The federal government and the Bundestag treated it as *nicht zustimmungsbedürftig* which the Bundesrat disputed but no Länder government went to the Constitutional Court. However, the uncertainty about how the Court would decide in 1992 caused the Bundestag to accommodate the wishes of the Länder to a large extent.

Greece: weak checks and balances
Unicameral parliament, but the directly elected president can veto a decision by the parliament. The parliament can override the veto by absolute majority.

Iceland: weak checks and balances
Unicameral parliament (with two divisions), but the directly elected president can veto a decision by the parliament. The president's veto can only be overridden by a referendum.

Ireland: weak checks and balances
Bicameral parliament with unequal power and unequal composition of each chamber.

Italy (before reform in 1994): no checks and balances
Bicameral parliament with equal power and equal composition of each chamber.

Comment   Before the reform in 1994, not only the Chamber of Deputies but also the Senate was elected by proportional representation. The terms of office are equal in both houses. Finally, the three largest parties have almost identical shares of seats in both chambers (1983 election).

Japan (before reform in 1994): no checks and balances
Bicameral parliament with unequal power and equal composition of each chamber.

Comment   Although both houses have different election rules and different terms, these are classified as equal because the Liberal Democratic Party had a majority in both houses from 1955–93 (Ramseyer and Rosentbluth, 1993).

Netherlands: weak checks and balances
Bicameral parliament with unequal power and equal composition of each chamber, but the executive can veto a decision by the parliament. This veto cannot be overridden.

New Zealand: no checks and balances
Unicameral parliament, no executive veto.

Norway: no checks and balances
Unicameral parliament (with two divisions), no executive veto.

Portugal (since 1976): weak checks and balances
Unicameral parliament, but the directly elected president can veto a decision by the parliament. The parliament can override the veto by an absolute majority.

Spain (since 1978): weak checks and balances
Bicameral parliament with unequal power and unequal composition of each chamber.

Sweden: no checks and balances
Unicameral parliament, no executive veto.

Switzerland: strong checks and balances
Bicameral parliament with equal power and unequal composition of each chamber. In addition, each legislative change can be vetoed by the majority of the people in a referendum if this is requested by 50 000 citizens.

United Kingdom: weak checks and balances
Bicameral parliament with unequal power and unequal composition of each chamber.

United States: strong checks and balances
Bicameral parliament with equal power and unequal composition of each chamber. In addition, the directly elected president can veto a decision by the parliament. The parliament can override the veto by a two-thirds majority in both chambers.

Sources: Inter-parliamentary Union, 1986; Mackie and Rose (1991); the *Europa Year Book*, various issues; Delury (1987); Mockli (1991).

NOTES

1. Attention is focused on OECD countries for two reasons. First, Cukierman (1992) found a negative relation between inflation rate and central bank independence only for industrialized countries and not for developing countries. Second, many developing countries are not characterized by stable democracies which explains this result (Cukierman and Webb, 1995). This implies that the veto players in the political systems of developing countries are not easily discovered by the study of the formal constitution.
2. As an illustration, consider the policy preferences of two fictitious legislators, Mr Ruhr and Ms Frankfurt (adapted from Grier, 1991). Mr Ruhr represents a district composed of workers with indexed labor contracts in highly cyclical industries and with high structural unemployment. Hence, he does not care much about inflation, but is greatly concerned about unemployment. On the other hand, Ms Frankfurt represents a district dominated by financial institutions holding fixed rate corporate and government debt. Other things equal, she prefers a low inflationary monetary policy and is less concerned with unemployment.

3. De Haan and van't Hag (1995) also find a significant impact of measures of political instability on central bank independence. These measures reflect the frequency of government changes or the frequency of significant government changes. Since both measures are highly correlated with the dummy variables for checks and balances, they could not be included simultaneously in the regressions. For example, the frequency of significant changes in countries with no checks and balances is three times as high as in countries with strong checks and balances. However, the adjusted R^2 in my regressions is always higher than their R^2 (ibid., Table 7) for the same number of observations.

4. In addition, a regression is run on a central bank independence index constructed by Eijffinger and Schaling (1993), and extended by Eijffinger and van Keulen (1995). For this index, no significant impact of the two dummy variables could be detected. However, this is not surprising since this index includes recent modification in central bank law due to the preparation for the European Monetary Union. Independent of their political system, member countries of the EU are forced by the Treaty of the European Community to install independent central banks.

5. Note that the regressions reported in Table 11.2 explain between 0.29 and 0.67 of the difference in legal independence. Hence, there remains some variance within the three groups of countries which allows the marginal impact of legal independence on the inflation rate to be tested.

6. In addition, a dummy variable is included for those countries that were the founding members of the European Monetary System (Germany, France, Italy, Netherlands, Belgium, Denmark and Ireland). However, this membership has no significant impact on average inflation, except for regression (5) in which European Monetary System (EMS) membership increases inflation at the 5.2 per cent level of significance. The coefficients of the variables reported in Table 11.4 and their levels of significance change only marginally with the inclusion of these additional variables.

7. A different behavioral pattern of the German Bundesbank is reported by Vaubel (1993, 1997). He claims to have found significant evidence that before elections, money supply rises if the party of the federal government also has a majority in the central bank council, otherwise money supply declines. Vaubel's empirical results are criticized by Neumann (1993). Lohmann (1998) could not find a significant impact of Vaubel's obstructionist hypothesis after controlling economic variables. However, she used a different method than Vaubel.

8. The importance of internal decision-making rules is revealed by the dispute among the federal government and the Lander in the reorganization of the Bundesbank in Germany in 1992 (Lohmann, 1998).

9. See von Hagen and Süppel (1994) for a discussion of the effects of different decision-making structures in a federal central bank.

Summary of Part IV

While an independent central bank is regarded as one way to mitigate the time-consistency problem in monetary policy, little attention has been paid to the conditions under which an independent central bank can be credibly supplied by politics. Steps have been taken in that direction by outlining a model that analyses the interaction between a central bank and two political decision bodies. Delegation is only credible if there are at least two veto players in the legislative process and if they disagree to some extent about monetary policy. Otherwise, the decision of the central bank could always be overturned by the legislators. The empirical investigation support this hypothesis: OECD countries whose legislative decision rules are characterized by extensive checks and balances are associated with significantly more independent central banks. Furthermore, central banks in countries with forms of checks and balances are behaviorally more independent, as reflected by a stronger negative correlation between legal central bank independence and average inflation than in countries with no checks and balances. These findings suggest that the design of political institutions has consequences for the choice of economic institutions and ultimately for the performance of economic policy. Particularly, this study provides an economic argument in favor of political systems with checks and balances: these systems have an advantage in credibly committing to a chosen policy.

Finally, the question why some countries have chosen legislative decision-making rules with checks and balances and others without such checks and balances has not been addressed here. Rather, the decision-making rules have been regarded as exogenous. However, considering the countries with extensive checks and balances, they are all characterized by a substantial degree of federalism. This seems to imply a correlation between the vertical structure of a state and its horizontal division of decision-making power at the central government. In other words, it may well be that federal systems, because they are characterized by stronger horizontal and vertical checks and balances, are better capable of credibly providing independent central banks.[1]

NOTE

1. In addition, federalism may promote a stable monetary policy by constraining fiscal policy (Busch, 1995) or by strengthening the influence of the financial opposition to inflation (Posen, 1993). Also Qian and Weingast (1997) argue that federalism may help the commitment to preserving market incentives.

Epilogue: Markets, checks and balances, and commitments

The starting point of this study was the economic argument that a market economy relies on a set of property rights which are regarded as stable or durable and which guarantee open markets. Collective decisions based on a simple majority rule are generally insufficient to meet these requirements for a market economy (Chapter 2). Rather, additional constraints are essential such that the risk of inconsistent collective choices (cycles) is reduced and the durability of policy decisions is increased (Chapter 3). Of course, such constraints are only a necessary but not a sufficient condition for a market economy, because they can provide durability to efficient as well as to inefficient allocations of property rights.

This study has concentrated on the contribution of political institutions to mitigating the problem of instability and the lack of durable policies caused by majority rule decisions. The main thesis of this research is that checks and balances are not only important in improving the quality of the discussion but also because checks and balances, which create several veto institutions, make it more likely that an equilibrium of collective choices in more dimensional issues exists. Chapter 4 reviewed a wide variety of legislative institutions that contribute to this purpose: committees, parties, coalition governments, multi-cameral legislatures, but also the combination of a representative with a direct democracy, as in the Swiss political system (Part II).

The design of checks and balances, particularly the allocation of agenda rights, influences the outcome of policy choices which, once chosen, cannot be modified easily. This point is revealed in the investigation of the cooperation procedure in the EU (Part III). The EP's right to suggest amendments gives policy influence to the Parliament only under certain conditions. If one of the constraints changes during the decision process, the Parliament can have significant influence on policy outcomes, as the case study on car emission standards exemplified (Chapter 9). Furthermore, this analysis provides new insights for the development of the theoretical approach. The conventional assumption of fixed restrictions can misguide the investigation whereas a careful analysis of restrictions and their modifications during the decision process can improve the predictions of rational or public choice models.

The existence of checks and balances has implications for legislative delegation to agencies. As discussed in Chapter 4, a regulatory agency can take advantage of stability-enhancing legislative institutions and choose its most preferred policy within the set of stable outcomes. On the one hand, legislators may want to constrain such agency discretion. On the other hand, such discretion may be to the advantage of legislators because it allows them to tie their hands. As analysed in Part IV, checks and balances permit legislators to commit themselves to a partially independent central bank. This argument points out that the design of political institutions has consequences for the choice of economic institutions and ultimately for the performance of economic policy. Particularly, this provides an economic argument in favor of political systems with checks and balances: these systems have an advantage to credibly commit to a chosen policy.

The positive analysis of political institutions can and should be extended in several ways. First, although the method has been applied to European institutions in recent years, the main focus of the literature is still on US institutions. As the analysis in Part III suggests, applications of these theories to the complex decision rules in the EU increase our understanding of these procedures considerably. However, many interesting questions are still open for further investigations. For example, the role of the European Court of Justice (Burley and Mattli, 1993; Garrett, 1995a), the decision making inside the Commission, or the expected behavior of the planned European Central Bank are issues of substantial interest.

A second extension of this research program should include the role of checks and balances in providing information and thereby improving the quality of policy decisions. While the informational aspects of committees have been investigated, it would be useful to extend these models to other forms of institutions and to generalize them to multidimensional choices. The work by Persson, Roland and Tabellini (1996) provides an interesting starting point.

Finally, a third extension should focus on the sustainability of institutions. For institutions to be credible, they have to be self-enforcing (Shepsle, 1991; Bendor and Lohmann, 1993; Calvert, 1993; North, 1993). Otherwise, the conflict over a policy choice will be transferred to a conflict over decision rules (Tsebelis, 1990). Some promising research has taken place with regard to this question. One approach is to regard a constitution as a convention that helps to coordinate the strategies of individual citizens against government transgressions in face of multiple coordination equilibria (Hardin, 1989; Wärneryd, 1990; Ordeshook, 1992; Weingast, 1993a, 1993b). Regular constitutional discussion becomes important since it allows the coordination of strategies and the possibility of an agreement on a set of limits whose violation will trigger a reaction by the citizenry. Regular popular referenda can be such a form of discussion (Frey and Kirchgässner, 1993). Furthermore, local governments in a federalist system may be able to limit the authority of the central government and thereby preserve open markets (Amar, 1987; Weingast, 1995; Qian and Weingast, 1997).

In summary, limits on majority rules or checks and balances are necessary to protect open markets, but some form of consent among the citizens is essential that such checks and balances are appropriate and necessary. It is hoped that this research program can contribute to the establishment and renewal of such a consent.

References

Alchian, Arman A. and Harold Demsetz (1972) 'Production, Information Costs, and Economic Organization,' *American Economic Review*, **62**, 777–97.

Alesina, Alberto and Roberta Gatti (1995) 'Independent Central Banks: Low Inflation at No Cost?', *American Economic Review*, **85**, 196–200.

Alesina, Alberto and Roberto Perotti (1994) 'The Political Economy of Growth: A Critical Survey of the Recent Literature', *The World Bank Economic Review*, **8**, 351–71.

Alesina, Alberto and Lawrence H. Summers (1993) 'Central Bank Independence and Macroeconomic Performance', *Journal of Money, Credit, and Banking*, **25**, 151–62.

Alesina, Alberto and Guido Tabellini (1990) 'A Positive Theory of Fiscal Deficits and Government Debt', *Review of Economic Studies*, **57**, 403–14.

Al-Marhubi, Fahim and Thomas D. Willett (1995) 'The Anti Inflationary Influence of Corporatist Structures and Central Bank Independence: The Importance of the Hump Shaped Hypothesis,' *Public Choice*, **84**, 153–62.

Alt, James E. and Robert C. Lowry (1994) 'Divided Government, Fiscal Institutions, and Budget Deficits: Evidence from the States', *American Political Science Review*, **88**, 811–28.

Amar, Akhil R. (1987) 'Of Sovereignty and Federalism', *Yale Law Journal*, **96**, 1425–520.

Arp, Henning A. (1992) 'The European Parliament in European Community Environmental Policy', Working Paper, European University Institute, Florence.

Arrow, K. [1951] (1963) *Social Choice and Individual Value*, 2nd edn., New Haven: Yale University Press.

Auer, Andreas (1991) 'Rückwirkungen der europäischen Integration auf die schweizerische Verfassungsgerichtsbarkeit', *Aussenwirtschaft*, **46**, 533–49.

Austen-Smith, David (1990) 'Information Transmission in Debate', *American Journal of Political Science*, **34**, 124–52.

Austen-Smith, David and Jeffrey Banks (1988) 'Elections, Coalitions, and Legislative Outcomes', *American Political Science Review*, **82**, 405–22.

Austen-Smith, David and Jeffrey Banks (1990) 'Stable Governments and the Allocation of Policy Portfolios', *American Political Science Review*, **84**, 891–906.

Austen-Smith, David and William Riker (1987) 'Asymmetric Information and the Coherence of Legislation', *American Political Science Review*, **81**, 897–918.

Austen-Smith, David and John R. Wright (1992) 'Competitive Lobbying for a Legislator's Vote', *Social Choice and Welfare*, **9**, 229–57.

Axelrod, Robert (1970) *Conflict of Interests*, Chicago: Chicago University Press.

Axelrod, Robert (1984) *The Evolution of Cooperation*, New York: Basic Books.

Banks, Jeffrey S. (1989) 'Agency Discretion, Cost Information, and Auditing', *American Journal of Political Science*, **33**, 670–99.

Banks, Jeffrey S. (1991) *Signaling Games in Political Science*, Chur: Harwood Academic Publishers.

Banks, Jeffrey S. and Barry R. Weingast (1992) 'The Political Control of Bureaucracies under Asymmetric Information', *American Journal of Political Science*, **36**, 502–24.

Baron, David P. (1991) 'A Spatial Bargaining Theory of Government Formation in Parliamentary Systems', *American Political Science Review*, **85**, 137–64.

Baron, David P. (1993) 'Government Formation and Endogenous Parties', *American Political Science Review*, **87**, 34–47.

Baron, David P. and John A. Ferejohn (1989a) 'Bargaining in Politics', *American Political Science Review*, **83**, 1181–206.

Baron, David and John A. Ferejohn (1989b) 'The Power to Propose', in Peter C. Ordeshook (ed.), *Models of Strategic Choices in Politics*, Ann Arbor: University of Michigan Press.

Barro, Robert J. and David B. Gordon (1983) 'Rules, Discretion and Reputation in a Model of Monetary Policy', *Journal of Monetary Economics*, **12**, 101–21.

Beck, Nathaniel (1990) 'Congress and the Fed: Why the Dog Does Not Bark in the Night', in Thomas Mayer (ed.), *The Political Economy of American Monetary Policy*, Cambridge: Cambridge University Press.

Becker, Gary S. (1983) 'A Theory of Competition among Pressure Groups for Political Influence', *Quarterly Journal of Economics*, **98**, 371–400.

Becker, Ulrich (1991) *Der Gestaltungsspielraum der EG-Mitgliedstaaten im Spannungsfeld zwischen Umweltschutz und freiem Warenverkehr*, Baden-Baden: Nomos.

Beetsma, Roel M.W.J. and Frederick van der Ploeg (1996) 'Does Inequality Cause Inflation? The Political Economy of Inflation, Taxation and Government Debt', *Public Choice*, **87**, 143–62.

Bendor, Jonathan and Susanne Lohmann (1993) 'Institutions and Credible Commitment', Manuscript, Graduate School of Business, Stanford University.

Bendor, Jonathan, Serge Taylor and Roland Van Gaalen (1985) 'Bureaucratic Expertise vs. Legislative Authority: A Model of Deception and Monitoring in Budgeting', *American Political Science Review*, **79**, 1041–61.

Bendor, Jonathan, Serge Taylor and Roland Van Gaalen (1987) 'Politicians, Bureaucrats, and Asymmetric Information', *American Journal of Political Science*, **31**, 796–828.

Bernholz, Peter (1973) 'Logrolling, Arrow Paradox and Cyclical Majorities', *Public Choice*, **15**, 87–95.

Bernholz, Peter (1974) 'Logrolling, Arrow Paradox and Decision Rules – A Generalization', *Kyklos*, **27**, 49–61.

Bernholz, Peter (1978) 'On the Stability of Logrolling Outcomes in Stochastic Games', *Public Choice*, **33**, 65–82.

Bernholz, Peter and Friedrich Breyer (1994) *Grundlagen der Politischen Ökonomie*, vol. 2, 3rd edn., Tübingen: J.C.B. Mohr.

Besley, Timothy and Stephen Coate (1998) 'Sources of Inefficiency in a Representative Democracy: A Dynamic Analysis', *American Economic Review*, **88** (1), 139–56.

Black, Duncan (1958) *The Theory of Committees and Elections*, London: Cambridge University Press.

Blankart, Charles B. (1992) 'Bewirken Referendum und Volksinitiative einen Unterschied in der Politik?' *Staatswissenschaften und Staatspraxis*, **3**, 509–23.

Blankart, Charles B. (1994) 'Club Governments versus Representative Governments', *Constitutional Political Economy*, **5**, 273–85.

Bohnet, Iris and Bruno S. Frey (1994) 'Direct-Democratic Rules: The Role of Discussion', *Kyklos*, **47**, 341–54.

Borner, Silvio, Aymo Brunetti and Thomas Straubhaar (1990) *Schweiz AG*, Zürich: Neue Zürcher Zeitung.

Borner, Silvio, Aymo Brunetti and Thomas Straubhaar (1994) *Die Schweiz im Alleingang*, Zürich: Neue Zurcher Zeitung.

Borner, Silvio, Aymo Brunetti and Beatrice Weder (1995) *Political Credibility and Economic Development*, Basingstoke: Macmillan.

Borner, Silvio, Michael E. Porter, Rolf Weder and Michael Enright (1991) *Internationale Wettbewerbsvorteile: Ein strategisches Konzept für die Schweiz*, Frankfurt: Campus.

Borner, Silvio and Hans Rentsch (eds), (1997) *Wieviel direkte Demokratie verträgt die Schweiz?*', Chur: Rüegger.

Bowler, Shaun and Farrell, David M. (1995) 'The Organizing of the European Parliament: Committees, Specialization and Co-ordination', *British Journal of Political Science*, **25**, 219–43.

Brennan, Geoffrey and James M. Buchanan (1985) *The Reason of Rules: Constitutional Political Economy*, Cambridge: Cambridge University Press.

Brunetti, Aymo (1998) 'Policy Volatility and Economic Growth: A Comparative Empirical Analysis', *European Journal of Political Economy*, **4**, 35–52.

Brunetti, Aymo and Beatrice Weder (1995) 'Political Sources of Growth: A Critical Note on Measurement', *Public Choice*, **82**, 125–34.

Buchanan, James M. (1971) *Limits of Liberty: Between Anarchy and Leviathan*, Chicago: University of Chicago Press.

Buchanan, James M. and Gorden Tullock (1962) *The Calculus of Consent*, Ann Arbor: University of Michigan Press.

Bueno de Mesquita, Bruce and Frans N. Stokman (eds) (1994) *European Community Decision Making: Models, Applications, and Comparisons*, New Haven: Yale University Press.

Bundesrat (1995) *Reform der Bundesverfassung: Verfassungsentwurf*, Bern: EDMZ.

Burley, Anne-Marie and Walter Mattli (1993) 'Europe Before the Court: A Political Theory of Legal Integration', *International Organization*, **47** (1), 41–76.

Busch, Andreas (1995) *Preisstabilitätspolitik: Politik und Inflationsraten im internationalen Vergleich*, Opladen: Leske und Budrich.

Calvert, Randell L. (1986) *Models of Imperfect Information in Politics*, London: Harwood Academic Publisher.

Calvert, Randell L. (1992) 'Leadership and Its Basis in Problems of Social Coordination', *International Political Science Review*, **16**, 7–24.

Calvert, Randell L. (1993) 'Rational Actors, Equilibrium, and Social Institutions', in J. Knight and I. Sened (eds), *Explaining Social Institutions*, Cambridge: Cambridge University Press.

Calvert, Randell L., Mathew D. McCubbins and Barry R. Weingast (1989) 'A Theory of Political Control and Agency Discretion', *American Journal of Political Science*, **33**, 588–611.

Caplin, Andrew and Barry Nalebuff (1988) 'On 64%-majority Rule', *Econometrica*, **56**, 787–814.

Carpenter, Daniel P. (1996) 'Adaptive Processing, Hierarchy, and Budgetary Control in Federal Regulation', *American Political Science Review*, **90** (2), 283–302.

Carter, John R. and David Schap (1987) 'Executive Veto, Legislative Override, and Structure-induced Equilibrium', *Public Choice*, **52**, 224–7.

Coase, Ronald (1937) 'The Nature of the Firm', *Economica*, **4**, 386–405.

Condorcet, Marquis de (1785) *Essai sur l'Application de l'Analyse à la Probabilité des Décisions Rendues à la Pluralité des Voix*, Paris.

Coughlin, Peter J. (1992) *Probabilistic Voting Theory*, Cambridge: Cambridge University Press.

Cox, Gary W. (1987) 'The Uncovered Set and the Core', *American Journal of Political Science*, **31**, 81–108.

Cox, Gary W. and Mathew D. McCubbins (1993) *Legislative Leviathan: Party Government in the House*, Berkeley: University of California Press.

Cox, Gary W. and Richard McKelvey (1984) 'Ham Sandwich Theorems for General Measures', *Social Choice and Welfare*, **1**, 75–83.

Crain, W. Mark (1990) 'Legislative Committees: A Filtering Theory', in W. Mark Crain and Robert D. Tollison (eds), *Predicting Politics: Essays in Empirical Public Choice*, Ann Arbor: University of Michigan Press, 149–66.

Crain, W. Mark, Donald R. Leavens and Robert D. Tollison (1990) 'Pork Barrel Paradox', in W. Mark Crain and Robert D. Tollison (eds), *Predicting Politics: Essays in Empirical Public Choice*, Ann Arbor: University of Michigan Press, 59–78.

Crain, W. Mark and Lisa K. Oakley (1995) 'The Politics of Infrastructure', *Journal of Law and Economics*, **38**, 1–17.

Crain, W. Mark and Robert D. Tollison (eds) (1990) *Predicting Politics*, Ann Arbor: The University of Michigan Press.

Crain, W. Mark and Robert D. Tollison (1993) 'Time Inconsistency and Fiscal Policy: Empirical Analysis of U.S. States, 1969–89', *Journal of Public Economics*, **51**, 153–9.

Crombez, Christophe (1996) 'Legislative Procedures in the European Community', *British Journal of Political Science*, **26**, 199–288.

Crombez, Christophe (1997) 'The Co-Decision Procedure in the European Union', *Legislative Studies Quarterly*, **22**, 97–119.

Cukierman, Alex (1992) *Central Bank Strategy, Credibility, and Independence: Theory and Evidence*, Cambridge, MA: MIT Press.

Cukierman, Alex (1994) 'Commitment through Delegation, Political Influence and Central Bank Independence', in J.O. de Beaufort Wijnholds, S. Eijffinger and L.H. Hoogduin (eds), *A Framework for Monetary Stability*, Boston: Kluwer Academic Publishers.

Cukierman, Alex, Pantelis Kalaitzidakis, Lawrence H. Summers and Steven B. Webb (1993) 'Central Bank Independence, Growth, Investment, and Real Rates', *Carnegie-Rochester Conference Series on Public Policy*, **39**, 95–140.

Cukierman, Alex and Steven B. Webb (1995) 'Political Influence on the Central Bank: International Evidence', *World Bank Economic Review*, **9**, 397–423.

Dashwood, Alan (1994) 'Community Legislative Procedures in the Era of the Treaty on European Union', *European Law Review*, August, 343–66.

Davis, O.A., M.H. DeGroot and M.J. Hinich (1972) 'Social Preference Ordering and Majority Rule', *Econometrica*, **40**, 147–57.

Dearden, James A. and David Schap (1994) 'The First Word and the Last Word in the Budgetary Process: A Comparative Institutional Analysis of Proposal and Veto Authorities', *Public Choice*, **81**, 35–53.

Delury, George E. (1987) *World Encyclopedia of Political Systems and Parties*, 2nd edn., New York: Facts on File Publication.

Demsetz, Harold (1990) 'Amenity Potential, Indivisibilities, and Political Competition', in James A. Alt and Kenneth A. Shepsle (eds), *Perspectives on Positive Political Economy*, Cambridge: Cambridge University Press, 144–60.

Denzau, Arthur and R. Mackay (1981) 'Structure Induced Equilibrium and Perfect Foresight Expectations', *American Journal of Political Science*, **25**, 762–9.

Denzau, Arthur and R. Mackay (1983) 'Gatekeeping and Monopoly Power of Committees: An Analysis of Sincere and Sophisticated Behavior', *American Journal of Political Science*, **27**, 740–61.

Dixit, Avinash (1996) *The Making of Economic Policy*, Cambridge, MA: MIT Press.

Donnelly, Martin and Ella Ritchie (1994) 'The College of Commissioners and their Cabinets', in Geoffrey Edwards and David Spence (eds), *The European Commission*, Harlow: Longman, 31–61.

Döring, Herbert (ed.) (1995) *Parliaments and Majority Rule in Western Europe*, Frankfurt: Campus Verlag.

Downs, Anthony (1957) *An Economic Theory of Democracy*, New York: Harper and Row.

Earnshaw, D. and D. Judge (1993) 'The European Parliament and the Sweeteners Directive: From Footnote to Inter-institutional Conflict', *Journal of Common Market Studies* **31** (March), 103–16.

Earnshaw, David and David Judge (1996) 'From Co-operation to Co-decision', in Jeremy J. Richardson (ed.), *European Union: Power and Policy-Making*, London: Routledge, 96–126.

Easton, Stephen T. and Michael A. Walker (1997) 'Income, Growth, and Economic Freedom', *American Economic Review*, **87** (May), 328–32.

Eichenberger, Reiner and Angel Serna (1996) 'Random Errors, Dirty Information, and Politics', *Public Choice*, **86** (1–2), 137–56.

Eijffinger, Sylvester and Jakob de Haan (1996) *The Political Economy of Central-Bank Independence*, Special Papers in International Economics, 19, Princeton University.

Eijffinger, Sylvester and Eric Schaling (1993) 'Central Bank Independence in Twelve Industrial Countries', *Banca Nazionale del Lavoro Quarterly Review*, **184**, 1–41.

Eijffinger, Sylvester and Eric Schaling (1997) 'Central Bank Independence: Theory and Evidence', in S.C.W. Eijffinger (ed.), *Independent Central Banks and Economic Performance*, The International Library of Critical Writings in Economics, Cheltenham: Edward Elgar.

Eijffinger, Sylvester and Eric Schaling (1998) 'The Ultimate Determinants of Central Bank Independence', in S.C.W. Eijffinger and H.P. Huizinga (eds), *Positive Political Economy: Theory and Evidence*, Cambridge: Cambridge University Press, 47–77.

Eijffinger, Sylvester and Martyn van Keulen (1995) ' Central Bank Independence in Another Eleven Countries', *Banca Nazionale del Lavoro Quarterly Review*, **192**, 39–83.

Enelow, James M. and Melvin J. Hinich (1984) *The Spatial Theory of Voting*, Cambridge: Cambridge University Press.

Enelow, James M. and Melvin J. Hinich (1989) 'A General Probabilistic Spatial Theory of Elections', *Public Choice*, **61**, 101–13.

Enelow, James M. and Melvin J. Hinich (eds) (1990) *Advances in the Spatial Theory of Voting*, Cambridge: Cambridge University Press.

Enelow, James M. and Melvin J. Hinich (1994) 'A Test of the Predictive Dimension Model in Spatial Voting Theory', *Public Choice*, **78**, 155–70.

Epstein, David and Sharyn O'Halloran (1994) 'Administrative Procedures, Information, and Agency Discretion', *American Journal of Political Science*, **38**, 697–722.

Epstein, David and Sharyn O'Halloran (1995) 'A Theory of Strategic Oversight: Congress, Lobbyists, and the Bureaucracy', *Journal of Law, Economics, and Organization*, **11** (2), 227–55.

Eskridge, William N. and John A. Ferejohn (1992) 'Making the Deal Stick: Enforcing the Original Constitutional Structure of Lawmaking in the Modern Regulatory State', *Journal of Law, Economics, and Organization*, **8**, 165–89.

Europa Year Book (various issues), London: Europa Publications.

Feld, Lars and Gebhard Kirchgässner (1999) 'Public Dept and Budgetary Procedures: Top Down or Bottom Up? Some Evidence from Swiss Municipalities', in James M. Poterba and Jürgen von Hagen (eds), *Fiscal Institutions and Fiscal Performance*, Chicago: Chicago University Press and NBER, 151–79.

Feld, Lars and Marcel Savioz (1997) 'Direct Democracy Matters for Economic Performance: An Empirical Investigation', *Kyklos*, **50** (4), 507–38.

Fenno, Richard (1973) *Congressmen in Committees*, Boston: Little Brown.

Fenno, Richard (1978) *Home Style: Representatives in Their Districts*, Boston: Little Brown.

Ferejohn, John A. (1974) *Pork Barrel Politics*, Stanford: Stanford University Press.

Ferejohn, John A. (1986) 'Logrolling in an Institutional Context: A Case Study of Food Stamp Legislation', in Gerald C. Wright, Leroy N. Rieselbach and Lawrence C. Dodd (eds), *Congress and Policy Change*, New York: Agathan, 223–53.

Ferejohn, John A. (1993) 'Law, Legislation, and Positive Political Theory', Manuscript, Stanford University.

Ferejohn, John A., Richard D. McKelvey and Edward W. Packel (1984) 'Limiting Distributions for Continuous State Markov Voting Models', *Social Choice and Welfare*, **1**, 405–16.

Ferejohn, John A. and Charles Shipan (1989) 'Congressional Influence on Administrative Agencies: A Case Study of Telecommunications Policy', in Lawrence C. Dodd and Bruce I. Oppenheimer (eds) *Congress Reconsidered*, 4th edn., Washington: Congressional Quarterly Press.

Ferejohn, John A. and Charles Shipan (1990) 'Congressional Influence on Bureaucracy', *Journal of Law, Economics, and Organization*, **6**, 1–20.

Ferejohn, John A. and Barry R. Weingast (1992) 'A Positive Theory of Statutory Interpretation', *International Review of Law and Economics*, **12**, 263–79.

Fiorina, Morris P. (1974) *Representatives, Roll Calls, and Constituencies*, Boston: Heath.

Fiorina, Morris P. (1977) *Congress: Keystone of the Washington Establishment*, New Haven: Yale University Press.

Fischer, Stanly (1980) 'Dynamic Inconsistency, Cooperation and the Benevolent Dissembling Government', *Journal of Economic Dynamics and Control*, **2**, 93–107.

Fitzmaurice, John (1988) 'An Analysis of the European Community's Co-operation Procedure', *Journal of Common Market Studies*, **26**, 389–400.

Frey, Bruno S. (1994) 'Direct Democracy: Politico-Economic Lessons from Swiss Experience', *American Economic Review*, **84**, 338–42.

Frey, Bruno S. and Gebhard Kirchgässner (1993) 'Diskursethik, Politische Oekonomie und Volksabstimmungen', *Analyse und Kritik*, **15**, 129–49.

Frey, Bruno S. and Gebhard Kirchgässner (1994) *Demokratische Wirtschaftspolitik*, 2nd edn., Munich: Oldenburg.

Frey, Bruno S. and Friedrich Schneider (1981) 'Central Bank Behavior: A Positive Empirical Analysis', *Journal of Monetary Economics*, **7**, 291–315.

Fudenberg, Drew and Eric Maskin (1986) 'Folk Theorems in Repeated Games with Discounting and Incomplete Information', *Econometrica*, **54**, 553–4.

Garfinkel, Michelle R. (1994) 'Domestic Politics and International Conflict', *American Economic Review*, **84** (5), 1294–309.

Garrett, Geoffrey (1995a) 'The Politics of Legal Integration in the European Union', *International Organization*, **49** (1), 171–81.

Garrett, Geoffrey (1995b) 'From the Luxembourg Compromise to Codecision: Decision Making in the European Union', *Electoral Studies*, **14** (3), 289–308.

Gärtner, Manfred (1994) 'Democracy, Elections, and Macroeconomic Policy: Two Decades of Progress', *European Journal of Political Economy*, **10**, 85–109.

Gärtner, Manfred (1997) 'Time-consistent Monetary Policy under Output Persistence,' *Public Choice*, **92**, 429–37.

Gely, Rafael and Pablo T. Spiller (1990) 'A Rational Choice Theory of Supreme Court Statutory Decisions, with Applications to the *State Farm* and *Grove City Cases*', *Journal of Law, Economics, and Organization*, **6**, 263–301.

Gely, Rafael and Pablo T. Spiller (1992) 'The Political Economy of Supreme Court Constitutional Decisions: The Case of Roosevelt's Court-Packing Plan', *International Review of Law and Economics*, **12**, 45–67.

Germann, Raimund E. (1990) 'Pour une Constitution fédérale "Euro-compatible"', *Zeitschrift für Schweizerisches Recht*, **I**, 1–15.

Germann, Raimund E. (1991) 'Die Europatauglichkeit der direktdemokratischen Institutionen der Schweiz', *Schweizerisches Jahrbuch für politische Wissenschaft*, **31**, 257–69.

Germann, Raimund E. (1994) *Staatsreform: Der Uebergang zur Konkurrenzdemokratie*, Bern: Haupt.

Gersbach, Hans (1992) 'Collective Acquisition of Information by Committees', *Journal of Institutional and Theoretical Economics*, **148**, 460–7.

Gersbach, Hans (1993) 'Politics and the Choice of Durability: Comment', *American Economic Review*, **83**, 670–3.

Gilligan, Thomas (1993) 'Information and the Allocation of Legislative Authority', *Journal of Institutional and Theoretical Economics*, **149**, 321–41.

Gilligan, Thomas and Keith Krehbiel (1987) 'Collective Decisionmaking and Standing Committees: An Informational Rationale for Restrictive Amendment Procedures', *Journal of Law, Economics, and Organization*, **3**, 287–335.

Gilligan, Thomas and Keith Krehbiel (1989) 'Asymmetric Information and Legislative Rules with Heterogeneous Committee', *American Journal of Political Science*, **33**, 459–90.

Gilligan, Thomas, Mark J. Moran and Barry R. Weingast (1989) 'Regulation and the Theory of Legislative Choice: The Interstate Commerce Act of 1887', *Journal of Law and Economics*, **32**, 35–61.

Glazer, Amihai (1989) 'Politics and the Choice of Durability', *American Economic Review*, **79**, S. 1207–13.

Glazer, Amihai (1993) 'Politics and the Choice of Durability: Reply', *American Economic Review*, **83**, 674–5.

Greif, Avner, Paul R. Milgrom and Barry R. Weingast (1994) 'Coordination, Commitment, and Enforcement: The Case of the Merchant Gilds', *Journal of Political Economy*, **102**, 745–76.

Grier, Kevin B. (1991) 'Congressional Influence on U.S. Monetary Policy', *Journal of Monetary Economics*, **28**, 201–20.

Grilli, Vittorio, Donato Masciandaro and Guido Tabellini (1991) 'Political and Monetary Institutions and Public Financial Policies in the Industrial Countries', *Economic Policy*, **13**, 342–92.

Grossman, Sanford and Oliver Hart (1986) 'The Costs and Benefits of Ownership', *Journal of Political Economy*, **94**, 691–719.

Grüner, Hans Peter (1996) 'Monetary Policy, Reputation and Hysteresis', *Zeitschrift für Wirtschafts- und Sozialwissenschaften*, **116**, 15–29.

Haan, Jakob de and Gert Jan van't Hag (1995) 'Determinants of Central Bank Independence: Some Provisional Empirical Evidence', *Public Choice*, **85**, 335–51.

Hall, Richard L. and Bernard Grofman (1990) 'The Committee Assignment Process and the Conditional Nature of Committee Bias', *American Political Science Review*, **84**, 1149–66.

Hall, Robert E. and Charles I. Jones (1997) 'Levels of Economic Activities Across Countries', *American Economic Review*, **87** (May), 171–7.

Hammond, Thomas H. and Jack H. Knott (1996) 'Who Controls the Bureaucracy? Presidential Power, Congressional Dominance, and Bureaucratic Autonomy in a Model of Multi-Institutional Policymaking', *Journal of Law, Economics, and Organization*, **12** (1), 119–66.

Hammond, Thomas H. and Gary J. Miller (1987) 'The Core of the Constitution', *American Political Science Review*, **81**, 1155–74.

Hansson, I. and C. Stuart (1984) 'Voting Competition with Interested Politicians: Platforms Do Not Converge to the Preferences of the Median Voter', *Public Choice*, **44** (3), 431–41.

Hardin, Russel (1989) 'Why a Constitution', in B. Grofman and B. Wittman (eds), *The Federalist Papers and the New Institutionalism*, New York: Agathon Press.

Hart, Oliver and Bengt R. Holmstrom (1987) 'The Theory of Contracts', in Trueman Bewley (ed.), *Advances in Economic Theory, Fifth World Congress*, Cambridge: Cambridge University Press.

Hart, Oliver and John Moore (1990) 'Property Rights and the Nature of the Firm', *Journal of Political Economy*, **98**, 1119–58.

Havrilesky, Thomas (1995) *The Pressures on American Monetary Policy*, 2nd edn., Boston: Kluwer Academic Publishers.

Hayek, Friedrich A. (1979) *Law, Legislation and Liberty*, vol. 3, London: Routledge.

Heinz, Kersten (1989) 'Nochmals: Die Fahrverbotsregelung der Smog-Verordnungen auf dem Prüfstand des EG-Rechts', *Neue Zeitschrift für Verwaltungsrecht*, **11**, 1035–9.

Herman, Valentino (1976) *Parliaments of the World: A Reference Compendium*, Berlin: de Gruyter.

Hibbs, Douglas C. (1992) 'Partisan Theory after Fifteen Years', *European Journal of Political Economy*, **8**, 1467–87.

Hill, Jeffrey S. and James E. Brazier (1991) 'Constraining Administrative Decisions: A Critical Examination of the Structure and Process Hypothesis', *Journal of Law, Economics, and Organization*, **7**, 373–400.

Hillman, Arye (1989) *The Political Economy of Protection*, Chur: Harwood Academic Publishers.

Holmstrom, Bengt R. (1979) 'Moral Hazard and Observability', *Journal of Economics*, **10**, 74–91.

Holmstrom, Bengt R. and Jean Tirole (1989) 'The Theory of the Firm', in R. Schmalensee and R.D. Willig (eds), *Handbook of Industrial Organization*, New York: North-Holland, 61–133.

Holzinger, Katharina (1994) *Politik des kleinsten gemeinsamen Nenners? Umweltpolitische Entscheidungsprozesse in der EG am Beispiel der Einführung des Katalysatorautos*, Berlin: Edition Sigma.

Hubschmid, Claudia and Peter Moser (1997) 'The Co-operation Procedure in the EU: Why was the European Parliament Influential in the Decision on Car Emission Standards?', *Journal of Common Market Studies*, **35** (2), 225–42.

Hug, Simon (1995) 'Uncertainty Causes Referendums,' Manuscript, University of Geneva.

Hug, Simon and Pascal Sciarini (eds) (1996) *Institutional Reforms*, special issue of the journal *Swiss Political Science Review*, **2** (2).

Ingberman, Daniel E. and Dennis A. Yao (1991) 'Circumventing Formal Structure Through Commitment: Presidential Influence and Agenda Control', *Public Choice*, **70**, 151–79.

Inter-Parliamentary Union (1986) *Parliaments of the World*, 2nd edn., Aldershot: Gower.

Iversen, Torben (1994) 'Political Leadership and Representation in West European Democracies: A Test of Three Models of Voting', *American Journal of Political Science*, **38**, 45–74.

Jacobs, Francis and Richard Corbett (1990) *The European Parliament*, Harlow, UK: Longman.

Jensen, Henrik (1997) 'Credibility of Optimal Monetary Delegation', *American Economic Review*, **87**, 911–20.

Jensen, Michael C. and William Meckling (1976) 'Theory of the Firm: Managerial Behavior, Agency Costs, and Capital Structure', *Journal of Financial Economics*, **3**, 305–60.

Judge, David, David Earnshaw and Ngaire Cowan (1994) 'Ripples or Waves: The European Parliament in the European Community Policy Process', *Journal of European Public Policy*, **1**, 27–52.

Kapteyn, P.J.G. and P. Verloren van Themaat (1989) *Introduction to the Law of the European Communities*, 2nd edn., Deventer: Kluwer.

Kelly, Jerry S. (1988) *Social Choice Theory: An Introduction*, Berlin: Springer Verlag.

Kiewiet, D.R. and Mathew D. McCubbins (1988) 'Presidential Influence in the Appropriations Process', *American Journal of Political Science*, **32**, 713–36.

Kiewiet, D.R. and Mathew D. McCubbins (1991) *The Logic of Delegation: Congressional Parties and the Appropriation Process*, Chicago: University of Chicago Press.

Kiewiet, D.R. and Kristin Szakaly (1996) 'Constitutional Limitations on Borrowing: An Analysis of State Bonded Indebtness', *Journal of Law, Economics, and Organization*, **12**, 62–97.

Kirchgässner, Gebhard (1992) 'Towards a Theory of Low-Cost Decisions', *European Journal of Political Economy*, **8**, 305–20.

Kirchgässner, Gebhard (1995) 'Geldpolitik und Zentralbankverhalten aus der Sicht der Neuen Politischen Ökonomie', in P. Bofinger and K.-H.Ketterer (eds), *Neuere Entwicklungen in der Geldtheorie und Geldpolitik. Implikationen für die Europäische Währungsunion*, Tübingen: Mohr (Siebeck), 21–41.

Kirchgässner, Gebhard (1996a) 'Bemerkungen zur Minimalmoral', *Zeitschrift für Wirtschafts- und Socialwissenschaften*, **116**, 223–51.

Kirchgässner, Gebhard (1996b) 'Probabilistic Voting and Equilibrium: An Impossibility Result', Discussion Paper of the Economics Department, no. 9618, University of St Gallen.

Klein, Benjamin, Robert G. Crawford and Armen Alchian (1978) 'Vertical Integration, Appropriable Rents, and the Competitive Contracting Process', *Journal of Law and Economics*, **21**, 297–326.

Klein, Benjamin and Keith Leffler (1981) 'The Role of Market Forces in Assuring Contractual Performance', *Journal of Political Economy*, **89**, 615–41.

Kleinewefers, Henner (1995) '"Verwesentlichung" der Politik durch Einschränkung der direkten Volksrechte? Eine Auslegeordnung der Probleme und ein Vorschlag aus ökonomischer Sicht', Manuscript, University of Freiburg.

Kölz, Alfred and Jörg Paul Müller (1990) *Entwurf für eine neue Bundesverfassung*, Basel: Helbling und Lichtenhahn.

Krämer, Ludwig (1993) 'Environmental Protection and Article 30 EEC Treaty', *Common Market Law Review*, **30**, 111–43.

Kramer, Gerald H. (1972) 'Sophisticated Voting over Multidimensional Choice Spaces', *Journal of Mathematical Sociology*, **2**, 165–80.

Kramer, Gerald H. (1973) 'On a Class of Equilibrium Conditions for Majority Rule', *Econometrica*, **41**, 285–97.

Krehbiel, Keith (1988) 'Spatial Models of Legislative Choice', *Legislative Studies Quarterly*, **13**, 259–319.

Krehbiel, Keith (1990) 'Are Congressional Committees Composed of Preference Outliners?' *American Political Science Review*, **84**, 149–63.

Krehbiel, Keith (1991) *Information and Legislative Organization*, Ann Arbor: Michigan University Press.

Krehbiel, Keith (1993) 'Where's the Party?' *British Journal of Political Science*, **23**, 235–66.

Krehbiel, Keith (1996) 'Institutional and Partisan Sources of Gridlock: A Theory of Divided and Unified Government', *Journal of Theoretical Politics*, **8**, 7–40.

Kreps, David (1990) 'Corporate Culture', in James A. Alt and Kenneth A. Shepsle (eds), *Perspectives on Positive Political Economy*, Cambridge: Cambridge University Press.

Kydland, Finn E. and Edward C. Prescott (1977) 'Rules rather than Discretion: The Inconsistency of Optimal Plans,' *Journal of Political Economy*, **85**, 473–91.

Laver, Michael and Ian Budge (1992) *Party Policy and Government Coalitions*, London: Macmillan.

Laver, Michael and Norman Schofield (1990) *Multiparty Government: The Politics of Coalition in Europe*, Oxford: Oxford University Press.

Laver, Michael and Kenneth A. Shepsle (1990) 'Coalitions and Cabinet Government', *American Political Science Review*, **84**, 873–90.

Laver, Michael and Kenneth A. Shepsle (eds) (1994) *Cabinet Ministers and Parliamentary Governments*, Cambridge: Cambridge University Press.

Laver, Michael and Kenneth A. Shepsle (1996) *Making and Breaking Governments*, Cambridge: Cambridge University Press.

Lenz, Carl Otto and Klaus-Dieter Borchardt (eds) (1994) *EG-Vertrag: Kommentar*, Basel: Helbling und Lichtenhahn.

Lindbeck, Assar and Jörgen W. Weibull (1993) 'A Model of Political Equilibrium in a Representative Democracy', *Journal of Public Economics*, **51**, 195–209.

Linder, Wolf (1994) *Swiss Democracy: Possible Solutions to Conflict in Multicultural Societies*, New York: St. Martin's Press.

Lockwood, Ben, Marcus Miller and Lei Zhang (1996) 'Central Bank Independence and the Role of Reputation', in Matthew B. Canzoneri, Wilfred J. Ethier and Vittorio Grilli (eds), *The New Transatlantic Economy*, Cambridge: Cambridge University Press, 236–60.

Lohmann, Susanne (1992) 'Optimal Credibility in Monetary Policy: Credibility versus Flexibility', *American Economic Review*, **82**, 273–86.

Lohmann, Susanne (1998) 'Federalism and Central Bank Autonomy: The Politics of German Monetary Policy, 1957–1992', *World Politics*, **50**, 401–46.

Lohmann, Susanne and Sharyn O'Halloran (1994) 'Divided Government and U.S. Trade Policy: Theory and Evidence', *International Organization*, **48**, 595–632.

Londregan, Jon and James M. Snyder (1994) 'Comparing Committee and Floor Preferences', *Legislative Studies Quarterly*, **19** (2), 233–66; reprinted 1995 in Kenneth A. Shepsle and Barry R. Weingast (eds), *Positive Theories of Congressional Institutions*, Michigan: University of Michigan Press, 139–72.

Lupia, Arthur (1992) 'Busy Voters, Agenda Control, and the Power of Information', *American Political Science Review*, **86**, 390–403.

Lupia, Arthur (1994) 'The Effect of Information on Voting Behavior and Electoral Outcomes: An Experimental Study of Direct Legislation', *Public Choice*, **78**, 65–86.

Macey, Jonathan R. (1992) 'Organizational Design and Political Control of Administrative Agencies', *Journal of Law, Economic, and Organization*, **8**, 93–110.

Mackie, Thomas T. and Richard Rose (1991) *The International Almanac of Electoral History*, Basingstoke: Macmillan.

Madison, James, Alexander Hamilton and John Jay [1788] (1987) *The Federalist Papers*, London: Penguin Books.

Marks, Brian A. (1988) 'A Model of Judicial Influence on Congressional Policymaking: Grove City v. Bell', Working Paper in Political Science, no. 88–7, Hoover Institution, Stanford.

Matsusaka, John G. (1995) 'Fiscal Effects of the Voter Initiative: Evidence from the Last 30 Years', *Journal of Political Economy*, **103**, 587–623.

Matthews, Steven A. (1989) 'Veto Threats: Rethoric in a Bargaining Game', *Quarterly Journal of Economics*, **104**, 347–69.

McCallum, Bennett T. (1995) 'Two Fallacies Concerning Central-Bank Independence', *American Economic Review*, **85**, 207–11.

McCarty, Nolan and Keith T. Poole (1995) 'Veto Power and Legislation: An Empirical Analysis of Executive and Legislative Bargaining from 1961 to 1986', *Journal of Law, Economics, and Organization*, **11** (2), 283–312.

McCubbins, Matthew D., Roger G. Noll and Barry R. Weingast (1987) 'Administrative Procedures as Instruments of Political Control', *Journal of Law, Economics, and Organization*, **3**, 243–77.

McCubbins, Matthew D., Roger G. Noll and Barry R. Weingast (1989) 'Structure and Process, Politics and Policies: Administrative Arrangements and the Political Control of Agencies', *Virginia Law Review*, **75**, 431–82.

McCubbins, Matthew D., Roger G. Noll and Barry R. Weingast (1990) 'Positive and Normative Models of Due Process: An Integrative Approach to Administrative Procedures', *Journal of Law, Economics, and Organization*, **6**, 307–32.

McCubbins, Matthew D. and Thomas Schwarz (1984) 'Congressional Oversight Overlooked: Police Patrols vs. Fire Alarms', *American Political Science Review*, **28**, 165–79.

McKelvey, Richard D. (1976) 'Intransitivities in Multidimensional Voting Models and Some Implications for Agenda Control', *Journal of Economic Theory*, **12**, 472–82.

McKelvey, Richard D. (1979) 'General Conditions for Global Intransitivities in Formal Voting Models', *Econometrica*, **47**, 1085–112.

McKelvey, Richard D. (1986) 'Covering, Dominance, and Institution Free Properties of Social Choice', *American Journal of Political Science*, **30**, 283–314.

Migue, J.-L. and G. Belanger (1974) 'Towards a General Theory of Managerial Discretion', *Public Choice*, **33**, 99–106.

Milesi-Ferretti, Gian Maria (1995) 'The Disadvantage of Tying Their Hands: On the Political Economy of Policy Commitments', *Economic Journal*, **105**, 1381–402.

Milgrom, Paul R, Douglass C. North and Barry R. Weingast (1990) 'The Role of Institutions in the Revival of Trade: The Law Merchant, Private Judges, and the Champagne Fairs', *Economics and Politics*, **2**, 1–23.

Milgrom, Paul R. and John Roberts (1992) *Economics, Organization and Management*, Englewood Cliffs: Prentice Hall.

Miller, Gary J. (1992) *Managerial Dilemmas: The Political Economy of Hierarchy*, Cambridge: Cambridge University Press.

Miller, Gary (1993) 'Formal Theory and the Presidency', in G.C. Edwards III, J.H. Kessel and R. Rockman (eds), *Researching the Presidency: Vital Questions, New Approaches*, Pittsburgh: University of Pittsburgh Press.

Miller, Nicholas R. (1980) 'A New Solution Set for Tournaments and Majority Voting: Further Graph-Theoretical Approaches to the Theory of Voting', *American Journal of Political Science*, **24**, 68–96.

Miller, Nicholas R., Bernhard Grofman and Scott L. Feld (1989) 'The Geometry of Majority Rule', *Journal of Theoretical Politics*, **1**, 379–406.

Möckli, Silvano (1991) 'Direkte Demokratie im Vergleich', *Aus Politik und Zeitgeschichte*, **23**, 31–43.

Möckli, Silvano (1993) 'Stärken und Schwächen der direkten Demokratie in der Schweiz', Beiträge und Berichte des Instituts für Politikwissenschaft an der Hochschule St. Gallen, no. 202.

Moe, Terry (1985) 'Control and Feedback in Economic Regulation: The Case of the NLRB', *American Political Science Review*, **79**, 1094–116.

Moench, Christoph (1989) 'Die Fahrverbotsregelung der Smog-Verordnungen auf dem Prüfstand des EG-Rechts', *Neue Zeitschrift für Verwaltungsrecht*, **4**, 335–8.

Money, Jeannette and George Tsebelis (1992) 'Cicero's Puzzle: Upper House Power in Comparative Perspective', *International Political Science Review*, **13**, 25–43.

Montesquieu, Charles-Louis de (1748) *De l'Esprit des Loix*, Geneva: Barrillot.

Moser, Peter (1990) *The Political Economy of the GATT with Application to U.S. Trade Policy*, Grüsch: Verlag Rüegger.

Moser, Peter (1991) *Schweizerische Wirtschaftspolitik im internationalen Wettbewerb*, Zürich: Orell Füssli.

Moser, Peter (1996a) 'The European Parliament as a Conditional Agenda Setter: What are the Conditions? A Critique of Tsebelis (1994)', *American Political Science Review*, **90** (4), 834–8.

Moser, Peter (1996b) 'Why is Swiss Politics so Stable', *Swiss Journal of Economics and Statistics*, **132** (1), 31–60.

Moser, Peter (1996c) 'Von der Immobilität zur Instabilität? Auswirkungen der Einführung der allgemeinen Volksinitiative und der Verfassungsgerichtsbarkeit in der Schweiz', *Schweizerische Zeitschrift für Politische Wissenschaft*, **2** (2), 227–49.

Moser, Peter (1997a) 'The Benefits of the Conciliation Procedure for the European Parliament: Comment to George Tsebelis' "Maastricht and the Democratic Deficit",' *Aussenwirtschaft*, **52** (1–2), 47–52; and in Peter Moser, Gerald Schneider and Gebhard Kirchgässner (eds) (2000), *Decision Rules in the European Union: A Rational Choice Perspective*, London: Macmillan.

Moser, Peter (1997b) 'A Theory of the Conditional Influence of the European Parliament in the Cooperation Procedure', *Public Choice*, **91** (3–4), 333–50.

Moser, Peter (1999a) 'Checks and Balances and the Supply of Central Bank Independence', *European Economic Review*, **43** (8), 1569–93.

Moser, Peter (1999b) 'The Impact of Legislative Institutions on Public Policy: A Survey', *European Journal of Political Economy*, **15** (1), 1–33.

Moser, Peter, Gerald Schneider and Gebhard Kirchgässner (eds) (2000) *Decision Rules in the European Union: A Rational Choice Perspective*, London: Macmillan.

Mueller, Dennis C. (1989) *Public Choice II*, Cambridge: Cambridge University Press.

Mueller, Dennis C. (1996) *Constitutional Democracy*, Oxford: Oxford University Press.

Neumann, Manfred J.M. (1993) 'Die Deutsche Bundesbank als Modell für eine Europäische Zentralbank?' in Dieter Duwendag and Jürgen Siebke (eds), *Europa vor dem Eintritt in die Wirtschafts- und Währungsunion*, Schriften des Vereins für Socialpolitik, **220**, 81–95.

Niskanan, William (1971) *Bureaucracy and Representative Government*, Chicago: Aldine-Atherton.

Nitzan, Shmuel (1994) 'Modelling Rent-Seeking Contests', *European Journal of Political Economy*, **10** (1), 41–60.

Noll, Roger G. (1989) 'Economic Perspectives on the Politics of Regulation,' in R. Schmalensee and R.D. Willig (eds), *Handbook of Industrial Organization*, vol. 2, New York: North Holland, 1253–87.

North, Douglass C. (1990) *Institutions, Institutional Change and Economic Performance*, Cambridge: Cambridge University Press.

North, Douglass C. (1993) 'Institutions and Credible Commitment', *Journal of Institutional and Theoretical Economics*, **149**, 11–23.

North, Douglass C. and Barry R. Weingast (1989) 'Constitutions and Commitment: The Evolution of Institutions of Public Choice in 17th Century England', *Journal of Economic History*, **49**, 803–32.

Olson, Mancur (1965) *The Logic of Collective Action*, Cambridge: Harvard University Press.

Ordeshook, Peter C. (1986) *Game Theory and Political Theory*, Cambridge: Cambridge University Press.

Ordeshook, Peter C. (1992) 'Constitutional Stability', *Constitutional Political Economy*, **3**, 137–75.

Ordeshook, Peter C. and Thomas Schwartz (1987) 'Agenda and the Control of Political Outcomes', *American Political Science Review*, **81**, 179–99.

Ostrom, Elinor (1986) 'An Agenda for the Study of Institutions', *Public Choice*, **48**, 3–25.

Peltzman, Sam (1976) 'Toward a More General Theory of Regulation', *Journal of Law and Economics*, **27**, 181–210.

Pernice, Ingolf (1990) 'Auswirkungen des europäischen Binnenmarktes auf das Umweltrecht – Gemeinschafts(verfassungs-)rechtliche Grundlage', *Neue Zeitschrift für Verwaltungsrecht*, **3**, 201–11.

Persson, Torsten and Lars E. O. Svensson (1989) 'Why a Stubborn Conservative would Run a Deficit: Policy with Time-inconsistent Preferences', *Quarterly Journal of Economics*, **85**, 325–45.

Persson, Torsten, Gerard Roland and Guido Tabellini (1996) 'Separation of Powers and Accountability: Towards a Formal Approach to Comparative Politics', *Working Paper no. 100*, Innocenzo Gasparini Institute for Economic Research.

Persson, Torsten and Guido Tabellini (1993) 'Designing Institutions for Monetary Stability', *Carnegie-Rochester Conference Series on Public Policy*, **39**, 53–84.

Plott, Charles R. (1967) 'A Notion of Equilibrium and its Possibility Under Majority Rule', *American Economic Review*, **57**, 787–806.

Pommerehne, Werner (1978) 'Institutional Approaches to Public Expenditures: Empirical Evidence From Swiss Municipalities', *Journal of Public Economics*, **9**, 163–201.

Pommerehne, Werner (1990) 'The Empirical Relevance of Comparative Institutional Analysis', *European Economic Review*, **34**, 458–69.

Pommerehne, Werner W. and Hannelore Weck-Hannemann (1996) 'Tax Rates, Tax Administration and Income Tax Evasion in Switzerland', *Public Choice*, **88**, 161–70.

Posen, Adam S. (1993) 'Why Central Bank Independence Does Not Cause Low Inflation: There is No Institutional Fix for Politics', in R. O'Brian (ed.), *Finance and the International Economy*, Oxford: Oxford University Press.

Potters, Jan and Randolph Sloof (1996) 'Interest Groups: A Survey of Empirical Models that Try to Assess their Influence', *European Journal of Political Economy*, **12**, 403–42.

Przeworski, Adam (1991) *Democracy and the Market*, Cambridge: Cambridge University Press.

Qian, Yingyn and Barry R. Weingast (1997) 'Federalism as a Commitment to Preserving Market Incentives', *Journal of Economic Perspectives*, **11**, 83–92.

Ramseyer, J. Mark and Frances McCall Rosenbluth (1993) *Japan's Political Marketplace*, Cambridge: Harvard University Press.

Rengling, Hans-Werner and Kersten Heinz (1990) 'Die Dänische Pfandflaschenregelung,' *Juristische Schulung*, **8**, 613–17.

Riker, William H. (1962) *The Theory of Political Coalitions*, New Haven: Yale University Press.

Riker, William H. (1982) *Liberalism Against Populism*, San Francisco: W.H. Freeman.

Riker, William H. (1992) 'The Justification of Bicameralism,' *International Political Science Review*, **13**, 101–16.

Riker, William H. and Peter C. Ordeshook (1973) *An Introduction to Positive Political Theory*, Englewood Cliffs: Prentice Hall.

Rodriguez, Daniel B. (1992) 'Statutory Interpretation and Political Advantage', *International Review of Law and Economics*, **12**, 217–31.

Rodrik, Dani (1991) 'Policy Uncertainty and Private Investment in Developing Countries', *Journal of Development Economics*, **36** (2), 229–42.

Rogoff, Kenneth (1985) 'The Optimal Degree of Commitment to an Intermediate Monetary Target', *Quarterly Journal of Economics*, **100**, 1169–89.

Rogoff, Kenneth (1987) 'Reputational Constraints on Monetary Policy', *Carnegie-Rochester Conference Series on Public Policy*, **26**, 141–82.

Rohde, David W. (1991) *Parties and Leaders in the Postreform House*, Chicago: University of Chicago Press.

Romer, David (1993) 'Openess and Inflation: Theory and Evidence', *Quarterly Journal of Economics*, **108**, 869–903.

Romer, Thomas and Howard Rosenthal (1978) 'Political Resource Allocation, Controlled Agendas, and the Status Quo', *Public Choice*, **33**, 27–43.

Root, Hilton (1989) 'Tying the King's Hands: Credible Commitments in Royal Fiscal Policy During Old Regime', *Rationality and Society*, **1**, 240–58.

Root, Hilton (1994) *The Fountain of Privilege: Political Foundation of Markets in Old Regime France and England*, Berkeley: University of California Press.

Root, Hilton (1996) *Small Countries, Big Lessons: Governance and the Rise of East Asia*, Hong Kong: Oxford University Press.

Rosenthal, Howard (1990) 'The Setter Model', in James M. Enelow and Melvin J. Hinich (eds), *Advances in the Spatial Theory of Voting*, Cambridge: Cambridge University Press, 199–234.

Sachs, Jeffrey D. and Andrew M. Warner (1997) 'Fundamental Sources of Long-Run Growth', *American Economic Review*, **87** (May), 185–8.

Schiemann, Jürgen and Stefan Alshuth (1994) 'Der Grad der Zentralbankautonomie und sein Einfluss im gesamtwirtschaftlichen Prozess: Eine international vergleichende Rangkorrelationsanalyse', *Aussenwirtschaft*, **49**, 579–600.

Schindler, Dietrich (1990) 'Auswirkungen der EG auf die schweizerische Staatsstruktur', *Wirtschaftspolitische Mitteilungen*, **2**, 1–18.

Schneider, Friedrich (1985) *Der Einfluss von Interessengruppen auf die Wirtschaftspolitik*, Bern: Haupt.

Schneider, Friedrich and Werner W. Pommerehne (1983) 'Macroeconomia della crescita in disequilibrio e settore pubblico in espansione: il peso delle differenze istituzionali', *Rivista Internazionale di Scienze Economiche e Commerciali*, **30** (4–5), 306–19.

Schneider, Gerald (1997) *Integration Games: Domestic Politics and Regional Cooperation in Europe*, Ann Arbor: University of Michigan Press.

Schofield, Norman (1978) 'Instability of Simple Dynamic Games', *Review of Economic Studies*, **45**, 575–94.

Schofield, Norman (1993) 'Political Competition and Multiparty Coalition Governments', *European Journal of Political Research*, **23**, 1–33.

Schofield, Norman (1995) 'Democratic Stability', in Jack Knight and Itai Sened (eds), *Explaining Social Institutions*, Ann Arbor: University of Michigan Press, 189–215.

Schwartz, Thomas (1986) *The Logic of Collective Choice*, New York: Columbia University Press.

Segal, Jeffrey A. (1997) 'Separation-of-power Games in the Positive Theory of Congress and Courts', *American Political Science Review*, **91** (1), 28–44.

Sen, Amartya K. (1986) 'Social Choice Theory', in Kenneth Arrow and M. Intriligator (eds), *Handbook of Mathematical Economics*, New York: North-Holland, 1073–81.

Sevenster, H. G. (1989) 'Van schone auto's en EEG-dingen, die voorbij gaan', *Nederlands Juristenblad*, 556–61.

Shepsle, Kenneth A. (1978) *The Giant Jigsaw Puzzle*, Chicago: Chicago University Press.

Shepsle, Kenneth A. (1979) 'Institutional Arrangements and Equilibrium in Multidimensional Voting Models', *American Journal of Political Science*, **23**, 27–59.

Shepsle, Kenneth A. (1986a) 'Institutional Equilibrium and Equilibrium Institutions', in Herbert F. Weisberg (ed.), *Political Science: The Science of Politics*, New York: Agathan Press, 51–81.

Shepsle, Kenneth A. (1986b) 'The Positive Theory of Legislative Institutions: An Enrichment of Social Choice and Spatial Models', *Public Choice*, **50**, 135–78.

Shepsle, Kenneth A. (1991) 'Discretion, Institutions and the Problem of Government Commitment', in Pierre Bourdrieu and James Coleman (eds), *Social Theory for a Changing Society*, Boulder: Western Press.

Shepsle, Kenneth A. and Mark S. Bonchek (1997) *Analyzing Politics: Rationality, Behavior, and Institutions*, New York: W.W. Norton.

Shepsle, Kenneth A. and Barry R. Weingast (1984) 'Uncovered Set and Sophisticated Voting Outcomes with Implications for Agenda Institutions', *American Journal of Political Science*, **28**, 49–74.

Shepsle, Kenneth A. and Barry R. Weingast (1987a) 'The Institutional Foundation of Committee Power', *American Political Science Review*, **81**, 85–104.

Shepsle, Kenneth A. and Barry R. Weingast (1987b) 'Why are Congressional Committees Powerful?' *American Political Science Review*, **81** (3), 935–45.

Shepsle, Kenneth A. and Barry R. Weingast (1994) 'Positive Theories of Congressional Institutions', *Legislative Studies Quarterly*, **19** (2), 149–80.

Shughart, William F, Robert D. Tollison and Brian L. Goff (1986) 'Bureaucratic Structure and Congressional Control', *Southern Economic Journal*, **52**, 962–72.

Snyder, James M. (1992) 'Artificial Extremism in Interest Group Ratings', *Legislative Studies Quarterly*, **17**, 319–45.

Snyder, James M. (1994) 'Safe Seats, Marginal Seats, and Party Platforms: The Logic of Platform Differentiation', *Economics and Politics*, **6**, 201–13.

Spiller, Pablo T. and Matthew L. Spitzer (1992) 'Judicial Choice of Legal Doctrines', *Journal of Law, Economics, and Organization*, **8**, 8–46.

Spulber, Daniel F. and David Besanko (1992) 'Delegation, Commitment, and the Regulatory Mandate', *Journal of Law, Economics, and Organization*, **8**, 126–54.

Steunenberg, Bernard (1992) 'Referendum, Initiative, and Veto Power', *Kyklos*, **45**, 501–29.

Steunenberg, Bernard (1994a) 'Regulatory Policymaking in a Parliamentary Setting', *Jahrbuch für Neue Politische Oekonomie*, **13** 36–57.

Steunenberg, Bernard (1994b) 'Decision Making under Different Institutional Arrangements: Legislation by the European Community', *Journal of Institutional and Theoretical Economics*, **150**, 642–69.

Steunenberg, Bernard (1996) 'Agency Discretion, Regulatory Policymaking, and Different Institutional Arrangements', *Public Choice*, **86**, 303–39.

Steunenberg, Bernard (1997) 'Commission Discretion, Parliamentary Involvement, and Administrative Policymaking in the European Union', Manuscript, University of Twente.

Steunenberg, Bernard, Christian Kobolt and Dieter Schmidtchen (1996) 'Policymaking, Comitology, and the Balance of Power in the European Union', *International Review of Law and Economics*, **16**, 329–44.

Steunenberg, Bernard, Christian Kobolt and Dieter Schmidtchen (1997) 'Beyond Comitology: European Policymaking with Parliamentary Involvement', *Aussenwirtschaft*, **52** (1–2), 77–102; and in Peter Moser, Gerald Schneider and Gebhard Kirchgässner (eds), *Decision Rules in the European Union: A Rational Choice Perspective*, London: Macmillan.

Stigler, George J. (1971) 'The Theory of Economic Regulation', *Bell Journal of Economics and Management Science*, **2**, 137–46.

Stratmann, Thomas (1996) 'Instability of Collective Decisions? Testing for Cyclical Majorities', *Public Choice*, **88**, 15–28.

Svensson, Jakob (1998) 'Investment, Property Rights and Political Instability', *European Economic Review*, **42**, 1317–241.

Svensson, Lars O. (1997) 'Optimal Inflation Targets, Conservative Central Banks, and Linear Inflation Contracts', *American Economic Review*, **87** (1), 98–114.

Tabellini, Guido and Alberto Alesina (1990) 'Voting on the Budget Deficit', *American Economic Review*, **80**, 37–49.

Tsebelis, George (1990) *Nested Games: Rational Choice in Comparative Politics*, Berkeley: University of California Press.

Tsebelis, George (1993) 'The Core, the Uncovered Set, and Conference Committees in Bicameral Legislatures', Manuscript, Hoover Institution.

Tsebelis, George (1994) 'The Power of the European Parliament as a Conditional Agenda Setter,' *American Political Science Review*, **88**, 128–42.

Tsebelis, George (1995a) 'Decisionmaking in Political Systems: Comparison of Presidentialism, Parliamentarism, Multicameralism, and Multipartism', *British Journal of Political Science*, **25**, 289–325.

Tsebelis, George (1995b) 'Decisionmaking Inside the European Parliament', in Barry Eichengreen, Jeffry Frieden and Jürgen von Hagen (eds), *Politics and Institutions in an Integrated Europe*, Berlin: Springer, 42–64.

Tsebelis, George (1996) 'More on the European Parliament as a Conditional Agenda Setter: Response to Moser', *American Political Science Review*, **90** (4), 839–43.

Tsebelis, George (1997) 'Maastricht and the Democratic Deficit', *Aussenwirtschaft*, **52** (1–2), 19–46; and in Peter Moser, Gerald Schneider and Gebhard Kirchgässner (eds) (1999), *Decision Rules in the European Union: A Rational Choice Perspective*, London: Macmillan.

Tsebelis, George and Jeannette Money (1997) *Bicameralism*, Cambridge: Cambridge University Press.

Tullock, Gorden (1967) 'The General Irrelevance of the General Impossibility Theorem', *Quarterly Journal of Economics*, **81**, 256–70.

Tullock, Gorden (1981) 'Why so much Stability?' *Public Choice*, **37**, 189–202.

Ursprung, Heinrich W. (1990) 'Public Goods, Rent Dissipation, and Candidate Competition', *Economics and Politics*, **2**, 115–32.

Ursprung, Tobias (1994) *Propaganda, Interessengruppen und direkte Demokratie*, Heidelberg: Physika-Verlag.

van den Bos, Jan M. (1994) 'The Policy Issues Analyzed', in Bruce Bueno de Mesquita and Frans N. Stokman (eds), *European Community Decision Making: Models, Applications, and Comparisons*, New Haven: Yale University Press, 33–65.

Vaubel, Roland (1993) 'Eine Public-Choice-Analyse der Deutschen Bundesbank und ihre Implikationen für die Europaische Wahrungsunion,' in Dieter Duwendag and Jürgen Siebke (eds), *Europa vor dem Eintritt in die Wirtschafts- und Währungsunion*, Schriften des Vereins für Socialpolitik, **220**, 23–79.

Vaubel, Roland (1997) 'The Bureaucratic and Partisan Behavior of Independent Central Banks: German and International Evidence', *European Journal of Political Economy*, **13**, 201–24.

von der Groeben, Hans, Jochen Thiesing and Claus-Dieter Ehlermann (eds) (1991) *Kommentar zum EWG-Vertrag*, Baden-Baden: Nomos.

von Hagen, Jürgen and Ralph Süppel (1994) 'Central Bank Constitution for Federal Monetary Unions', *European Economic Review*, **38**, 774–82.

Waller, Christopher J. (1992) 'The Choice of a Conservative Central Banker in a Multisector Economy', *American Economic Review*, **82**, 1006–12.

Walsh, Carl E. (1995a) 'Optimal Contracts for Central Bankers and the Inflation Bias of Monetary Policy', *American Economic Review*, **85**, 150–67.

Walsh, Carl E. (1995b) 'Is New Zealand's Reserve Bank Act of 1989 an Optimal Central Bank Contract?' *Journal of Money, Credit, and Banking*, part 1, November, **27** (4), 1179–91.

Wärneryd, Karl (1990) 'Conventions: An Evolutionary Approach', *Constitutional Political Economy*, **1**, 83–107.

Weingast, Barry R. (1981) 'Regulation, Reregulation, and Deregulation: The Political Foundation of Agency Clientele Relationship', *Law and Contemporary Problems*, **44**, 147–77.

Weingast, Barry R. (1984) 'The Congressional-Bureaucratic System: A Principal Agent Perspective (with Applications to the SEC)', *Public Choice*, **44**, 147–91.

Weingast, Barry R. (1989a) 'Floor Behavior in the U.S. Congress: Committee Power Under the Open Rule', *American Political Science Review*, **83**, 795–815.

Weingast, Barry R. (1989b) 'The Political Institutions of Representative Government: Legislatures', *Journal of Institutional and Theoretical Economics*, **145**, 693–703.

Weingast, Barry R. (1989c) 'Fighting Fire With Fire: Amending Activity and Institutional Change in the Post-Reform Congress', *Working Paper in Political Science 89–11*, Hoover Institution, Stanford University.

Weingast, Barry R. (1993a) 'The Political Foundations of Democracy and the Rule of Law', Manuscript, Hoover Institution, Stanford University.

Weingast, Barry R. (1993b) 'Constitutions as Governance Structures: The Political Foundation of Secure Markets', *Journal of Institutional and Theoretical Economics*, **149**, 286–311.

Weingast, Barry R. (1995) 'The Economic Role of Political Institutions: Market-Preserving Federalism and Economic Development', *Journal of Law, Economics, and Organization*, **11** (1), 1–31.

Weingast, Barry R. and William Marshall (1988) 'The Industrial Organization of Congress; or, why Legislatures, like Firms, are not Organized as Markets', *Journal of Political Economy*, **96**, 132–63.

Weingast, Barry R. and Mark J. Moran (1983) 'Bureaucratic Discretion or Congressional Control? Regulatory Policymaking by the Federal Trade Commission', *Journal of Political Economy*, **91**, 765–800.

Wessel, Wolfgang (1991) 'The EC Council: The Community's Decisionmaking Center', in Robert O. Keohane and Stanley Hoffmann (eds), *The New European Community: Decisionmaking and Institutional Change*, Boulder: Westview Press, 133–54.

Westlake, Martin (1994) *The Commission and the Parliament: Partners and Rivals in the European Policy-making Process*, London: Butterworth.

Williamson, Oliver (1979) 'Transaction-cost Economics: the Governance of Contractual Relations', *Journal of Law and Economics*, **22**, 233–61.

Williamson, Oliver (1985) *The Economic Institutions of Capitalism*, New York: Free Press.

Williamson, Oliver E. (1989) 'Transaction Cost Economics', in R. Schmalensee and R.D. Willig (eds), *Handbook of Industrial Organization*, New York: North-Holland, 135–82.

Wittman, Donald A. (1983) 'Candidate Motivation: A Synthesis of Alternative Theories', *American Political Science Review*, **77**, 142–57.

Wittmann, Walter (1992) *Marktwirtschaft für die Schweiz*, Frauenfeld: Huber Verlag.

Ziegler, Andreas (1996) *Trade and Environmental Law in the European Community*, Oxford: Oxford University Press.

Index